D0225516

The Dragon Looks South

The Dragon Looks South

China and Southeast Asia in the New Century

Bronson Percival

PRAEGER SECURITY INTERNATIONAL
Westport, Connecticut • London

Library of Congress Cataloging-in-Publication Data

Percival, Bronson.
The dragon looks south : China and Southeast Asia in the new century / Bronson Percival.
p. cm.
Includes bibliographical references and index.
ISBN 978–0–275–99426–6 (alk. paper)
1. Southeast Asia—Relations—China. 2. China—Relations—Southeast Asia. I. Title.
DS525.9.C5D73 2007
327.51059—dc22 2007008457

British Library Cataloguing in Publication Data is available.

Library of Congress Catalog Card Number: 2007008457
ISBN-13: 978–0–275–99426–6
ISBN-10: 0–275–99426–0

First published in 2007

Praeger Security International, 88 Post Road West, Westport, CT 06881
An imprint of Greenwood Publishing Group, Inc.
www.praeger.com

Printed in the United States of America

The paper used in this book complies with the Permanent Paper Standard issued by the National Information Standards Organization (Z39.48–1984).

10 9 8 7 6 5 4 3 2 1

Contents

Preface and Acknowledgments

This book is an introduction to China's relationships with Southeast Asia and the implications of these relationships for the United States. Although it would have been easier to organize the book around such notions as a struggle for power between China and the United States in this region or American "hard power" set against Chinese "soft power," it quickly became clear that these approaches would be more misleading than informative. Eleven Southeast Asian states, ranging from giant Indonesia to tiny and newly independent East Timor, are tied into a complex web of relationships among themselves. The region is remarkably open to many different external economic and cultural influences, and the major states now seeking to influence the region include not only China and the United States, but also Japan and India.

When initially approached to write this book, I was concerned that most published material on the China-Southeast Asia relationship was written by scholars versed in Chinese foreign policy and that my academic and professional background had focused not on China but on Southeast Asia. Moreover, despite a lifetime of analysis and writing as an American diplomat and a few years teaching at the U.S. Naval War College, I had no experience writing a book. In conducting my research I was able to draw on my background to interview a wide variety of officials, diplomats, and semi-official strategic studies experts in Washington, D.C., and in Southeast Asia from September 2004 to May 2006. These interviews were conducted on a confidential basis and the names of the interviewees are not provided. I was helped through my long education in the process of writing a book by, among others, Professors Zachary Abuza, Robert Sutter, and Brantly Womack, who kindly reviewed and commented on drafts of the manuscript. In addition, a former colleague from the Foreign Service, Mathew Daley, provided a balanced practitioner's viewpoint. Dr. Ellen Frost offered particularly timely encouragement.

I am also indebted to Admiral Michael McDevitt and to Dr. David Finkelstein at the Center for Strategic Studies at the Center for Naval Analyses. They demonstrated extraordinary patience and confidence as I struggled to transform bits and pieces of accumulated knowledge into a manuscript for the foundation that had provided a research grant to write on China's growing influence in Southeast Asia. That manuscript, revised and updated, was the basis for this book.

Finally, I would like to thank Mr. Allan Song of the Smith Richardson Foundation for his encouragement and the Foundation for a research grant.

The mistakes are my responsibility.

Bronson Percival
Bethesda, Maryland

Abbreviations

ACFTA	ASEAN-China Free Trade Agreement (also know as CAFTA)
ADB	Asian Development Bank
AFP	Armed Forces of the Philippines
AFTA	ASEAN Free Trade Area
APEC	Asia Pacific Economic Cooperation Forum
ARF	ASEAN Regional Forum
ASC	ASEAN Security Community
ASEAN	Association of Southeast Asian Nations
ASEAN+3	ASEAN plus China, Japan and South Korea
BFA	Boao Forum for Asia
CAFTA	China-ASEAN Free Trade Agreement (also know as ACFTA)
CCP	Chinese Communist Party
CLMV	Cambodia, Laos, Myanmar (Burma), Vietnam
CSCAP	Councils for Security Cooperation in the Asia-Pacific
EAS	East Asian Summit
EHP	Early Harvest Program
EPA	Economic Partnership Agreement
FDI	Foreign Direct Investment
FPDA	Five Power Defense Arrangement (Australia, Malaysia, New Zealand, Singapore, United Kingdom)
FTA	Free Trade Agreement
GDP	Gross Domestic Product
GMS	Greater Mekong Subregion
IMF	International Monetary Fund
JI	Jema'ah Islamiyah

LNG	Liquefied Natural Gas
MILF	Moro Islamic Liberation Front (Philippines)
NSC	New Security Concept
ODA	Official Development Assistance
PLA	People's Liberation Army (China)
PRC	People's Republic of China
RMSI	Regional Maritime Security Initiative
SARS	Severe Acute Respiratory Syndrome
SCS	South China Sea
SOM	Senior Officials Meeting
TAC	Treaty of Amity and Cooperation
TIFA	Trade and Investment Framework Agreement
VFA	Visiting Forces Agreement (U.S.–Philippines)
WTO	World Trade Organization

Introduction

This book seeks to explain China's growing influence in Southeast Asia. It is important to understand China's impact there because more than half a billion people live in Southeast Asia, because that region is the fifth largest trading partner of both the United States and China, and because Southeast Asia sits astride China and the rest of East Asia's energy windpipe. The most consistent and predictable component of the complicated relationship between China and Southeast Asia has been Beijing's comprehensive strategy for that region over the past decade. Since this is the one variable that can be held most constant, this book analyzes the impacts of China's current strategy, rather than speculating on what might happen if Beijing adjusted this strategy.

A central argument is that China's success is inexplicable without exploring the politics, economics, cultures, and foreign policies of the states of Southeast Asia. This region is among the world's most ethnically, politically, and economically diverse, and is divided into eleven independent states. Any attempt to treat this region as one state or economy in relation to China distorts reality. It also fails to explain why China has been more successful in one state or part of the region than in another.

China's approach and its appeal to the region has remained remarkably consistent over the past decade. The most significant change has been a decision by Beijing, in early 2001, to avoid direct criticism of or opposition to American policies in Southeast Asia. To achieve its goals China needs non-confrontational relations with the United States.

Working from the assumption that China is the driver in the relationship and that a black box called Southeast Asia or ASEAN is the dependent variable, some scholars and officials have attempted to understand the relative weight of the components of China's influence by asking how an important internal change in China—for example, a banking crisis that halted China's rapid economic growth for a few years—might affect its influence in Southeast Asia. This book does not take this approach for two reasons. First, the author is not a China scholar and is incapable of judging the likelihood of internal changes in China. Second, the relationships between China and the States of Southeast Asia vary significantly and are interactive. Attempts to track the possible impact of a change in Chinese internal affairs on China's relationships in Southeast Asia would be extremely complex and inevitably speculative.[1]

Neither does this book speculate on China's motivations, an approach which is implicit in some lists of alternative futures. Among these possible motivations is that China is in pursuit of hegemony in the region, albeit employing more sophisticated policies than in the past. Another possibility is that Beijing's campaign in the region is primarily defensive, an attempt to "neutralize" the region while China focuses on internal priorities. A third possibility is that China seeks to establish a cooperative structure—to include several states outside the region that have traditionally exercised influence within Southeast Asia—which would prove beneficial for all involved. Whatever China's motivations may be, the expectations in China and Southeast Asia that have led to a "honeymoon" may prove unrealistic and inevitably fade. Since the crystal ball is murky, this book will not attempt to assign one motivation to Beijing.

Instead, the approach is to explore China's influence in Southeast Asia from several perspectives. The first chapter provides an overview of the history of China's policies toward Southeast Asia and outlines China's current key goals. China's rising influence in the new century has significantly affected Southeast Asia's relations with Taiwan—and, to a lesser extent, its relations with Japan—but not this region's relations with the United States. Chapter 2 reviews the utility of particularly relevant or prominent international relations "schools of thought" against reality in China's relationships in Southeast Asia. The intent is not to explore international relations theory or to confuse the reader with academic terminology. Instead, the goal is to suggest the assumptions that underlie many of these analytic "schools of thought," and—much like trying on glasses with different prescriptions—to see whether they help us better understand China's relationships. The third and fourth chapters focus, respectively, on mainland and maritime Southeast Asia, and include individual sections on China's relations with each Southeast Asian country. A central contention of this book is that these regions of Southeast Asia constitute individual political and cultural subsystems, and that China's influence is, and will likely continue to be in the foreseeable future, qualitatively different in these different parts of Southeast Asia. Chapter 5 reviews China's political and security relations with the region as a whole and Beijing's turn to multilateral diplomacy, including its decision to shelve conflicting territorial claims in the South China Sea. Economics, which many observers see as the most important component of the relationship, are addressed in Chapter 6. Chapter 7 explains the roles of different aspects of "soft power," and reviews the reactions to China's rise in Southeast Asia's ethnic Chinese communities. The interests and policies of the United States in Southeast Asia are explored in Chapter 8. Finally, in the conclusion the analytic strands are drawn together to suggest the implications of China's rise for the United States and Southeast Asia.

Beijing's ultimate intentions—that is, its motivations—are not clear. However, its current goals are. They include, in rough priority order: to stabilize its southern periphery; to tap Southeast Asian funds and resources to contribute to China's economic modernization; to isolate Taiwan; and to increase China's influence, in part to forestall the "containment" of China.

In pursuit of these goals, over the past decade China's leaders and officials have replaced assertiveness with a search for common interests and "win-win" solutions to conflicts. China's leaders have assured Southeast Asian elites of their support for the political and territorial status quo. In most, but not all, Southeast Asian eyes, China has transformed itself from the state most often feared into a perceived partner. This feat has been accomplished primarily through attentive and accommodating Chinese diplomatic leadership. In addition, a booming trade relationship, which may shortly surpass that between Southeast Asia and the United States, and expectations that China's economic growth will continue to contribute to their own prosperity, have moderated resentment in Southeast Asian countries over competition for foreign direct investment (FDI) and export markets in developed countries. In response, all Southeast Asian states have grasped at the opportunity to participate in China's economic growth, through trade, investment, and the negotiation of a China-ASEAN Free Trade Agreement (CAFTA).

China's comprehensive approach, however, has also provoked different responses in different parts of Southeast Asia. For most of mainland Southeast Asia, China looms as the primary external force and influence. Geography, culture, poverty, and authoritarian governments in much of mainland Southeast Asia all play a role in explaining China's influence. Thailand retains its renowned ability to bend with the prevailing wind, but a hesitant response to requests by its American "treaty ally" over the past few years suggests that this wind blows increasingly from the north. Myanmar is condemned to dependence on China absent a democratic revolution that would attract international support, and the Cambodian and Laotian regimes look first to Beijing. A wary Vietnam, even as it tries to cautiously develop alternatives, will always be looking over its shoulder at China, even if its political system liberalizes. China's most basic security interest in Southeast Asia is to have friendly regimes on its southern borders.

Maritime Southeast Asia is a different world, an island world peopled predominantly with Muslims and Christians and governed by democratically elected leaders for whom China is a relatively distant, if increasingly important, trade partner.[2] U.S. security interests in the region are centered in the Strait of Malacca, the world's most important maritime chokepoint, not in Myanmar or even Bangkok. American investments and trade are overwhelmingly in and with maritime Southeast Asia. Malaysia's response to China is similar to Thailand's, but contains less of a strategic component and is less deferential. Singapore hosts the U.S. military, and invests in China's economy. Indonesia and the Philippines are the latest participants in the region's booming trade with China, but are also the states most wary of China's intentions. Indonesia, which is almost as large as the United States, considers itself the natural leader of the region.

No assessment of the implications for the United States of China's increasing influence in Southeast Asia is possible without an understanding of American interests in the region. Washington has been reluctant to define these interests with precision for over a hundred years—from the acquisition of the Philippines in the late nineteenth century to the American "return to Southeast Asia" to combat terrorism at the beginning of the twenty-first century. Instead, ad hoc responses and laundry lists of U.S. interests have alternated with deep intervention. The most prominent example of intervention by the United States was the war to prevent the unification of Vietnam under Communist leadership.

Core U.S. interests, however, have been clear at least since the Japanese attack on Pearl Harbor launched the United States into World War II in the Pacific. They are: to prevent the domination of the entire region by one other power, to assure control when necessary of the critical sea-lanes connecting the Pacific and Indian Oceans, and to compete on equal terms for commercial opportunities. To these basics have been added, although the commitment waxes and wanes, support for democracy and human rights and, more recently, the eradication of international terrorism.

In 2006, China's influence in Southeast Asia has little direct impact on America's core interests in the region. Indirectly, China's "rise" affects broader U.S. interest in East Asia by undermining Southeast Asian support for Taiwan. Arguably, this could indirectly increase the costs to the United States of continuing to support the current status quo between Beijing and Taipei. In addition, Japan's fading clout in the region has the potential to increase the burden on the United States when it seeks the support of Southeast Asian elites for specific American policies supported by Japan but opposed by China.

Some analysts, particularly those focused on mainland Southeast Asia, stress China's support for authoritarian regimes in mainland Southeast Asian states. They argue that the Chinese model of strong economic growth and political repression, undercuts democratization, human rights, good governance, and anticorruption in the region. China's rise does directly constrain U.S. efforts to promote human rights and democracy in the three poorest countries of mainland Southeast Asia—Myanmar, Cambodia, and Laos—but these countries are of marginal strategic significance to the United States. It may also slow internal reform in Vietnam.

China's growing influence in Southeast Asia may also eventually contribute to the exclusion of the United States from an emerging East Asian network of multilateral institutions, which now, however, appears unlikely to evolve into a meaningful East Asian "community." Moreover, if the broad China-ASEAN Free Trade Agreement (CAFTA) is fully implemented in the next decade, that agreement will lead to trade diversion affecting American economic interests in both China and Southeast Asia.

However, the balance of influence among the major outside powers involved in Southeast Asia is in a period of rapid change. If China continues to rise at the same pace it has recently achieved, there will be significant implications for Japan, and possibly for the United States, within in the next decade.

CHAPTER 1

China's Strategy in Southeast Asia

CHINA'S CURRENT STRATEGIC GOALS

1. Maintain a stable environment on its periphery.
2. Encourage economic ties that contribute to China's economic modernization and thus to regime stability.
3. Further isolate Taiwan and block moves toward its de jure independence.
4. Convince others that China is not a threat.
5. Increase China's influence in East Asia, in part to prevent "containment" of China in the future.
6. In Southeast Asia, secure recognition as the most influential external Asian power.

HISTORY

Over the course of the past sixty years, China's strategic goals have varied, adapting to both internal political change and China's changing external environment. For more than a quarter of a century after 1949, the People's Republic of China pursued policies driven primarily by ideological considerations, which were often also seen to have pragmatic strategic benefits for China. Most Southeast Asian elites and their countries were prime targets of Communist China's campaigns to export revolution. China considered itself the leader in Asia of the revolutionary Communist movement, part of whose mission was to replace the post-independence nationalist, and often conservative, Southeast Asian leadership. It provided moral and organizational support and limited assistance to revolutionary insurgent groups when and where possible. Emerging in Southeast Asia from the oppression, deprivation, and subsequent chaos of the Japanese occupation during World War II were major Communist-led insurgencies in Malaya, the Philippines, and Vietnam, and one of the largest Communist movements in the world in Indonesia. In addition, China supported smaller insurgencies in Burma, Thailand, and Laos.[1] China's pragmatic national interest in a secure periphery did trump ideological fervor when, during the Geneva Conference of 1954, Chinese Foreign Minister Zhou Enlai agreed to the temporary partition of Vietnam despite the protest of Vietnam's Communist leaders. The war to unify Vietnam under Vietnamese Communist leadership lasted another twenty years and cost over a million Vietnamese lives.

During the early 1960s, Mao Zedong's revolutionary worldview drove Chinese support for insurgencies and "wars of national liberation." Mao pressed Vietnamese Communist leader Ho Chi Minh to make greater efforts to "liberate" South Vietnam. In 1965 Chinese Defense Minister Lin Biao proclaimed his "Long Live the Victory of People's War," which claimed that the "countryside" of the world, including China and the countries of Southeast Asia, would surround and defeat the "cities" of the world—that is, the United States and Western Europe. At the same time, Beijing's goal of driving the United States out of the region, the growing Sino-Soviet rivalry, and fear of encirclement interacted with ideology to produce an unpredictable Chinese foreign policy. One result was a heated debate outside China about the balance between ideology and pragmatism as factors in China's foreign policy decision making.

At that time, a much larger prize than southern Vietnam was Indonesia, where President Sukarno balanced precariously between a 3 million strong Parti Kommunis Indonesia (PKI) and anticommunist military officers. In 1965 the army blamed the murder of several generals on the PKI and the new military government in Indonesia asserted that Beijing had been complicit in an attempted Communist coup d'etat. Hundreds of thousands of Communists and alleged Communists, including many ethnic Chinese, died in the subsequent repression in Indonesia. Diplomatic ties between Jakarta and Beijing were severed for more than twenty-five years. Indonesia's subsequent search for internal stability, increasing U.S. involvement in Vietnam, and China's descent into its Cultural Revolution played a role in the formation of the Association of Southeast Asian States (ASEAN) in 1967 by the leaders of Indonesia, Malaysia, Singapore, the Philippines, and Thailand.[2] ASEAN was born to shelter, as much as possible, Southeast Asian states from the ideological and strategic conflicts that had brought external powers into their region.

By the early 1970s, Beijing had begun to view Southeast Asia primarily through the prism of Sino-Soviet rivalry and alleged Soviet encirclement and "hegemonism," in which Vietnam became an important link. The withdrawal of U.S. forces from Vietnam and the subsequent final collapse of the regime in Saigon in 1975 eventually led to the Soviet-Vietnamese treaty of friendship and cooperation and to Hanoi's bid to control all of Indochina. By the latter half of the decade, even Beijing's support for the genocidal Khmer Rouge in Cambodia was based not on ideology, but on power politics. The Khmer Rouge opposed Vietnam, the Soviet Union's ally in Southeast Asia.

Mao Zedong died in 1976. By 1979 a more moderate leadership under Deng Xiaoping had consolidated power. Chinese leaders then began to also focus on economic development and reform as a means to legitimize their continued rule from Beijing. After the United States established diplomatic relations with China, Beijing's relations with Southeast Asian states also began to improve. Beijing slowly halted support to fading communist insurgencies. By the end of the decade, Beijing had established diplomatic relations with all but Indonesia, Singapore, and Brunei. In 1979, it launched an armed attack "to teach Vietnam a lesson" and remind its old ideological ally of China's enduring geopolitical interests in Indochina.

During the 1980s Beijing achieved a tacit alliance with Thailand. This helped convinced ASEAN (despite Indonesian preferences) to oppose Vietnam's occupation of Cambodia. Afraid that Vietnam would consolidate its position in Indochina, China harassed Vietnam whenever it initiated offensives against the Khmer Rouge. In 1988, an armed clash in the Spratly islands left eighty Vietnamese sailors dead. Only with the collapse of the Soviet Union in 1991 and Vietnam's withdrawal from Cambodia, did China welcome talks to normalize relations with Vietnam.

As China's "four modernizations" increasingly came to dominate national policy, China also began to develop significant economic relationships in Southeast Asia, mostly through ethnic Chinese connections in Thailand and Singapore. In 1989 China passed its Nationality Law, which finally ended its claims to authority over the ethnic Chinese populations in Southeast Asia. Beijing appreciated Southeast Asian reticence while much of the rest of the world denounced the brutal suppression of demonstrations at Tiananmen in June 1989.[3] By the end of the decade China's accelerating economic development and its cooperation against Vietnam's occupation of Cambodia had put Beijing on the threshold of acceptance as a legitimate player in the international relations of those Southeast Asian states then grouped under the ASEAN banner.[4]

Throughout most of the 1990s, Chinese relations in Southeast Asia waxed and waned. Diplomatic relations with Indonesia, and subsequently with Singapore and Brunei, were normalized in 1991. High-level contacts increased. China was welcomed by ASEAN members as first an observer and then, in 1995, as a formal ASEAN dialogue partner. In 1994, China cautiously participated in the Asian Regional Forum (ARF), a new ASEAN-inspired "security" forum. But in 1992 China decided to issue its Law of the Territorial Sea and Contiguous Zones, reiterating Beijing's claim to most of the South China Sea. This threw a spanner in the works. Moreover, China began active exploration for oil in offshore areas also long claimed by Southeast Asian countries. The Philippines, Vietnam, Malaysia, and Indonesia—all claimants to parts of the South China Sea—reacted with alarm, particularly after China occupied Mischief Reef in 1995. Beijing refused to deal collectively with the Southeast Asian claimants to islets, reefs, and rocks in the South China Sea (who all had their own disagreements) and only reluctantly agreed to informal confidence-building meetings. No progress was achieved on resolving sovereignty issues or even on temporarily shelving territorial disputes while resources were developed jointly.

In addition Taiwan, with whom many Southeast Asians had old business and personal connections, launched a major investment and diplomatic campaign in the region in 1989. Moreover, China's military pressure on Taipei in 1996—which included launching missiles off Taiwanese waters—and the dispatch of U.S. naval carrier battle groups in response, worried most Southeast Asian elites deeply. Southeast Asian leaders have long viewed a military confrontation over Taiwan as a potential disaster for their region as a whole. In the mid-1990s, many officials and scholars predicted growing tensions between Beijing and several Southeast Asian states.

In response, Beijing initiated its own high-level diplomacy: such leaders as President Jiang Zemin, Premier Li Peng, and Vice Premier Zhu Rongji began to routinely visit Southeast Asian capitals. And diplomacy was supplemented with trade and investment, which began to take off. By 1995, trade between Southeast Asia and China had jumped to $20 billion. In addition, by the end of 1996, Southeast Asians had pumped almost $10 billion in investments into China's economic expansion. Particularly prominent was a multibillion-dollar Singaporean investment at Suzhou in Jiangsu. A judicious observer assessing the state of the relationship across the board in late 1996 could have made a reasonable case for predicting either improvement or deterioration in China's ties with Southeast Asian states.

The Asian Financial Crisis of 1997 turned the world upside down in Southeast Asia.[5] It led to the removal of Indonesia's President Suharto after more than thirty years of authoritarian rule and eventually to the emergence of a new democracy. It thoroughly scared the old, established elite coalitions then governing Thailand, Indonesia, and Malaysia, and shattered the assumption that the Southeast Asian economic boom of the 1980s and early 1990s would continue forever.

Ultimately, China benefited, not just from its responses to the crisis but also from the glow that quickly came to surround its actions. Beijing refused to devalue its own currency; contributed to IMF rescue plans; and it agreed to provide additional financial support to Thailand. These measures were helpful in dealing with the economic side of the crisis but even more important was China's public sympathy in contrast with the perception of American support for the International Monetary Fund's (IMF) "harsh" terms.

CHINA: THE "FRIENDLY ELEPHANT"[6]

Over the past decade, Chinese leaders and officials have turned their approach to Southeast Asia on its head, replacing the assertiveness that characterized pre-1997 Chinese policy with accommodation. This concerted campaign has not only assuaged Southeast Asians' fears but also paved the way for Southeast Asians and Chinese to participate in and profit from their rapidly expanding economic ties.

Chinese leaders and officials have gradually learned to smoothly employ diplomacy, executed by leaders from the President and Premier on down, in innumerable meetings with their Southeast Asian counterparts to slowly and carefully win greater influence in Southeast Asia. The Chinese foreign policy community has made a concerted effort to represent China's reemergence as a regional power—after an absence from much of the area for almost two centuries—as essentially an economic, rather than a strategic, development. It has also learned to portray recent trends as aligned with the economic and security interests of its southern neighbors. Crucial has been Beijing's impressive transformation of itself into the external power most supportive of the current political status quo in Southeast Asia states. In the past decade, Beijing has convinced most Southeast Asians that China is not a "threat."

The same formula—that is the same set of instruments of Chinese national security policy—has been employed at both the multilateral level with ASEAN and the bilateral level with individual Southeast Asian states, and with all Southeast Asian countries, albeit with differing effects in the countries concerned depending on their individual circumstances. China has thoroughly adjusted to the "ASEAN Way."[7] It places contentious issues (such as conflicting claims in the South China Sea) temporarily to the side, places process before product, and welcomes efforts to build an East Asian "community." Beijing has repeatedly advanced new proposals to bind Southeast Asia to China. Some are filled with platitudes but others are substantive, and they range across the spectrum of economic, political, and cultural life. It has also advanced security proposals but wisely allowed security ties to follow at a pace that individual Southeast Asian countries find comfortable. Although sometimes derided as a "charm offensive," this intensive diplomacy has proven effective.

As Beijing's leadership courted its southern neighbors, China supplemented diplomacy with economic ties, most dramatically in terms of trade and economic investment. Early on, Beijing "opened" China to "overseas" ethnic Chinese and invited ethnic Chinese Southeast Asians to invest in China. It subsequently went out of its way to also include indigenous Southeast Asians. The collective response has been a cumulative investment of as much as $40 billion from Southeast Asia. Moreover, rapid increases in Sino-Southeast Asian trade helped pull the region out of the 1997 Asian Financial Crisis, while Southeast Asian exports to its traditional markets stagnated. In many ways, its economic success has been as impressive as its diplomatic campaign, because China and the Southeast Asian states are often direct economic competitors, both for foreign direct investment (FDI) and for developed markets in Japan, Europe, and the United States. Beijing has worked assiduously to provide Southeast Asian economies with a stake in China's economic expansion, thus both stabilizing China's periphery and contributing to China's own economic growth.

In part to address concerns about China's accession to the World Trade Organization (WTO), Beijing first floated the idea of a China-ASEAN Free Trade Area (CAFTA) in 2000. All parties have agreed that the goal is to remove all tariffs by 2015, and negotiations are moving forward on the specifics. This planned "free trade" area contains almost 2 billion people, with a combined GDP of over $3 trillion and trade of over $1.5 trillion. In addition, China has agreed to "early harvest" measures, which are widely perceived to provide some Southeast Asian products with earlier and easier access to the Chinese market. The actual value of Sino-ASEAN trade is exaggerated because between one-third and one-half of this trade is "processing" trade, particularly subject to multiple counting as components of networked producers cross borders several times until the final product is exported. Nonetheless, most experts believe that trade statistics will show that technically the value of this trade surpassed ASEAN-U.S. trade in 2006.[8]

Southeast Asia also plays a key role in assuaging China's angst about its growing dependence on imported energy to fuel continued economic growth. China now imports 40 percent of its oil and will soon start importing Liquefied Natural Gas (LNG) from Australia and Indonesia. Though Southeast Asia does not have sufficient proven reserves to meet more than a small percentage of China's energy requirements, China's primary energy supply routes from the Middle East and Africa pass through Southeast Asian chokepoints. Since China's energy imports are predicted to continue their rapid growth, energy is likely to assume an increasingly prominent role in Beijing's diplomacy with its southern neighbors.

As China has become more confident, Beijing has progressively limited the issues on which it seeks the support of Southeast Asian states. Most notable since 2001 has been a moderation of China's anti-American message. With improved U.S.-Chinese bilateral ties, Beijing has taken few discernible steps since 2002 that can be portrayed to have had a direct impact on U.S. interests in Southeast Asia. While Southeast Asian officials usually agree that no change has taken place in the "balance of power" between the United States and China in Southeast Asia, many now argue that the "balance of influence" among China, Japan, India, and the United States is shifting to China's advantage.[9]

If the key components in this "balance of influence" are diplomacy and economics, Beijing is on a roll. It cannot compete with the United States in terms of traditional military power in Southeast Asia and has not sought to do so, but China has, with considerable success, sought to change the nature and rules of the game to emphasize its strengths and to redefine the meaning of the term "security." Moreover, China is incrementally replacing Japan as the most influential Asian state in Southeast Asia. Thus, China is stabilizing its periphery, forging economic ties that contribute to its own economic growth and modernization, and reassuring its Southeast Asian neighbors. As it increases its relative influence in Southeast Asia, Beijing is also securing China's territorial integrity, primarily by isolating Taiwan.

SECURING CHINA'S TERRITORIAL INTEGRITY[10]

Taiwan

In the 1990s, Taiwan had great hopes in Southeast Asia.[11] Substantial Taiwanese investment in Southeast Asia complemented a pragmatic "Go South" diplomatic campaign. In 1989 Taiwanese President Lee Teng-hui launched his "informal diplomacy" with a visit to Singapore, and by 1995 Taiwan had established offices throughout Southeast Asia. Throughout the decade Taiwan conducted a campaign of informal visits by its President and other officials and received some, albeit fewer, reciprocal visits by Southeast Asian leaders. In mid-1999, Taiwanese investment in the region may have reached nearly $40 billion.[12]

In the wake of the spreading Asian Financial Crisis of 1997, Taipei saw a golden chance to enhance its Southeast Asian connections and reacted quickly. The idea was to entice Southeast Asian leaders from the affected countries with a rapid injection of aid from Taiwanese entrepreneurs connected to the ruling Nationalist Party. Taiwanese leaders met with their Indonesian, Malaysian, Singaporean, and Filipino counterparts. Beijing realized that a harsh reaction could be counterproductive and refrained from criticism of Southeast Asian leaders. More dramatically, Beijing stepped forward to assist Thailand and Indonesia. Down south in Southeast Asia, it has been downhill for Taiwan ever since.

Now Taiwan is in trouble in Southeast Asia, for several reasons. Since 1998 Chinese policymakers have slowly turned the screws on Southeast Asian states to sever their remaining political links to Taiwan. Southeast Asia's ethnic Chinese minorities have turned from Taiwan to China (and Hong Kong) as their primary source for Chinese cultural, educational, and economic links. Taiwanese companies retain large investments in Southeast Asia, but new investments in the region have declined as Taiwanese investment has flowed increasingly across the Taiwan Strait to the Chinese mainland.[13]

In 2000, Taiwan elected Chen Shui-bian, whose party platform espoused movement toward Taiwanese independence. This cut many of the old, informal links between senior Southeast Asian officials and their Taiwanese counterparts. Southeast Asian leaders have rebuked President Chen for his statements and initiatives that have challenged the status quo between Beijing and Taipei, and in March 2004 the ASEAN Foreign Ministers collectively warned Taiwan to avoid a referendum on independence.[14] The difference between the 1996 confrontation between China and Taiwan discussed earlier and 2006 is not that ASEAN states would now chant Beijing's "One China" slogan more loudly. Rather, it is that private sympathy for Taiwan in Southeast Asia has largely dried up. As one Southeast Asian academic recently said, in a crisis involving Beijing and Taipei, Taiwan will be blamed.[15]

Moreover, as Southeast Asian trade with China zoomed past its trade with Taiwan ($45 billion compared to $15 billion by 2001) and as China became more influential in Southeast Asia, Chinese officials became increasingly firm regarding Taiwan.[16] By the start of the new century, Beijing was in a position to block all visits by Taiwan's President to Southeast Asia and no head of state or government in Southeast Asia visited Taiwan. Moreover, Southeast Asian leaders and officials were increasingly reluctant to meet with their lower ranking Taiwanese counterparts. During Taiwanese Vice President Annette Lu's (Lu Hsiu Lien) alleged "vacation" in 2002 in Indonesia, an embarrassed Jakarta issued a statement that she had not visited in her "supposed capacity" as vice president of an "entity" known as the "Republic of China."[17] In January 2003, just before a senior Chinese official arrived in Bangkok, Thailand scrambled to withdraw the visas it had issued to Taiwanese legislators led by the vice president of Taiwan's parliament.[18] One recent exception to the virtual embargo on visits by Southeast Asian cabinet members to Taiwan was when the Indonesian Minister of Manpower and Transmigration Fahmi Idris traveled to Taipei in May 2005 for talks with his Taiwan counterpart, Chen Chu, on Taiwan's practice of bringing Indonesian laborers to the island.[19] The most dramatic intervention by Beijing involved a visit to Taiwan by Singapore's Prime Minister-designate, who is also the son of former Prime Minister Lee Kuan Yew, in June 2004. The precise reasons for Beijing's "explosion of anger" have since been hotly debated in the region, but China's reaction was unprecedented. It publicly cancelled several planned visits by Chinese officials and negotiations for a China–Singapore Free Trade Agreement.[20]

In addition to continued pressure to deepen the virtual embargo on contacts between Taiwanese officials and Southeast Asians, Beijing may again seek to convince Singapore to abrogate its arrangement with Taiwan that permits the Singaporean Armed Forces to conduct division level army training on that island. When Beijing recently raised this issue with Singapore and offered alternative training facilities on Hainan, the offer was politely refused.[21]

INCREASING CHINESE INFLUENCE

Perceptions of China's goals in Southeast Asia are often colored by a larger debate within academic and official communities about whether China's strategy is designed to assert regional dominance in East Asia as a whole. Opinions range widely. Some scholars see the removal of the United States from East Asia as the primary driver in a Chinese grand strategy, while others argue that Chinese leaders have come to appreciate the traditional U.S. role in East Asia as contributing to China's peaceful rise through economic growth and interdependence. Still others argue that, "continued anti-U.S. tendencies in Chinese policy . . . are currently held in check by circumstances, especially the predominance of U.S. power and influence in Asia . . . China's strategy is contingent, and U.S. power and policies play a large role in determining Chinese policy in the region."[22] In support of the argument that China's strategy is contingent, tactical, and based on a cost-benefit analysis, this school acknowledges that U.S.-Chinese relations are better than they have been since the end of the cold war and notes the "abrupt falloff in mid-2001 of the wide-ranging and often very harsh public Chinese criticism of U.S. policy that prevailed throughout the previous decade."[23] Nonetheless, proponents of this analysis question the belief that China's views of the United States have undergone a fundamental shift. In support of this cautious appraisal, they cite deeply rooted suspicions of the United States, efforts to weaken American influence around China's periphery, nationalism and "anti-American conditioning," and China's opposition to U.S. policy, particularly with regard to Taiwan.

Some American (and Singaporean) analysts and officials have extrapolated from a presumed "strategic competition" between the United States and China in Asia to suggest that this competition extends to Southeast Asia. Whether or not one believes that such competition exists, or that competition is either inevitable or contingent, any assessment of Chinese-U.S. competition in Southeast Asia must factor in the reactions of Southeast Asian states when calculating costs and benefits for China and the United States. Although the reaction to China's rising influence varies widely in Southeast Asia, all these states seek to avoid participation in competition or conflict between Beijing and Washington. Although the influence that Southeast Asian states can bring to bear on Chinese and American decision making is limited, these states are actors in their own right. Their antipathy to the importation of Chinese-American competition suggests that, whether or not China's current approach is primarily tactical, China has good reasons to avoid direct conflict with the United States in Southeast Asia.[24]

Despite Beijing's sensitivity to Southeast Asian preferences, an argument has been made that since 2001 Beijing has continued trying to increase Chinese influence in Southeast Asia at America's expense, albeit more subtly than before. This effort apparently has continued despite the fact that the American-Chinese relationship is now often referred to as a "strategic partnership."[25] Nonetheless, tensions remain over trade imbalances, currency revaluation, intellectual property rights, and several other bilateral issues, including China's continued military buildup. However, U.S.-Chinese bilateral economic issues and U.S. concerns about China's growing military capabilities, which are primarily directed at Taiwan, have not spilled over into Southeast Asia. In fact, whether China's intentions with regard to the United States are ultimately malign or benign, there is scant evidence that China and the United States now compete directly with each other in Southeast Asia. Instead, China, Japan, India, and the United States pursue their different interests in Southeast Asia, at one time competing and another cooperating, in a complex dance that seldom brings the United States and China face to face.

India

India is seeking an expanded role in Southeast Asia. New Delhi's "Look East" policy, driven in part by its balance of payments crisis of 1991, attempts to mirror China's successful effort to woo Southeast Asia with fewer resources and comparatively anemic trade ties. This policy has several objectives: to provide a diplomatic alternative to China, to tap into Southeast Asia's dynamic economic growth, to secure energy supplies, and to build ties as India extends its naval power in the Indian Ocean.

In economic terms, India has a long way to go before it catches up with China in Southeast Asia. Nonetheless, despite decrepit infrastructure and continued protectionism at home, India's trade with Southeast Asia is growing by as much as 30 percent annually. Still, India's trade with Southeast Asia is only 15 percent of China's. Nonetheless, taping into the Indian Diaspora, New Delhi has built trade ties with Singapore and Malaysia. It is also looking to build links between India's unstable northeast and Myanmar and Thailand.

Myanmar is a special case for India. New Delhi made a conscious decision a decade ago to modify its antipathy to the Myanmar's military regime to check Chinese influence. In addition, New Delhi wants Myanmar to deny refuge to insurgents who flee across the common border. India has also kept an eye fixed on Myanmar's natural gas.

India scrambles to match China as an avid participant in Asia's expanding network of multilateral organizations and commercial free trade agreements. It will not cede these links to China. In 2001, Singapore persuaded ASEAN to hold an ASEAN+1 summit with India. New Delhi has also signed ASEAN's Treaty of Amity and Cooperation (TAC), and pushed a framework for a free trade zone by 2013.

The rapid warming of Indian-U.S. relations has led to speculation that the developing Indian-U.S. strategic partnership might encourage India to become a counterweight to China in Southeast Asia. But New Delhi is pursuing its own goals for its own purposes, which do not always mesh with Washington's.

Thus far, Beijing has adopted a relaxed response to the Look East policy, though it opposed India's participation in the first East Asian Summit (EAS). China does not appear to view India as an impediment to the implementation of its strategy in Southeast Asia and, in fact, India is the least influential of the four major powers that pursue their national goals in the region.[26]

Japan

In the first years of the twenty-first century, Sino-Japanese rivalry has been riveted on direct bilateral issues—the Yasukuni Shrine and other historical disputes—and northeast Asia.[27] Within Japan, elites debate how to adjust to China's growing wealth and power.[28] Meanwhile, Beijing's campaign to woo Southeast Asia caught Tokyo flatfooted. Ambivalent and burdened with a glacial decision-making process, Japan has allowed such traditional issues as trade, investment, and aid to continue to dominate Japanese-Southeast Asian bilateral issues. However, it has simultaneously paid Beijing the ultimate diplomatic compliment by attempting to play catch-up with China in regional multilateral organizations and in proposing free trade areas. The contest in Southeast Asia pits Japan's massive economic stake against China's comprehensive campaign to increase its influence in the region.[29] The links between the overall Sino-Japanese rivalry for leadership in East Asia and the competition now underway in Southeast Asia are not always direct, but China is gradually replacing Japan as the most influential external Asian regional power in Southeast Asia.

In 1977, Japanese Prime Minister Fukuda arrived in Southeast Asia with $1 billion in gifts and promises of substantial official development assistance (ODA). By the late 1980s, officials and pundits alike talked and wrote of Southeast Asia as part of a new Japanese "co-prosperity sphere." Japan was also compared to a "leading goose" in the region's "flying geese" pattern of development as it provided capital and technology while it shed labor-intensive industries to Southeast Asia. Moreover, Japan played a major role in the reconstruction of war-torn Cambodia, using its clout to broker a peace agreement between competing Cambodian factions in 1997. In addition, it often distanced itself from Washington on the efficacy of multilateral institutions and on sanctions against Myanmar, while it cautiously expanded the role of the Japanese Self-Defense Forces in peacekeeping operations.[30] But initiatives that were touted in Tokyo often received a blasé reception in Southeast Asia, particularly after Japanese economic growth stalled. Moreover, Tokyo's reaction to the 1997 Asian Financial Crisis shredded Japan's remaining credentials as a leader of and model for Asian development.[31]

As the Japanese economy sputtered at home, Japan's prestige in Southeast Asia waned. Nonetheless, its economic footprint in Southeast Asia remains impressive. Though its official development assistance has declined by a third since 1995, Japan's cumulative ODA to the region totals more that $20 billion and it continues to be the region's major aid donor.[32] Japan and the United States remain the largest investors and trade partners.[33] Tokyo has played a leadership role on currency swap agreements (Chiang Mai Initiative) and an Asian bond market initiative. However, Japanese aid, trade, and investment, adjusted for inflation, are static or in decline.[34] Moreover, there is little evidence that the investments and trade by Japanese companies have left a lasting positive legacy, or that Japan's cultural influence extends much beyond the appeal of its commercial products. The key constraint on Japan's influence in Southeast Asia, however, has often been Tokyo's reluctance to leverage its economic clout to promote other interests.

In the new century, Japan has presented to Southeast Asia the uninspiring picture of a country usually trailing in China's wake. In 2000, Beijing proposed a comprehensive China-ASEAN Free Trade Agreement (CAFTA); Tokyo responded hesitantly by floating the idea of bilateral free trade arrangements, renamed economic partnership agreements (EPAs), that would exclude Southeast Asian agricultural products. China's President and Premier often toured Southeast Asia. In 2002, Japan's Prime Minister Koizumi responded through visits to the Philippines, Thailand, Singapore, Malaysia, and Indonesia. But he traveled empty-handed, constrained by Tokyo's decision to cut aid and the Japanese agricultural lobby's fierce opposition to arrangements that would pry open Japan's protected agricultural market.[35] In 2003, China signed ASEAN's Treaty of Amity and Cooperation; Japan followed suit a year later. As of 2006, Tokyo's "diplomacy by EPA" also includes a proposal for a wider free trade zone, but this commercial diplomacy appears to have become a substitute for policy coordination at home. Few Southeast Asians are impressed.

Japan's economic diplomacy leaves Tokyo with remarkably little ability to influence Southeast Asian governments' foreign or domestic policies. For example, 80 percent of Japan's energy imports flow through Southeast Asian straits. However, for several years Southeast Asian governments have routinely deflected Japanese efforts, including those by a succession of Japanese prime ministers, to press for improved antipiracy efforts to protect shipping passing through Southeast Asian waters. Only now, almost six years after Japan launched its initiative for a Regional Cooperation Agreement on Combating Piracy and Armed Robbery Against Ships in Asia (ReCAAP) has the agreement come into force, which has led in turn to the establishment of a piracy information center located in Singapore.

The Japanese also face other challenges to their influence. Tokyo's assistance in the wake of the Indian Ocean tsunami that devastated parts of Southeast Asia in December 2004 was generous, and several times that of China. It was appreciated if scarcely noticed in the region.[36] Even more striking has been Tokyo's inability to profit politically from its multibillion dollars in aid for the development of the Mekong River basin, which has primarily benefited China. In the summer of 2005, as China voiced opposition to Tokyo's efforts to secure a permanent seat on the United Nations Security Council, Tokyo turned to Southeast Asia to drum up diplomatic support. The Japanese Foreign Ministry was "shocked to learn they have almost no friends in Southeast Asia."[37] Indeed, in the past six years, Japan's lone clear political success in Southeast Asia has been in working with Singapore and Indonesia to expand the list of invitees to the Malaysian-hosted EAS in December 2005 to include Australia, New Zealand, and India, over China's and Malaysia's objections.

In sum, most Southeast Asians welcome Japan's transition to a "normal country" and its potential to serve as a counterweight to China,[38] as long as Japan's role in the region is not cast in anti-Chinese terms. But as one Southeast Asian official put it, "The Japanese have done practically nothing right since 1995. The Japanese don't know what they want. They have no consensus on what their role is."[39]

United States

Although relations between the United States and China were normalized during President Nixon's second administration, tension and détente have alternated as the dominant themes in U.S.–China relations for another thirty years. The ebb and flow of bilateral relations was occasionally reflected in Southeast Asia, though each power often pursued its own interests in the region with little regard for the overarching Sino-U.S. relationship. But 2001 was a pivotal year in both U.S.–China relations and Southeast Asia's ties to the major powers. After a Chinese F-8 fighter confronted and collided with a U.S. EP-3 patrol plane in mid-air off the coast of China's Hainan island in April 2001, it looked as if Sino-U.S. strategic rivalry might become a dominant theme in Southeast Asia. But the September 11, 2001 terrorist attacks on the United States and the subsequent discovery of terrorist networks in Southeast Asia brought renewed U.S. attention to the region not to compete with China, but to combat terrorism. At the same time, Beijing sought to mend relations with Washington, and in Southeast Asia to avoid direct competition, much less conflict, with the United States. Since 2001, China has consistently downplayed its opposition to the American presence in Southeast Asia.

As Sino-U.S. tension has faded, human rights issues have become the most prominent source of contention in Sino-U.S. relations in Southeast Asia. In 1989, Beijing supported a brutal crackdown against pro-democracy forces by Myanmar's repressive military regime. Since then, it has supported that regime's resistance to external pressures for recognition of the results of democratic elections won by opposition leader Aung San Suu Ki and for the restoration of minimal human rights. Beijing's support for this repression has been based on China's traditional opposition to interference in another state's internal affairs. It also widely believed to have encouraged the Cambodian Hun Sen regime's tactics to postpone the establishment of an international court to try Khmer Rouge leaders, whom China supported in the 1970s and 1980s, for crimes against humanity. These actions continue to compromise efforts by the United States to promote human rights in these Southeast Asian countries. If human rights in Cambodia and Myanmar, where U.S. economic and security concerns are minimal, are at the forefront of America's purpose throughout Southeast Asia, then a case can be made that Beijing's Southeast Asian policy is clearly anti-American.[40]

A noted American scholar has provided a list of additional Chinese actions since 2001 that have demonstrated its "continued sensitivity regarding U.S. military deployments and leadership in Southeast Asia." These include[41]:

- Tried in vain to use an arrangement with ASEAN over the South China Sea to regulate U.S. exercises in the area.
- Voiced sharp criticism of U.S. policy in Iraq.
- Competed with U.S., Japanese, and other free trade arrangements in the region.
- Voiced concern over reported U.S. interest in military access to Vietnam.
- Cast a critical eye on U.S. military deployments in the Philippines and U.S.-backed efforts to encourage Japanese military actions in Southeast Asia.

Examined carefully, however, these actions are not impressive indicators of China's opposition to America's continued presence and traditional roles in Southeast Asia.

China's most recent overtly anti-American action was made during Chinese-Southeast Asian negotiations on a "Code of Conduct" for the South China Sea in 2002. Beijing raised the possibility of regulating military exercises, including those involving the United States, in the waters to be covered by the Code of Conduct. However, it also quickly deferred to ASEAN opposition to this proposal.

China has indeed voiced criticism of U.S. policy in Iraq, but China's criticism has been mild compared to that of several Southeast Asian states. Muslims constitute almost half the region's population and have, on the whole, been vehemently opposed to the U.S. invasion of Iraq and subsequent American counterinsurgency operations in that country. This public antipathy to America's actions in Iraq has, in fact, severely complicated efforts by several Southeast Asian states to cooperate with the United States against international terrorism in Southeast Asia.[42] Even America's treaty allies, the Philippines and Thailand, have withdrawn their token forces from Iraq.

Southeast Asians have welcomed Beijing's proposed CAFTA, and have contrasted Beijing's eagerness to accommodate Southeast Asian concerns with the United States' reluctance to negotiate free trade agreements with ASEAN or with any Southeast Asian countries other than its three wealthiest states. Moreover, U.S. negotiations require more intrusive economic reforms in the Southeast Asian country affected than the CAFTA. Thus far, the United States has concluded a free trade agreement with Singapore. Its difficult negotiations with Thailand have yet to produce such an agreement, and proposed negotiations with Malaysia are likely to prove contentious. No evidence has come to light that Beijing has sought to interfere with or complicate U.S. free trade negotiations with individual Southeast Asian states.[43]

China has expressed concern over U.S. interest in military access to Vietnam in the past, but Hanoi has now also welcomed American ship visits to Vietnamese ports. Vietnam also recently agreed to participate in the U.S. International Military Education and Training Program (IMET), without eliciting public comment from China. Hanoi would probably not have agreed to these measures if China had strenuously objected in private.

China's criticism of U.S. military deployments in the Philippines pre-date the post-9/11 "global war on terror," which has in fact brought the United States and China together in opposition to international terrorism. The post-9/11 deployment of American military forces to assist the Armed Forces of the Philippines (AFP) in defeating the Abu Sayyaf Group (ASG) terrorists in the southern Philippines appears to have provoked little public comment by China.[44]

Turning from the list of China's actions that demonstrate its sensitivities, it is important to note that Beijing has been supportive of U.S. counterterrorism policies in the region as a whole. Moreover, despite China's growing dependence on energy imported through Southeast Asian maritime chokepoints, Beijing has carefully modulated its response to the U.S. Regional Maritime Security Initiative (RMSI), announced in 2004 as a plan to help littoral Southeast Asian countries counter piracy and potential maritime terrorism in the Strait of Malacca.[45] In addition, "even as the United States consolidated defense cooperation with Japan, Singapore, and the Philippines and expanded its naval and air presence throughout the region, China has offered only minimal opposition."[46] China did send only lower-level functionaries to a conference usually attended by the U.S. Secretary of Defense in Singapore, but Taiwan's presence was the primary reason for Beijing's stance. China has advanced a proposal for ASEAN-wide security and defense cooperation, which ASEAN turned down, agreeing only to an inaugural defense ministerial meeting.[47]

Another American scholar has written that "China has become an important provider of security assistance, and the presence of its military far from home is becoming commonplace. If Beijing has its way and Washington continues to neglect Southeast Asia, American military and security guarantees will soon be redundant to the Chinese presence."[48] There is, however, little basis for that claim. In fact, Chinese naval deployments to the region have not increased over the past six years and its new security assistance relationships with Malaysia, the Philippines, and Indonesia are unimpressive when examined in detail.[49] Neither is there evidence that these first steps toward adding a security component to China's bilateral relationships in maritime Southeast Asia are directed at the United States.

Turning from China's alleged anti-American actions in the "security" arena to "diplomacy," China has become increasingly active in an expanding list of Asia-only multilateral organizations that exclude the United States. This trend culminated in the December 2005 "East Asia Summit" in Malaysia. But ASEAN countries, not China, set the terms for participation in this summit (which the United States declined to meet), and the Summit, in the end, did not meet Beijing's initially high expectations. Beijing, which had hoped to host the 2006 summit, had to bow to ASEAN's decision to host future summits in ASEAN countries.[50]

It is also possible that China's rising influence in the region encourages a perception—particularly among those Southeast Asian leaders who continue to assume Sino-U.S. strategic rivalry—that they can leverage Beijing against Washington. If so, this could potentially increase the costs to Washington of securing Southeast Asian elites' support for specific American policies. There is, however, little evidence that Washington feels pressured to compete with China in Southeast Asia. For example, there is no discernible China "factor" or "angle" in the economic and other assistance that the United States has provided to several Southeast Asian states since 9/11, primarily to facilitate their cooperation in the American-led campaign against international terrorism.

In conclusion, Beijing may have gained influence in Southeast Asia but there is scarce evidence to support the contention that China's leaders or officials have sought to deepen Chinese influence in Southeast Asia at the expense of the United States in the past five years.[51]

SUMMARY

Beijing's current strategic goals in Southeast Asia are to maintain a stable environment on its periphery, to assure others that China is not a threat, and to encourage economic ties that contribute to China's economic modernization and thus regime stability. The foreign policy instruments that Beijing has employed to secure its goals are consistent throughout most of Southeast Asia, but the priorities assigned to these different strategic goals vary depending on China's interests in different parts of the region. China is also seeking support for its territorial integrity and to increase its influence more broadly among its Southeast Asian neighbors. Although Beijing has asked little from Southeast Asians in response to its campaign to court them, it has successfully sought to accelerate the decline of Taiwan's political profile in the region. In an era of improving U.S.-Chinese relations, Beijing has been careful to avoid direct conflict with Washington. Chinese-Japanese rivalry has spilled over into Southeast Asia.

In Washington, some officials have recently claimed that China is "eating America's lunch in Southeast Asia." This Americanism misses the mark. China has now joined the United States and Japan, and often India, at the head table for countries external to the region. But if China is nibbling anyone else's lunch, it is nibbling sushi, not steak. Moreover, in Southeast Asia Beijing is focused on its primary goals—a stable periphery and economic development—rather than strategic competition with other outsiders.

CHAPTER 2

How to Think About China and Southeast Asia

Southeast Asia is often viewed through glasses that seem to help us see a bit better. Actually, glasses can also distort reality if the prescription is not quite right. Acting much like glasses are preconceived notions of the region, and of the role of external powers in Southeast Asia. These notions are often based on assumptions embedded in international relations schools of thought that seek to predict the behavior of states.[1] For example, old cold warriors and traditional power-oriented "realists" tend to assume that China's "rise" is leading to a transition of power in which Southeast Asian states will be compelled to choose between the rising regional challenger and the current dominant world power. A second assumption is that most countries will eventually align with the United States as the only state with sufficient power to "balance" China. These assumptions would have greater validity if China posed a military threat to the stability or sovereignty of Southeast Asia states, as it was once often perceived to do. But even in that case, not all Southeast Asian states would seek to align with the United States. Instead, the two basic, underlying subsystems in Southeast Asia, on the mainland of Southeast Asia and in maritime Southeast Asia, would emerge from the shadows.

A second factor that contributes to the tendency to view Chinese-U.S. "power" in the region in zero-sum terms is the attempt to simplify reality by portraying Southeast Asia as one state, often referred to as ASEAN, over which external powers compete. This misunderstanding of the nature and role of a regional organization, the Association of Southeast Asian Nations (ASEAN), is reinforced by Southeast Asians' own genuflection to the claim that ASEAN forms a united community. ASEAN, however, is a regional organization designed primarily to reinforce the individual sovereignty of each of ASEAN's ten member states.

Moreover, the asymmetry in the instruments of power and influence that China and the United States bring to the table dampens potential rivalry between these two countries in the region. China, for example, has no ability to challenge U.S. naval power in Southeast Asian waters, while the United States has little ability to compete with China's allure as the assumed next great economic opportunity for many Southeast Asian businesses. Southeast Asian elites have, moreover, often been adept in disaggregating the various components of Chinese, American, Japanese, and Indian power, and responding to the different external powers' specific strengths.

Recognizing that the "realists" school of thought fails to explain current reality on the ground, some Southeast Asian scholars and government leaders have turned to attempts to distinguish between "power" and "influence."[2] Thus one Singaporean scholar writes that "while the current distribution of hard power in favor of the United States will not change for some time, more fluid and challenging is the shifting 'balance of influence' within Southeast Asia with the steady development of China's multilayered relationships with the region."[3] This is useful, though the problem is distinguishing between power and influence. However, whether subjected to either the power or the influence of either China or the United States, most states in Southeast Asia do not believe they are faced with the stark choice of either balancing against or aligning with one of these external states. Instead, there is an emerging consensus that many, if not all, countries are able to engage China while also encouraging other external powers to remain involved in the region.

The term most often used to describe Southeast Asian states' reactions to the rise of China is "hedging." But "hedging" is a broad concept. In Southeast Asia the idea is that it consists of persuading the United States to act as potential counterweight to China, while engaging China to "socialize" it in regional norms, and generally trying to enmesh all external powers to give them a stake in the system. In theory, this layering differentiates hedging from simple neutrality, but "hedging" requires a complicated, dynamic set of policies, which may not always be understood or recognized by other states. Moreover, "hedging" theory assumes a level of foreign policy sophistication and coordination that does not exist in all Southeast Asian states, where elites are focused on regime stability and on economic growth as a contributor to that stability.

If "hedging" is so broad as to provide only a general framework for understanding Southeast Asian reactions to China's rise, perhaps a particularly Asian model offers an additional intellectual framework. One model is based on the argument that East Asia historically exhibits a system of hierarchy, where China receives deference in exchange for providing legitimacy for a regime and guaranteeing autonomy for another East Asian state. This idea harks back to the precolonial "tribute system." However, the Chinese tribute system mainly involved mainland, not maritime, Southeast Asian kingdoms, and even then in a spasmodic fashion. Moreover, modern ideas of nationalism and state sovereignty would seem to make this system antiquated. A more useful idea may be that of "asymmetry," largely based on the Chinese-Vietnamese relationship, which, in part, stresses the larger states' responsibility to reassure the smaller.

In addition, some Southeast Asian leaders, journalists, and academics implicitly reject traditional calculations of "power" in the hands of states, turning instead to a vague concept of "soft power." The term "soft power," originally conceived of to include the appeal of American political values, is also often conflated with "influence." It is used in Asia in a wide variety of ways, ranging from shorthand for all aspects of life but military power to more narrowly defined concepts such as the appeal of a particular culture.

It means so many different things to so many different people, that it has little explanatory value. If the concept is to contribute to understanding China's relationships with Southeast Asia, we will need to modify its formulation by its primary intellectual advocate to fit Southeast Asian perceptions of "soft power," and to explain how the individual components of "soft power" increase China's influence with specific constituencies in Southeast Asia.

Finally, political economists might argue that the comparatively small size of Southeast Asian economies determines that they will inevitably be integrated into the larger Chinese economy. The rapid growth in Chinese-Southeast Asian trade in recent years would appear to provide support for this view. But this argument would make more sense if the Chinese economy were the only alternative for Southeast Asians, or at least dominant. In fact, China is only one of four major trade partners and a comparatively minor source of foreign direct investment (FDI) in Southeast Asia. Neither does China's reemergence in Southeast Asia yet provide much support for economic interdependence theorists, who argue that economic links create an interest in stable, cooperative political relations and increase the opportunity cost of conflict. They may do so, but extraordinary growth in Chinese-Southeast Asian trade mostly followed—it did not precede—political accommodation facilitated by an intense Chinese diplomatic campaign to woo Southeast Asian states.

There is no one answer. Moreover, instead of only looking deductively from various "schools of thought," it might also be useful to examine China's contribution to meeting Southeast Asian priorities. To help us better understand China's rise in Southeast Asia, an assessment of how China's policies have contributed to regime maintenance in Southeast Asia may be as illuminating as ideas about how states exert power and influence. This chapter will take a closer look at the prescriptions we have mentioned above, and touch on the Southeast Asian concept of "comprehensive security."

THE LIMITATIONS OF "REALISM"

Southeast Asia has been a site of great power competition, due to its natural resources and strategic location. Japan launched its surprise attack on Pearl Harbor in 1941 in an attempt to neutralize American power, the only effective constraint on achieving its primary goal in World War II—to secure the resources of Southeast Asia. Until 1975, the United States invested tens of thousands of lives and hundreds of billions of dollars in an effort in Vietnam that was justified, at least in part, as resisting Chinese Communist domination of Southeast Asia. However, thirty years have now passed and no state is threatening to use military force to change the status quo in Southeast Asia. Neither China's nor the United States' future intentions in the region are predictable. A decade or two from now, should China both build the military capabilities to challenge American military, primarily naval, dominance and demonstrate an intention to do so in Southeast Asia, "realism" may appear to have greater explanatory power. Should the United States cast China as its strategic opponent in a new cold war, and undertake a concerted campaign to "contain" China throughout Southeast Asia, particularly by expanding military ties to and "bases" in Southeast Asian states, "realists" may also look back on the 1990s and first half decade of the twenty-first century as an interregnum.

In the meantime, "realism," which assumes that relative "power" determines relationships between states, is of little explanatory value in Southeast Asia. Realists differ as to what determines secondary states responses to rising great powers, but basically realism assumes that the military power is determinant. The strong dominate the weak and weaker states will seek to balance the threat of domination by forming alliances. With the rise of China's power, the countries of Southeast Asia should have moved to balance China by allying with third countries. ASEAN should have emerged strengthened, with a new security component, and ties with the United States should have been strengthened. Alternatively, some Southeast Asian states could have decided to submit to Chinese domination and "bandwagon" with Beijing. China should have discouraged regional cohesion and penalized balancing, while the United States should have encouraged both.[4] But as Womack has pointed out, none of these predicted outcomes have taken place. Instead, as China's and Southeast Asia's relative "power" in terms of military capabilities and the size of their economies shifted in China's favor throughout the 1990s and early twenty-first century, both Beijing's relations with Southeast Asian states and its influence and reputation with Southeast Asian populations improved.

A STABLE BALANCE OF POWER

In a variant on the realist school, Robert Ross in his 1999 article, "The Geography of Peace," postulates that a bipolar regional power balance has emerged in East Asia.[5] This balance is also premised on the assumption that smaller Asian states will seek to compensate for their own vulnerability by aligning with either China or the United States.[6] Ross contends that China is the dominant land power while the United States is the primary maritime power in the Asia-Pacific region. These two countries are the only regional actors that possess sufficient material and nonmaterial means to project power. He concludes that, "Simply put: the United States and China are destined to be great power competitors."[7] However, although the Sino-U.S. relationship is competitive, the complementary geopolitical strengths of the two countries simultaneously prevent them from forcefully interfering in one another's respective sphere of influence. In short, the geographic positions of China and the United States, and the evolution of their interests and military capabilities accordingly, make it unlikely that either country would seek to project "power" into the other's respective sphere.

Ross therefore postulates that the emerging bipolar structure is potentially stable and enduring. He also notes that the "US strategic interest in a divided East Asia does not require a US military presence on the East Asian mainland."[8] Washington has accordingly turned to consolidating its maritime presence in East Asia, including with such U.S. "security partners" in Southeast Asia as the Philippines and Singapore, under the current Bush administration.[9]

A variant on Ross's conclusions as they apply to Southeast Asia argues that although Southeast Asian states seek a closer relationship with the great power they perceive to be geopolitically dominant at a given time, they do not actually align with that power. According to Shannon Tow, they instead seek to maximize their maneuverability and hedge against what they view as regional domination by any one state. Tow claims that:

> They will adopt this policy approach, however, only so long as they believe that the Sino-U.S. relationship affords them sufficient leverage and strategic latitude to do so . . . Geographic proximity informs Southeast Asian states' foreign policy behavior more than the "hedging" theorists suggest, but its relative influence on such behavior is contingent on their ongoing perceptions of the Sino-U.S. relationship.[10]

Tow's approach may better reflect Southeast Asian reality, but when does the perception that "the Sino-U.S. relationship affords them sufficient leverage and strategic latitude" apply and how does this perception interact with domestic political constraints and opportunities? Moreover, the examples used to buttress the argument are the 1998 addendum to the U.S.-Singapore Memorandum of Understanding, the 1999 U.S.-Philippines Visiting Forces Agreement, and the 1999 Sino-Thai Plan of Action for the twenty-first century, all of which predate improved Sino-U.S. relations. The author concludes that the relevant Southeast Asian countries "alluded to geopolitical dominance as a principal factor in their decisions to forge agreements with the great powers," but also that "Washington and Beijing will confront difficulties in cultivating decisive influence among these countries because of the leverage the ASEAN states derive from competitive Sino-U.S. relations."[11] But in the absence of competitive Sino-U.S. relations, how central is geopolitics to Southeast Asian states' security calculations? Do balance of power theorists place undue emphasis on military power?

There is no doubt that China exerts more influence in most of mainland Southeast Asia, much of which shares borders with China, than the United States.

Vietnam is acutely aware of China's presence on its northern borders and of a history of intermittent Chinese armed intervention in Vietnam. In addition, Thailand—a treaty ally of the United States—has accorded Beijing a role as the primary, but by no means exclusive, external influence on its foreign policy decision making under the current Thai administration. However, Beijing's influence in Vietnam is not simply a reflection of geography and disparities in military capabilities. Communist party-to-party ties, as well as an evolving economic relationship, are crucial to understanding the current relationship, as are different perceptions of history in China and Vietnam and a post-1975 history of war and reconciliation. Moreover, Vietnam, more than any other state in Southeast Asia, has historically resisted Chinese domination, despite the disparity in their "power" for more than a thousand years. In addition, as Vuving has pointed out, Hanoi's current policy is the product of a balance of power within the Vietnamese leadership, and thus combines confusing and mutually contradictory elements of "balancing, bandwagoning, and accepting hierarchy." Finally, Hanoi's attempts to reassure Beijing have not eliminated Beijing's suspicions of Hanoi's real intentions.[12]

Myanmar (Burma) has sought to accommodate China since it achieved independence after World War II, but Chinese influence has fluctuated over the past decade and a half due more to domestic political developments in Myanmar than to geography. Chinese influence also exceeds that of the United States in Laos and Cambodia, again a reflection of recent history and the nature of the current leadership of the latter countries, as well as their poverty and the absence of American interest. Thailand, famous for its sensitivity to shifts in the balance of power and its willingness to "shift with the wind" accordingly, will be addressed later in this chapter.

On the other side of the coin, Ross argues that "the Philippines, Indonesia, Singapore, and Malaysia all remain within a stable U.S. military region."[13] However, U.S. influence in maritime Southeast Asia is similarly constrained by domestic political factors. Malaysian Prime Minister Mahathir combined a twenty-year record of strident anti-Western rhetoric with a low-key, largely unacknowledged military-to-military relationship with the United States. This approach, however, had little to do with China or balancing power; rather, it reflected his desire to improve the capabilities of the Malaysian military. Similarly, in 2006 Indonesia and the United States are reknitting traditional military-to-military ties that were originally broken for domestic U.S. political reasons. At the same time, Indonesia and China, albeit from a low base, are forging new economic ties. Since the American invasions of Afghanistan (in response to the 9/11 attacks) and Iraq (to remove Saddam Hussein), the political elites of Indonesia and Malaysia, both predominantly Muslim democracies, must accommodate increasing popular distrust of the United States. Not China's military modernization, but identification with the worldwide Muslim community, now affects their security cooperation with the United States in its global war on terror.

But "realists" would point to Singapore and the Philippines as the prime examples of ASEAN countries "balancing" China by further aligning with the United States. In fact, Ross notes that "since 2001 annual US military assistance to the Philippines increased from $1.9 million to a projected $126 million in 2005."[14] But the increase in U.S. military assistance reflects the fact that President Arroyo quickly jumped on the bandwagon of counterterrorism after 9/11; it does not indicate Manila's participation in some presumed balance of power between the United States and China. Indeed, the United States has declined to be drawn by Filipino suggestions that it might back Philippine claims in the South China Sea in opposition to China. Instead, Washington has stressed improved U.S./Filipino cooperation against terrorists and insurgents within the Philippines.

Singapore would appear to best fit the criteria of the twin dominance of geography and security. In 2001, Singapore constructed a facility designed to accommodate a U.S. aircraft carrier and it has been Washington's closest ally in combating terrorism in the region since 9/11. But Singapore is only secondarily balancing against the potential of Chinese power. Singapore's primary concern has always been its vulnerability as a small, predominantly ethnic-Chinese island in a Malay Muslim sea. Singapore is balancing primarily against its neighbors. Besides, Singapore is the prime exponent of "hedging," not balancing, between the United States and China.

The relevance of "realism" increases with rising military competition between China and the United States and a concomitant increase in threat perceptions in Southeast Asia. This competition has, in fact, declined significantly since the early 2001 incident between a Chinese fighter and a U.S. EP-3 plane off the coast of the Chinese island of Hainan, and even more since the 9/11 al Qaeda terrorist attacks in the United States, which reinjected the United States into Southeast Asia in ways not seen since 1975. China has not, in fact, objected to American military participation in the U.S. counterterrorism campaign in the region, including the dispatch of U.S. military forces, in a "training" role, to the southern Philippines and U.S. efforts to enhance maritime security in the strategic Strait of Malacca. Despite the fact that some realists recognize the division of Southeast Asia into two subsystems, they misunderstand the reasons for this division.

THE ASIAN PARADIGM AND ASYMMETRY

Several authors have begun to suggest that any international relations theory based on Western examples, is fundamentally flawed in its analysis of Chinese-Asian relations.[15] They argue that East Asia historically exhibits a system of hierarchy, in which China requires deference in exchange for guarantees of autonomy for other East Asia states. The idea often harks back to East Asia's precolonial-era tribute system. Under this system certain states in Asia, including in Southeast Asia, sent "tribute" missions to China's court. In return the current ruler in that kingdom would receive the Chinese Emperor's approval, thus strengthening a particular Southeast Asian ruler's claim to legitimacy. However, this "tribute system," which Southeast Asians viewed as primarily a means to conduct profitable trade relations with China, only operated, and then in a spasmodic fashion, with established kingdoms in mainland Southeast Asia and, for a short time, with the a major emporium based on the Strait of Malacca. The latter fell to Portugal 500 years ago. The last time China sought to protect a tributary state with military force, in Vietnam in 1885, France defeated China and its "tributary state." In 2006 Beijing may harbor nostalgia for such unequal relationships, and Myanmar, Thailand, Vietnam, and even Malaysia have occasionally used older brother/younger brother terminology to describe their relationships with China. But the tribute system, though perhaps recalled fondly by some in Beijing, has no resonance in maritime Southeast Asia and little on the mainland. Instead, Southeast Asian states are vehement defenders of individual states' sovereignty and much of China's current influence in Southeast Asia is based precisely on Beijing's unstinting support for that national sovereignty.

A more relevant variant on "hierarchy" is Womack's theory of asymmetry, based primarily on the example of the China-Vietnam relationship. Due to the great disparity between the stronger and weaker states, the weaker side will be more attentive to the relationship than the stronger because proportionally it is it is more exposed to risks and opportunities. Because the relationship has different meanings for the different sides, misperception of the other state is likely. This can lead to vicious circles of misunderstanding, particularly in times of crisis, requiring deft management by both sides. In explaining his theory, Womack writes:

> The larger power, in this case China, has a particular responsibility for leadership because the smaller powers are more at risk and therefore the larger power has their full attention. China has some advantages in its role of regional leadership because of its imperial tradition, its own status as a victim of larger powers, its retreat from revolutionary politics, and its reform-era emphasis on peaceful economic cooperation. As a result, China's increasing prominence in regional trade, investment and tourism is treated by Southeast Asia as a challenge of how to engage China rather than how to protect itself from China.[16]

He argues that China's striking recent success in Southeast Asia has been due primarily to the quality of its diplomatic leadership. As China's reassessment of its interests and goals vis-à-vis Southeast Asia has progressed since the 1980s, Chinese leaders have assiduously cultivated and repeatedly reassured Southeast Asian elites, adjusting even the style of Chinese diplomacy to Southeast Asian norms. Bilateral ties have been supplemented with close attention to Southeast Asians' desire to bolster ASEAN's credibility. This multilayered, sustained diplomatic campaign, sometimes labeled a "charm offensive," has gradually transformed China from a perceived threat to a perceived partner.

"HEDGING"

The application of the theoretical construct called "hedging" has been most thoroughly articulated for Southeast Asia by academics in Singapore. "Hedging" has become the intellectual construct through which some Southeast Asians seek to explain their states' goals and behavior.

> Hedging refers to taking action to ensure against undesirable outcomes, usually by betting on multiple alternative positions. In our case, hedging may be defined as a set of strategies aimed at avoiding (or planning for contingencies in) a situation in which states cannot decide upon more straightforward alternatives such as balancing, bandwagoning, or neutrality. Instead, they cultivate a middle position that forestalls or avoids having to choose one side at the obvious expense of another. The term has been applied to Japanese and Southeast Asian strategies to cope with China—ranging from their efforts to maintain and deepen security ties with the United States to their emphasis on developing

> multilateral institutions as a means to stimulate constructive Chinese participation in regional security issues. Different states—including China—appear to be engaged in hedging behavior toward a variety of ends: against potential Chinese aggression; against a possible American drawdown in the region; but also against an all-out containment policy by Washington vis-a-vis Beijing.[17]

Articulated and practiced most by such states as Singapore, Malaysia, and Thailand, hedging seems to be an ideal, but its relevance for Myanmar , thoroughly dominated by a repressive regime supported by China, or Indonesia, which views itself as the region's natural leader, is questionable.[18] However, Singapore's most articulate academic on hedging, Evelyn Goh, has attempted to probe the nature of the Southeast Asian regional security dynamic by investigating the regional security strategies of three key states: Singapore, Thailand, and Vietnam. Goh investigates each state's perception of the American role in regional security and discusses how each implements its hedging policies against a potential U.S. drawdown in the region, as well as the different degrees to which each uses its relationship with the United States as a hedge against potential Chinese domination. Theoretically, we should be able to identify the nature and breadth of "hedging" by comparing and contrasting the "multipronged hedging strategies" of the three countries that Goh selected as case studies. Particularly elucidating should be a comparison of Vietnam, at heart the Southeast Asian state most acutely aware of the potential Chinese threat to its security, and Thailand, which has maintained the closest strategic relationship with China of any regional state since the late 1970s.

From an examination of these two cases, it appears that the effectiveness of "hedging" as a national security strategy depends on a state's geography, military and economic power, and threat perceptions. The successful "hedger" is a state that is able to establish and maintain close strategic relations with both the United States and China at the same time, and separate the classic security and economic instruments of power. In Goh's words,

> Thailand favors a strong hedging strategy by trying to find a true balance between maintaining its security relations with the United States without jeopardizing its growing political and economic ties with China. Vietnam's security strategy, in contrast, depends heavily on the China variable: it can only afford the weak and long-term hedging plan of rebuilding its national strength by economic development with U.S. help.[19]

Perhaps "hedging" should be viewed as both an offensive and defensive strategy—in Thailand's case, playing off external powers against each other to persuade them to raise their antes for the Southeast Asian state's support and, in Vietnam's case, carefully calculating the costs and benefits of seeking help to balance one dominant external power.

Of all the states in Southeast Asia, Thailand is best known for its long and sophisticated record of appeasing, accommodating, and aligning with major external powers to protect its independence. Now Thailand views "hedging" as a means to maximize the benefits it receives from competing external powers. Goh writes that Thai "officials and analysts are explicit in explaining that the aim of deeper Sino-Thai relations is to persuade the Americans to improve relations with Thailand." Bangkok starts with the proposition that China is not a threat, but the most important engine of growth for Southeast Asian economies now and into the foreseeable future. This assertion dovetails with China's effort over the past fifteen years to present itself in the region as an economic opportunity, rather than a long-term security threat. Although Thailand and China do not share borders, either on land or at sea, and have no territorial disputes that could form the basis for conflict, the two nations have shared a close strategic relationship since the 1970s. Indeed, Thailand has maintained a closer strategic relationship with China than any other Southeast Asian country.

Despite its relationship with China, Thailand has also been careful to maintain the form of a security alliance with the United States, while with equal care it has calculated the minimum requirements necessary to do so. The formal Thai-U.S. alliance relationship, now more than forty years old, boils down to varying levels of intelligence cooperation, joint military exercises, and the occasional dispatch of small contingents of Thai troops to participate in U.S.-led conflicts outside the region. From Bangkok's point of view, it is a way to maintain American engagement in the region, but contains no anti-Chinese component. Thai officials have portrayed it as a "fallback" or "psychological reassurance."[20]

Bangkok's ambivalent response to the post-9/11, American-led war against terrorism reflects the Thai assumption that "the Americans need us" and the tendency to view security issues through a domestic lens that is focused on economic growth. Prime Minister Taksin's well-known declaration of neutrality after 9/11 if Washington went to war in Muslim countries, though subsequently modified following strenuous U.S. efforts to bring Thailand on board in its "global war against terrorism," reflected a threat perception that accorded international terrorism a low priority. Indeed, Thai officials have been at pains to distinguish the Muslim insurgency that exploded in Thailand's southern provinces in 2004, largely due to Bangkok's inattention and subsequently heavy-handed response until former Prime Minister Taksin was deposed in a coup in September 2006, from the larger issue of transnational terrorism. This is because Bangkok sought, under the populist Thaksin government, to refocus on the Thai elite's primary concern, economic growth.

Thus, the Thai continue to raise the Thai financial crisis of 1997, and contrast China's quick offer of aid and pledge not to devalue its currency during what evolved into the Asian Financial Crisis, with America's perceived indifference and support for painful IMF-led reforms. The aim has been to shift the discourse to the economic realm, and to suggest that the United States should seek to "win back Thai trust" by balancing China through economic concessions to Thailand. This would, of course, further diversify the Thai economy while Thailand focuses on its own priority, that is linking itself to the presumed benefits of greater participation in the Chinese market.

Several hundred miles away in Hanoi, "hedging" takes on a different complexion. Vietnam, for good historical reasons, views its neighbor China as a state bent on asserting hegemony. Moreover, the perceived Chinese political/military threat that led to Vietnam's alliance with the Soviet Union two decades ago has now been supplemented by Chinese economic competition. Hanoi has no choice but to assiduously cultivate close ties with Beijing, as it has since the two countries normalized relations in 1991, and enmesh other states when and where possible.

The United States is Vietnam's obvious partner, but for historical and ideological reasons, Vietnamese leaders have deep reservations about creating a close strategic relationship with the United States. They also question the reliability of external powers based on their experience with the Soviet Union. Thus Hanoi will continue to emphasize the economic side of its relations with the United States, while following China's lead in terms of such military-to-military ties as U.S. navy ship visits.

Since the development of a strategic partnership with the United States is blocked for a number of internal and external reasons, Hanoi has placed enormous emphasis on multilateral institutions, particularly ASEAN. In particular, by enmeshing ASEAN in the maritime territorial claims by four ASEAN members and China in the South China Sea, Vietnam hoped to temper China's temptation to assert its claims through force, an approach that appears to have had some success with the 2002 Declaration on the Conduct of Parties in the South China Sea. In addition, Hanoi has sought to construct a low-key strategic relationship with India and encourage Japanese investment and aid. This is defensive hedging, fundamentally different from Thailand's hedging, and aimed primarily at managing a perceived threat from China.

ECONOMICS

According to Goh, "The concept of power in a Southeast Asian context places equal emphasis on hard military might and soft political-economic influence."[21] On the same theme, Sutter states: "The rapid growth of trade and other economic interchanges was the most important indication of Chinese-Southeast Asian cooperation in the post-Cold War period."[22]

Southeast Asians' awe and infatuation with China's booming economy, and their anticipation that China may prove to be the engine for rapid economic growth throughout East Asia, play a major role in explaining China's rising influence in Southeast Asia. But economic ties alone do not explain the transformation of Southeast Asian perceptions of and relations with China. China does not yet possess a sufficiently dominant economy to integrate the comparatively smaller Southeast Asian economies into its own. Even if it did, economic relationships with China hold as much potential for conflict as for cooperation. Even then, as the Japanese model in Southeast Asia has proven, economics alone is insufficient to transform bilateral relationships with Southeast Asian states, Finally, trade is at the heart of China's relationship with maritime Southeast Asia, but is only one factor in its relationships with the states of mainland Southeast Asia.

Although China's gross domestic product (GDP), computed in terms of purchasing power parity (PPP), is more than twice that of all Southeast Asian countries combined, China does not dominate any of the Southeast Asian national economies. These economies recovered from the Asian Financial Crisis of 1997 in part by exporting to the China market,[23] and trade has continued to grow so rapidly that the value of China-Southeast Asia trade is expected to surpass U.S.-Southeast trade in 2006. But trade with China was still only 10 percent of ASEAN's total trade in 2004. In addition, Chinese investment in Southeast Asia is miniscule compared to American and Japanese investments, and Beijing's development assistance (despite substantial loans to some countries) remains smaller than that provided by Washington and Tokyo. In short, Southeast Asian economies have not become primarily suppliers to a dominant Chinese economy.

The Japanese experience in the region may also be instructive. Twenty years ago, many Southeast Asians believed they would be drawn into a new Japanese economic "Co-Prosperity Sphere." Japan was then the dominant outside economic power in Southeast Asia. However, its position declined in the post–cold war period as economic weakness at home drained Japan's influence in Southeast Asia. Moreover, as explained in Chapter 1, Japan has been singularly ineffective, in times of both boom and stagnation, in translating its economic clout into an ability to affect Southeast Asian decision making outside the economic sphere.[24]

The Chinese and most Southeast Asian economies compete directly for markets and FDI. There is some benefit from increasing intra-industry interdependence as both China and the region serve as platforms for the integrated production networks for multinational firms. However, China has emerged as the manufacturing hub, attracting more FDI than Southeast Asia. This has increased worries among Southeast Asian elites that China's low-cost production will flood their domestic markets with cheaper Chinese goods, and that they will gradually become providers of raw resources for China's manufactures. In some sectors, Chinese expansion is already undermining domestic businesses. In addition, in Indonesia, Malaysia, and Thailand, complaints have begun to be heard that jobs are being lost to China. The difficulty of negotiating, and local complaints about implementing, the "early harvest" provisions of the China-ASEAN Free Trade Agreement (CAFTA) do not augur well for smooth integration of Southeast Asian economies into an integrated, Chinese-dominated East Asian economy.

Moreover, economic ties appear to depend in large measure on political conditions in Southeast Asia. There governments, either through government-owned firms or particularly close relations between political and economic elites, play a more important role in economic decision-making than they do, for example, in the United States. Thus, while minority ethnic Chinese Southeast Asian citizens were early investors in China, a review of the history of Chinese bilateral relations in Southeast Asia shows that diplomacy to assuage Southeast Asians' fears paved the way for the accelerating trade relationship. Trade and diplomacy now go hand in hand, but it is not clear that economic ties are yet sufficiently dense for economic considerations to drive political or security decisions.

Although it will need refinement, one idea that might help explain the reasons for China's influence in Southeast Asia is that domestic coalitions commit themselves to "grand strategies" composed of linked domestic and foreign policies. China's "peaceful development" strategy for the region may be particularly appealing to Southeast

Asian elite coalitions because it supports their continued hold on power. In Southeast Asia, most states are now committed to "internationalizing" strategies "which involve the crafting of domestic economic policies that are compatible with global access, including foreign markets, capital, investments, and technology (and) require cooperative (non-violent) policies allowing stable investment environments, appropriate macroeconomic conditions, and the avoidance of detrimental arms races."[25] For these states, participating in China's economic boom supports their "grand strategies."

On the other hand, Beijing supports the status quo in Southeast Asia, whether it is represented by "internationalizing" domestic political coalitions or by their polar opposites, "backlash" coalitions such as in Myanmar. Thus, we still need a concept that relates different types of domestic political coalitions to their receptivity to specific kinds of external support, from traditional security goods to "soft power," from China.

Finally, perhaps as important as the reality of growing economic ties, is anticipation of the benefits to flow from an increasingly dense economic web. In a pattern reminiscent of Southeast Asian's assumptions in the 1980s of their inevitable inclusion in a Japanese-led East Asian economy, many of even the region's most hardheaded businessmen and government leaders have been caught up in the excitement of the China's economic boom, and the assumption that China will be Asia's engine of economic growth in the future. This aspect of economic relations, which might best be termed infatuation, is also an aspect of "soft power."[26]

THE LIMITATIONS OF "SOFT POWER"

What is soft power? Its primary intellectual advocate defines it as "the ability to get what you want through attraction rather than coercion or payments. It arises from the attractiveness of a country's culture, political ideals, and policies."[27] In a section on Asia in one of his books, he provides examples of Asian countries impressive resources for soft power, ranging from "arts, fashion and cuisine" to "rapid economic growth."[28]

One basic problem with soft power is its analytic vagueness. A second question is the content of "soft power" once it has been removed from its original American context? In the original sense in which it was first articulated in the United States, including the enduring appeal of certain political and cultural values, it is ridiculous as an explanation of China's growing influence in the region. Few Southeast Asians find the values of the Chinese Communist Party (CCP) in the least appealing. In the sense of an appeal to similar Asian values and norms, it suffers from the same problems that bedeviled the use of the term "Asian values" by Southeast Asian leaders in the 1990s in their response to American pressure in support of universal human rights.

In short, we need to attempt to outline a Southeast Asia version of "soft power." The term has so many different meanings in Asia that any definition will necessary be subjective and imprecise. However, by "soft power," Southeast Asians usually mean some mixture of economics and norms of state behavior in a regional system, combined with extensive "networking" with implied reciprocal obligations. The emphasis is on style in the conduct of foreign policy. The export of democracy and human rights so prominent in the American idea of "soft power" is a pale shadow in the Southeast Asian version. Moreover, most of the evidence for "soft power" is more anecdotal and impressionistic and less measurable than it would be in developed countries such as the United States. Nonetheless, if we can identify the components of "soft power" in the Chinese-Southeast Asian relationships, perhaps we can get a better handle on this idea. Because this effort is so complicated, "soft power" will be addressed in its own chapter (see Chapter 7).

SUMMARY

No one school of thought captures the complexity of China's relationships with the different Southeast Asian states, which are located in a region where several other countries, including the United States and Japan, provide alternatives to China. However, several different lenses, or schools of thought, do contribute to an understanding of these relationships. Those "realists" who argue that a stable balance of power has emerged in Asia, while they overemphasize military power, recognize the basic division of Southeast Asia into mainland and maritime worlds. Hedging, though vague, provides a guide to Southeast Asian states' efforts to increase their room to maneuver among external actors. The common term "soft power" is analytically useless, but can be helpful if its components are examined within its regional context. Finally, economic, particularly trade, ties are key to explaining Southeast Asia's growing willingness to take into account Chinese preferences, although the Japanese experience demonstrates the limitations of economics as a means of exercising influence. Economic ties alone are an insufficient explanation for China's "rise." Instead, economic factors need to be tied to their contribution to political stability and regime maintenance in Southeast Asia.

Missing from this review has been a conceptual model that relates China's external policies to domestic, not foreign, policy priorities in Southeast Asia. One place to start is the Southeast Asian idea of "comprehensive security," which shifts the focus from "defense" against an external threat to the means to promote internal stability. Domestic political considerations, rather than the external environment, largely define threat perceptions. Viewed from this perspective, the Asian Financial Crisis of 1997 was the most severe threat—to economic growth and thus regime stability—that much of Southeast Asia had faced since the 1960s. As one academic noted that "the attainment of performance legitimacy through economic development is a key element of the comprehensive security doctrines found in ASEAN."[29] Thus, an assessment of how China's policies have contributed to the maintenance of elite coalitions in individual Southeast Asian states may help us better understand China's "rise" in the region. As this book will show, China's influence, in essence, is based neither on the exercise of military or economic power to threaten Southeast Asian states, nor on the "soft power" of attraction. Instead, the book argues that Chinese "influence" rests on China's restraint in requesting adjustments in Southeast Asian policies, China's contribution to the political stability of Southeast Asian regimes, and Southeast Asians' anticipation of additional benefits to be derived from closer relations with China in the future.

CHAPTER 3

China and Its Neighbors in Mainland Southeast Asia

Mainland Southeast Asia is China's backyard. Several factors contribute to making China the most influential external state in the countries of mainland Southeast Asia. These include history, culture, religion, authoritarian regimes, fear of neighbors, poverty and dependence, expectations for the future, Beijing's political support and economic assistance, and China's sheer looming presence either on these countries borders or close by to the north. These elements combine in different concoctions in each country. The depth of China's influence varies from state to state. Two thousand years of close, though unequal, ties between China and Vietnam make this relationship especially dense and complex.[1]

Myanmar's isolated military regime and Cambodia's rulers, sitting atop two of the world's poorest countries, depend on Beijing for support. Vietnam's circumspection, the result of centuries of Chinese interference, blends pragmatism with a core of deep nationalism. Laos is slowly slipping from Vietnam's embrace into China's. Thailand—famous for playing one foreigner off against another and free to pick and choose among external influences—is enamored with China.

These are not tributary relationships in modern dress. The modern language of deference may occasionally sound eerily familiar to historians, but the old "tributary" relationships involved Chinese confirmation of local leaders' legitimacy in exchange for formal deference, all greased by profitable trade relations for the country that was allegedly paying "tribute." Modern nationalism—strong in all but Laos but often directed against Southeast Asian neighbors (Vietnam excepted)—precludes the form, and much of the substance, of traditional tributary relations.

Myanmar, Laos, and Cambodia were the last states to join ASEAN in the late 1990s. They are largely wards of the international development community (Cambodia and Laos) or economic basket cases (Myanmar) of little economic benefit to China.

Supporting them has numerous costs, including the flow of drugs from Myanmar to Chinese addicts and the further compromise of China's reputation on human rights and transparency issues. The countries are, however, strategically placed, potentially for political and military but now largely for economic reasons. They provide outlets to the sea (Myanmar to the Indian Ocean, Cambodia through Laos to the Gulf of Siam) for landlocked southwestern China, which suffers from underdevelopment compared to China's wealthy coastal provinces.[2]

The cost of buying influence is low. It comes largely in the form of partial forgiveness for small loans, new loans at low rates, and perhaps as much as $3 billion in military, economic, and infrastructure aid for Myanmar over the past decade and a half. The influence of official aid is supplemented by about a million new Chinese migrants, principally to northern Burma, who maintain a network of business and family connections back into China. These countries also provide Beijing with an insider's window on ASEAN deliberations. These countries' principal value to China, however, is as transportation routes and as part of the massive Asian Development Bank (ADB) supported Greater Mekong Subregion (GMS) involving China, Laos, Cambodia and Thailand, and more peripherally Myanmar and Vietnam. Improved roads and railways, and especially an oil pipeline through Burma, would provide an alternative means for China to import energy supplies, the need for which is expected to continue to grow at exponential rates, from the Middle East and Africa. As one Chinese academic commented, China's "cooperation is a comprehensive security strategy which helps to maintain stability and cohesion of the region by way of economic cooperation with the peripheral states of mainland China."[3] As is so often the case in the poorer states of mainland Southeast Asia, the cost to China is small indeed.

THE MEKONG RIVER

For almost half of its length, the Mekong (Lancang, in China) river flows through China before it continues on through Southeast Asia to the sea. Beijing has been widely criticized by scholars, journalists, and especially environmentalists for its construction of dams on the Mekong, its support for the clearance of reefs and rapids to improve navigation on the river in Laos, and its disregard for the environmental consequences of its actions downriver in Laos, Cambodia, and Vietnam. It has also declined to join the Mekong River Commission, but participates in the Greater Mekong Sub-Region (GMS). Meanwhile, Chinese plans include the construction of eight large dams on the Mekong, two of which are now completed. Downriver in Southeast Asia itself, several smaller dams have been constructed and channels are being dredged in the river.[4] The negative impact of these dams on fish resources in Cambodia received considerable attention in the international media during the summer of 2005.[5] Despite the fact that China's actions have measurably, if perhaps only temporarily, impoverished the lives of people living downriver, the governments of Laos, Cambodia, Thailand, and Vietnam have failed to publicly raise their concerns with Beijing. Initially at least, China appears to have decided that it has the right to exploit the river for power generation within its own borders whatever the consequences may be for its neighbors to the south. China's generally accommodating diplomacy in Southeast Asia has not been echoed in its attitude toward the downstream impact of its independent exploitation of the upper Mekong.

Even more intriguing than China's actions is the question of whether China's attitude should be taken as an indication of its preferred approach to Southeast Asia when it is in the driver's seat, as it is especially with Laos and Cambodia. While it is true that Beijing has been particularly determined to build dams on the river within its borders, the Chinese attitude toward the Mekong seems to be more reminiscent of Chinese assertiveness on South China Sea issues in the 1990s than it is of China's current approach to Southeast Asia as a whole.

Another relevant issue, in addition to the environmental one, is how Beijing has dominated the exploitation of the river, while others, principally Japan, have paid the bills. The GMS program, into which the ADB and Japan have poured several billion dollars, was founded under ADB auspices in 1992. It seeks to construct a major road network and a regional power distribution system, and to improve navigation along the river from the Chinese province of Yunnan southward. Beijing has used summit meetings in Cambodia and Yunnan to promote development through the GMS, through which it stands to reap the greatest benefit, particularly from electricity production surplus to current requirements. The province of Yunnan has been part of the tangle of institutions and countries involved since 1992, and has also received $400 million from the ADB for highway construction. Although the picture is complicated, involving the GMS, the Mekong River Commission, bilateral aid programs, and several states, the bottom line is apparently that Japan and the ADB, in which Japan has great influence, are paying the bulk of the costs for a massive development scheme that primarily benefits China.

CHINA–THAILAND–VIETNAM TRIANGLE

In mainland Southeast Asia, Beijing can leverage neighbor against neighbor. Ties to Thailand can be used to constrain Vietnam, as they were during the Vietnamese occupation of Cambodia in the 1980s. Beijing can also use its influence in Myanmar to reward or punish Bangkok, which sees Myanmar as a serious external threat to Thai security.[6] Laos and Cambodia are squeezed between Vietnam and Thailand, and China has served as a referee. Beijing tries to avoid being drawn into small quarrels. However, much to Thai annoyance it reportedly interjected itself after Cambodia's political leadership encouraged anti-Thai rioting in Phnom Penh in 2002, and Bangkok intervened to withdraw its citizens and demand compensation for the damage to their properties.[7] But China no longer needs to expend the effort it did two decades ago to moderate Thai and Vietnamese ambitions. Vietnam's attempt to dominate Indochina collapsed after Hanoi's withdrawal from Cambodia in 1989, and its influence in Laos rests primarily on old ties to the aging Communist leadership. Bangkok's primary goal is to serve as the economic hub of mainland Southeast Asia, not to compete with China for political influence in Laos, Cambodia, or Myanmar. In short, the previously harsh hand is no longer required. Instead, the political costs of ensuring stability in its "backyard" are low, and the potential benefits in terms of bringing southwestern China into the nation's modern economy are high. But Beijing is not concerned solely with moderating Vietnamese and Thai ambitions in mainland Southeast Asia; bilateral ties with these key states take precedence. Hanoi's bilateral relationship with China is primarily defensive; Bangkok's is Thailand's own free choice.

OVERVIEW

If mainland Southeast Asia is China's "backyard," how does Beijing exercise influence to achieve its goals, as spelled out in Chapter 1, and what less does its record in mainland Southeast Asia suggest that Beijing might do if China's definition of its periphery were to expand to take in more of Southeast Asia? The record in this part of Southeast Asia would suggest that China's primary concern is stability. Beijing is prepared to invest considerable diplomatic capital and limited economic and military assistance where required, and to insist (except with Thailand, with whom it requests) that China's interests be considered before those of other major external states. Among those interests is the development of transportation and power networks which will contribute to the economic development of Yunnan and Guangxi provinces. There is no evidence of an attempt to establish Soviet-style satellites or military bases. Beijing deeply appreciates deference, but is usually careful to maintain the appearance of compromise and to avoid provoking a nationalist response.

CHINA–MYANMAR (BURMA)

Myanmar is often described as a Chinese "client state," but if it is, it is a difficult, xenophobic client. From China's point of view, geopolitical and energy supply considerations dominate, trumping minor trade ties. Yet this alliance, which reflects Beijing's pragmatism, complicates relations with other ASEAN countries embarrassed by Myanmar's intransigence on human rights issues. Thus it fits uncomfortably with China's comprehensive strategy for the region.

Most Southeast Asian leaders hoped that Myanmar's inclusion in ASEAN in 1997 would moderate the military regime's internal policies and eventually lead to internal political reconciliation. If the old saying that when "China spits, Burma swims" applies no matter who rules in Rangoon, Beijing also might prefer a more predictable, and in international eyes more legitimate, partner. It would benefit from one at least capable of bringing Myanmar's dysfunctional economy into the modern world.

In June 2003, ASEAN modified its traditional reluctance to interfere in the domestic affairs of other countries and condemned Myanmar's human rights practices, in particular its detention of the pro-democracy leader Aung San Suu Kyi and attacks on her supporters. In April 2004, China surprised its neighbors by supporting a resolution in the United Nations Human Rights Commission urging the government of Burma to restore democracy.[8] Though Malaysian, Indonesian, and other special envoys pressing for internal reform have been annoyed with the military regime's intransigence, China and ASEAN apparently worked together to convince Myanmar to skip its turn as ASEAN's chair in 2005.[9] More recently, the

UN Security Council met to discuss the situation in Myanmar in response to a U.S. initiative as part of the Bush administration's new "democracy campaign," an effort that Beijing has neither supported nor, thus far, opposed in public.[10] In short, China and ASEAN are reluctant to endorse interference in another state's internal affairs ("flexible engagement" in ASEAN terminology), but share an interest in sufficiently moderating Myanmar's behavior to avoid embarrassment in the international community.

Myanmar provides China with access to the Indian Ocean. Military-minded observers focus on China's potential challenge to Indian naval predominance in these waters and on potential Chinese force projection capabilities from Myanmar into the Andaman Sea and the Bay of Bengal. They also stress reports about the presence of Chinese military personnel and communications facilities at Myanmar's naval bases, though there is not much hard evidence on exactly what the Chinese are up to along Myanmar's coast.[11] Observers also note that China has provided more than $1 billion in weapons, including fighters, tanks, and naval vessels, to the military regime since it refused to accept the results of the national election won in a landslide by Aung San Suu Kyi in 1990. This assistance was used to more than double the size of the Myanmar's military, which has in turn crushed minority groups and intimidated other political opponents.

However, in the early twenty-first century, with improving Sino-Indian relations and Beijing's focus on internal economic development, Myanmar's role as a transportation corridor between Yunnan province and other parts of China's comparatively underdeveloped southwestern interior and the sea, may take precedence. China has already helped Myanmar build a road to Bhamo (and perhaps Mandalay), which may be part of the old Burma Road of World War II fame, and part of the planned Kunming-Singapore railroad will pass through Myanmar. Myanmar has a small role to play in the ambitious GMS development scheme, into which the ADB has already poured funds for many years. On the other hand, China has apparently offered to help improve navigation on the Irrawady River. The gleam in Chinese leaders' eyes, however, is the possibility of an oil pipeline through Myanmar, which could provide an alternative for some of the 80 percent of China's skyrocketing oil imports that now pass through the Strait of Malacca chokepoint between Malaysia and Indonesia.[12]

Myanmar has substantial natural gas resources, in which the China National Offshore Oil Company (CNOOC) has expressed interest. One concession has long been held by UNOCAL. If CNOOC had been successful in its $18.5 billion dollar bid to acquire the California-based UNOCAL in 2005, it also would have acquired the last significant link between the United States and Myanmar. As it is, Burmese natural gas flows to neighboring Thailand, India is negotiating to import natural gas from an offshore field in which a South Korean company is heavily invested, and Indian, Chinese, and Singaporean companies are exploring several other potential fields. Total gas exports are already estimated to be "more than $1 billion a year."[13]

In many ways, however, China treats Myanmar as just another desperately poor country that happens to sit on its southern border. Despite the constant reference to a brotherly love, or "paukwaw," relationship between the two, Beijing's economic assistance, outside the military sphere, is modest. It advanced a much-needed loan of

$200 million to purchase Chinese goods in the wake of Aung Sang Suu Kyi's house arrest and subsequent additional Western sanctions in 2003. As it did with Laos, Vietnam and Cambodia, Beijing has cancelled repayment of parts of some previous loans. Total trade, including legal border trade, runs only $1 billion a year, scarcely more than a few weeks' worth of the China-Malaysia trade. Moreover, Burma undermines China's economy through the drug trade, much of which feeds the habits of Chinese addicts. China and Myanmar do back each other on international issues, with Rangoon parroting China's line on such issues as the 2001 confrontation between a Chinese fighter and a U.S. EP-3 patrol plane and Beijing denouncing Western sanctions against Myanmar. Also, senior Chinese military leaders often travel to Myanmar, while China plays host to leaders of Myanmar's military regime. Nonetheless, the last Chinese president to visit Myanmar was Jiang Zemin, in December 2001.

One potential problem in the relationship may be tension between traditional Burmese xenophobia and the flow of ethnic Chinese across the porous border into northern Burma. The number most often cited is 1,000,000 "new" Chinese immigrants to Burma, scattered throughout what has been referred to as "Yunnan south." Mandalay is believed to host 200,000, who dominate local business and have reportedly escalated prices so much that the center of the city has become a Chinese town. Chinese currency is used to pay the bills, and communications links run through Kunming in Yunnan.[14] The most serious exception to good bilateral relations since 1950 was anti-Chinese rioting in Rangoon and elsewhere at the height of the Chinese Cultural Revolution in the 1960s. Some observers believe that Myanmar's current close relations with China rest on a fragile marriage of convenience, largely the result of the military regime's isolation. In the unlikely event that the military regime started to crumble, popular resentment of China's patronage of the military could mix with long-suppressed anti-regime sentiment.

CHINA–CAMBODIA

China is the predominant foreign influence in Cambodia. In July 1997, Hun Sen took power in Cambodia in a bloody coup. Widely condemned and facing a suspension of international assistance, Hun Sen traveled to Beijing after he threw Taiwan's unofficial representation out of Cambodia. Chinese Premier Li Peng assured him that Beijing would "never interfere" in Cambodia's internal affairs, and dispatched military equipment to help Hun Sen prevail against his domestic political opponents. China has, of course, often interfered in this Southeast Asian state, which may have suffered the most since formal independence. The one constant Chinese goal has been to prevent the emergence of an Indochina dominated by Vietnam. To accomplish this, China attacked Vietnam in response to Hanoi's invasion of Cambodia in 1979, supported the genocidal Khmer Rouge, and belatedly put its money on Hun Sen. China is the prime guarantor of Cambodia's national security.

Phnom Penh has staunchly supported Beijing's "One China" policy, banned the Falun Gong, and blocked a visit by the Dalai Lama. It took China's side after the

U.S. bombing of the Chinese Embassy in Belgrade and later supported Beijing's stance during China's confrontation with the United States after the mid-air collision of the two countries' airplanes in 2001. Cambodia backs China's position on the disputed Spratly islands in the South China Sea. Taipei's cultural and economic office has been expelled. In addition, Phnom Penh has banned all meetings between Cambodian officials and their Taiwanese "counterparts," blocked direct air links with Taiwan, and supported China's passage of its controversial March 2004 antisecession law.[15] It is also widely believed that Beijing and Phnom Penh have worked closely together to postpone the trials of the "perpetrators of the Cambodian holocaust." Only in December 2003 did Hun Sen agreed to allow the United Nations to join with Cambodia in a trial of former Khmer Rouge leaders, who are rapidly dying off. As of 2006, this trial has not yet taken place.

Meanwhile, Cambodian and Chinese leaders have routinely exchanged visits. In early 2005, for example, Chinese Vice-Premier Wu Yi visited Cambodia, and signed a package of trade and other economic agreements; Hun Sen arrived in Beijing, and received a preferential loan; and Chinese President Hu Jintao welcomed Cambodia's new King Sihamoni to Beijing. In early 2006, Chinese Premier Wen Jiabao visited Cambodia bearing a $600 million loan. If any modern relationship between China and a Southeast Asian country smacks of the old "tributary system," it is the one between Beijing and Phnom Penh.[16]

China appreciates Cambodia's acquiescence as it upgrades transportation links and dams the Mekong.[17] Although international aid institutions and "the West" (including Japan) keep Cambodia's economy afloat (through an estimated $7 billion in economic assistance since 1991), this economic assistance provides minimal political leverage for these donors, who are in any case focused on internal reforms that do not compete directly with China's foreign policy goals. Other donors have tried to make future aid dependent on internal reform; China claims that its aid comes with no strings attached. China has provided $18.3 million in foreign assistance "guarantees" and $200 million in no-interest loans for infrastructure projects. In 2002, Premier Zhu Rongji announced that China had cancelled all of Cambodia's debt. China is the largest investor in Cambodia; bilateral trade reached $482 million in 2004. In 2006, China extended a $600 million loan for infrastructure, including bridges, roads, and a hydropower plant. A Chinese company may have been awarded the right to explore for oil in Cambodian waters. Moreover, ethnic Chinese, whose numbers decline from 430,000 in 1975 to 215,000 by 1979 during the Khmer Rouge era, again dominate the economy and have established a large network of Chinese-language schools.[18]

In recent years, the United States has taken 80 percent of Cambodia's exports, primarily due to a special quota established in 1999 in return for Cambodia's recognition of labor rights in the textile industry. The global textile quota system expired in January 2005, and most observers expected a substantial shrinkage of the Cambodia textile industry, which paradoxically continues to flourish.[19] But even while this crucial economic tie was in place, it had no discernible impact on Cambodian-Chinese relations.

China plays a "security" role in Cambodia, as the United States once did in the Philippines. It demonstrated in 1979 that it will use force to guarantee Cambodia's continued independence. It provides steady, if modest, aid for the Cambodian army. For several years, speculation has continued that China might be interested in a naval presence on the Gulf of Thailand at the Cambodian port of Sihanoukville. Thus far, there is no indication that this speculation has a basis in fact. Beijing's leverage is likely to continue to grow, as donor fatigue finally prevails among the traditional aid-givers and as China's booming economy draws Cambodia like a moth to the light.

CHINA–LAOS

Isolated and poor, Laos does not enjoy the luxury of competition among major powers for influence, within the country. Instead, it is caught between a rising China, slowly fading Vietnamese patronage, some Thai economic and cultural influence, and growing donor fatigue as the old communist regime resists pressures for reform. As elsewhere in the region, Japan's role as the largest source of economic assistance buys little political influence.[20] Beijing has combined high-level political attention and the usual mix of trade, investments, and loans. Hanoi can't compete with Beijing's generosity, and China is likely to gradually become the dominant external influence in Laos.

In their "charm offensive" throughout the region, China's leaders have not ignored Laos, which has hosted both Jiang Zemin and Wen Jiabao. Leaders of the Lao People's Revolutionary Party and the government routinely travel to Beijing to be received by their Chinese counterparts, from Hu Jintao on down. China helped maintain the value of the Laotian currency in 1997 and canceled much of Laos' debt of $1.7 billion (according to Chinese figures) in 2003. China still competes with Vietnam and Thailand as an investor and trade partner for Laos, but Chinese investments, and, according to anecdotal evidence, Chinese citizens have crossed into Laos in increasing numbers in recent years.[21] China's goals, according to a leading academic, are to eventually displace Vietnam and Thailand as political influences, to develop Laos' transportation infrastructure to open up connections between Southwest China and Thailand, and to exploit Laos' natural resources.[22]

Chinese dams on the upper Mekong (Lancang) River and the dynamiting of rapids on the river in Laos to facilitate the transportation by water of Chinese goods, which are flooding into the country, have also made the Laotian population more dependent on decisions made in China. Laos will also play a role in the Mekong River power grid that is under development, and a $1.3 billion International Bank for Reconstruction and Development (IBRD)-funded dam is under construction on a major Mekong River tributary in Laos.[23]

CHINA–VIETNAM

Vietnam's relationship with China is fundamentally different from that of any other Southeast Asian state. The last time China sought to protect a tributary state with military force was in Vietnam in 1885, when France decisively defeated China and its "tributary state." But Vietnam is the only Southeast Asian country that, for historical reasons, views China not as a protector, but primarily as a threat.[24] However, if it is true that throughout history the Vietnamese have "despised, dreaded, and rejected Chinese political domination,"[25] it is also true that they have found ways to accommodate China while preserving their autonomy. In a pattern familiar in the history of these two states, China launched an attack on Vietnam's northern provinces in 1979 to teach Vietnam "a lesson," failed to immediately do so, but used its "weight" to eventually convince Hanoi to seek to reestablish "normal" relations. These "normal relations" were reestablished in 1990 and 1991. The old asymmetric relationship was reasserted. Vietnam retains its independence, but pays close attention to and respects China's core interests.

Since 1990, Vietnam accordingly has assured China that relations with others will not disrupt progress in resolving major differences with China. Confidence-building measures included deliberately delaying final negotiation of the Bilateral Trade Agreement with the United States in the late 1990s while Vietnam negotiated a border agreement with China. When Russia relinquished its lease in 2002, Hanoi also went out of its way to reassure Beijing that these facilities at Cam Ranh Bay would be turned to commercial, not military, purposes. Moreover, Vietnamese officials are frank in stating that they have concluded that security treaties with powerful distant states are not a reliable way to balance against China. Appeasing and reassuring Beijing is thus a top foreign policy priority. As noted scholar Wang Gungwu has said, "Ultimately, a good relationship with China and other neighbors is the key to security."[26]

In several ways Beijing has Hanoi boxed in. Beijing's influence in the rest of mainland Southeast Asia limits Hanoi's options, as does unresolved internal debate within the Vietnamese leadership over how to manage the China relationship. The United States is a potential partner, but Vietnamese leaders have deep reservations about appealing to Washington, for ideological and several other reasons. Instead, Vietnam has sought to practice a "hedging" strategy, but its hedging is defensive and weak. The first priority is to try to ensure that China doesn't add economic dominance to "the tyranny of geography" and its current political leverage. Vietnam's answer is to have a trade relationship with the United States that surpasses that with China.[27] Secondarily, Hanoi looks to its membership in ASEAN to constrain China and strengthen its own hand, though China's growing influence in Southeast Asia and ties to ASEAN make reliance on this regional organization problematic.

One obvious answer is to compromise, and to improve relations primarily on Beijing's terms. This approach has been eased through party-to-party ties and by a stalemate within the Vietnamese leadership among those who would balance against, align with, or accept a more traditional hierarchy in the overall relationship.[28] So Vietnamese leaders have reached out, China has reciprocated, and both play down their differences, at least in public.

Progress has been reached on contentious territorial issues, both on land and at sea. A Sino-Vietnamese land border agreement was reached in 1999, and an agreement on the sea boundary and fisheries cooperation in the Gulf of Tonkin in 2000.[29] Though Hanoi unsuccessfully sought to include the Paracel islands in the 2002 Declaration on the Code of Conduct in the South China Sea, it has reason to be pleased with a deal that shelves the issues for the moment, since Vietnam occupies more islets other than claimants in the more important Spratly islands.[30] In March 2005, China, Vietnam, and the Philippines agreed to conduct joint seismic research, though one Vietnamese scholar said that this agreement does little more than prepare the way for further progress on other South China Sea issues several years down the road.[31] In November 2005 Vietnam's President and Communist Party General Secretary agreed on "all suggestions made by Hu Jintao," including joint exploration for natural gas in the Gulf of Tonkin.[32]

Diplomacy

Despite conflicting claims in the South China Sea and lingering Vietnamese resentment over border concessions,[33] relations between China and Vietnam have been improving for over a decade, and are likely to continue to improve as long as China continues its current campaign to reassure Southeast Asians of its pacific intentions and offer them a way to participate in China's economic growth. On a regular basis, the heads of state hold annual meetings, as do Vietnamese communist party leaders. In addition, there are about one hundred ministerial or vice-ministerial working visits a year, and on the party side, exchanges between the respective parties' external relations departments and party schools.[34] Vietnamese leaders often express their gratitude to China and their travel to China, especially after they have met with Western officials, sometimes take on the appearance of pilgrimages.

During a 2002 visit by Jiang Zemin, a "framework to develop ties" was agreed on. It includes "political exchanges at a variety of levels; the exchange of experiences with economic development, and the strengthening of cooperation in international and regional forums."[35] The mantra in bilateral relations is that the two sides have now defined guidelines for "friendly neighborliness, comprehensive cooperation, long-lasting stability, and looking toward the future."[36]

The tone of the relationship was conveyed during a July 2005 visit by Vietnam's President, who met with Hu Jintao, with references to "mutual understanding and trust between the two parties and two countries, especially to boost win-win relations in economic and trade cooperation" and to continue Chinese-Vietnamese negotiations on Vietnam's accession to the World Trade Organization (WTO).

Taiwan

Vietnam supports the "One China" policy. During a recent visit, the Vietnamese government reaffirmed its strong opposition to any activity aimed at separating Taiwan from China and its support for China's Anti-secession Law. Bilateral intelligence talks may continue with Taiwan.[37] Taiwan-Vietnam annual economic talks at the ministerial level were suspended in 1995. In terms of disbursements, Taiwan was the largest investor in Vietnam ($1.2 billion) in 1998[38] and the second largest source of foreign investment in Vietnam in 1999, but new Taiwanese investment in Southeast Asia has been declining for several years.[39]

Economics

Hanoi has long looked to Beijing for guidance on how to simultaneously retain Communist party control and accelerate economic growth, though the Vietnamese regime has trailed China in implementing market reforms. Economic ties between the two countries have expanded through increased trade, modest investments, and highly touted but limited Chinese aid. In 2006, Vietnam's economic growth rate of 8.4 percent trailed only China's in Asia.

Since normalization in 1991, trade between the two countries increased from almost nothing to $8.2 billion in 2005. The agreed-upon "target" is $10 billion by 2010, and may be reached more quickly. Vietnam runs a large deficit with the PRC. Although China's exports to Vietnam increased by 20 percent while imports from Vietnam rose by 80 percent in the first eight months of 2004, the trade deficit is still a significant problem. One source noted that because it is "difficult for Vietnam to overcome (its relative economic underdevelopment) because of the structure of trade, Vietnamese leaders have consistently asked the Chinese to buy more Vietnamese goods, but without result."[40] Vietnam is also deeply concerned with the (legal) influx of cheap Chinese consumer goods and the implications for its manufacturing industries. Illicit border trade also remains a problem, but some reports suggest that Beijing has cracked down on local Chinese provincial authorities. In addition, China and Vietnam compete in foreign markets, particularly to export their textiles.

Vietnamese academics point out that their country continues to play a role as a "bridging country" for Southwestern China. Despite plans to construct several major new transportation links to Thailand, products from Southwestern China are still transported to the world market more rapidly through Vietnam than through current alternative routes. Moreover, compared to the 1990s, Beijing and Hanoi now appear to be more inclined to work together on plans to construct two "economic corridors" linking the provinces of Yunnan and Guangxi with Vietnam.

China's alleged cumulative investment in Vietnam is $540 million, and its investment in 2003 reached $146 million.[41] Another source states that China has invested $330 million in joint venture projects.[42] UNCTAD statistics record a total FDI flow into Vietnam in 2004 at $1.61 billion.

During Vietnamese President Pham Van Khai's meetings with Chinese President Hu Jintao at the APEC Summit in 2003, China offered to write off part of Vietnam's debt. Beijing has provided small amounts of aid, including a loan of $36 million for the Thai Nguyen Steel Complex and another for $40 million for a copper mining project. In 2002, China provided a low-interest loan of $120 million. Vietnamese leaders have been effusive in their praise for China's generosity.[43] During his November 2005 visit to Hanoi, Hu Jintao may have offered substantial new loans for economic development projects.

Soft Power

Vietnam is the one country in Southeast Asia with a Chinese (as opposed to Indian) cultural background, yet Chinese "soft power" may be limited both by history and deeply rooted nationalism. Despite an increased flow of Chinese tourists (from 672,000 in 2001, to 778,000 in 2004)[44] and the departure of more Vietnamese students to China (from 2,336 in 2002, to 4,382 in 2004), over familiarity with Chinese culture may limit China's soft power. As one well-placed Vietnamese observer commented, China's new "cultural invasion" is "kind of boring Chinese music, TV and so forth all the time."[45]

A lingering issue in bilateral relations is the problem of the ethnic Chinese, many of whom were driven out of, or left, Vietnam to China, particularly in 1978. As one academic puts it, "the issue of ethnic Chinese from Vietnam, estimated at 280,000, living in China remains a potential source of friction,"[46] as does compensation for the property they left behind. In addition, the Vietnamese government did not appreciate the 2005 demonstrations in Hanoi against Japan during similar demonstrations in China.[47]

Security

Senior Vietnamese and Chinese military leaders routinely "exchange views" during structured rounds of visits and meetings. Vietnam's relative military power, compared to China's, has declined considerably since Vietnamese militia thrashed the invading Chinese People's Liberation Army more than twenty-five years ago.

Overlapping territorial disputes in the South China Sea remain the most significant problem in Sino-Vietnamese relations (for information on the South Chinas Sea dispute, see Chapter 5). In 2001 a Chinese navy ship made a port call in Vietnam.[48] A recent step by Vietnam has been to promote "tourism" to the Spratlys, apparently with an eye on developing an "exercise of authority" claim over at least some of the islands and eventually taking its case to the International Court.[49]

CHINA–THAILAND[50]

Thailand eagerly snuggles up to China. Thailand accords China the respect it craves. But some observers argue that Bangkok is just trying "to make sure it is not left behind" as a new China-centered Asian economic order emerges.[51]

The Asian Financial Crisis of 1997 shook the complacency of the Thai elite. Disappointed with one old patron's response, Thailand turned to another, linking Thai hopes and expectations to China's growing wealth and patronage. Although Thailand is probably the best-positioned Southeast Asian state to balance external pressures, under the Thaksin Shinawatra government Bangkok slipped ever closer to China. The peaceful coup that removed Taksin in September 2006 is unlikely to alter the fundamentals of the Sino-Thai relationship.

The top priority of Thailand's elite is economic growth. China is widely assumed to provide a golden opportunity to get rich. In a situation with some similarities to

South Korea's, Beijing is also potentially useful in managing security problems—for example, drug smuggling from Burma—posed by neighbors over whom China exerts influence. Bangkok, with ambitions to serve as mainland Southeast Asia's economic hub, but no longer illusions of successfully competing for political influence in neighboring Myanmar, Cambodia, or Laos, has good reasons to flatter Beijing by treating it as Thailand's main patron.

China, in turn, sees its relationship with Thailand as a model for the region: strong personal ties and a dense and growing network of cultural and security linkages complement booming trade relations. Moreover, Thailand continues to serve as a potential political counterweight to Hanoi should Vietnam's ambitions in Indochina revive. In addition, Thailand can help improve transportation routes essential to the rapid development of landlocked Southwestern China.

Nonetheless, Thai expectations for the future of its China relationship may be too rosy, particularly if Chinese competition forces too many Thai businesses to the wall. Thus, despite periodic tensions with Washington, Thailand has sensibly retained an old alliance with the United States as an "insurance policy" and encouraged new connections with New Delhi.

Diplomacy

Thai diplomacy is famous for "bending before the wind blows," that is adjusting to shifts in power and influence to protect Thailand's room for maneuver and, in the nineteenth century, its independence. Bangkok now appears to be basking in a warm breeze from China, but in fact the relationship is build on an old and solid foundation of mutual ties and interests.

China and Thailand normalized relations in 1975, and the security interest of China and Thailand converged soon thereafter with the Vietnamese invasion of Cambodia in late 1978. An informal security alliance then emerged in the 1980s in opposition to Vietnam's occupation of Cambodia. After Vietnam's withdrawal from Cambodia in 1991, Beijing and Bangkok could have gone their separate ways. Instead, both focused on their deep historical, cultural, and ethnic ties, and Thailand's role adjusted to promoting China's links with Southeast Asian regional organizations. As a senior Thai military officer commented "Thailand saw its role as one of 'mentor' in helping China overcome problems as its presence in Southeast Asia grew."[52]

Now Bangkok and Beijing have supplemented their mutually beneficial partnership with economic and diplomatic cooperation, buttressed by cultural and other "soft power" links and the language of a family relationship. With no territorial disputes and an ethnic Chinese minority thoroughly integrated into Thai society, both sides can indulge in such verbiage as Zhu Rongji's comment that a trip to Thailand was a "family visit to a relative" and Thai Prime Minister Thaksin's claim that Bangkok is Beijing's "closest" and "most sincere" friend. Moreover, the Thai public supports this relationship, as demonstrated by a 2003 poll in which 76 percent of Thais responded not that Thailand was China's "closest friend" but that China was Thailand's closest friend.

The sense that Thai-Chinese relations are a family affair was further strengthened during the Asian Financial Crisis of 1997, which led to a more than 11 percent contraction in Thailand's real GDP. Although Beijing's role was modest, consisting of a contribution of $1 billion to the $17 billion IMF rescue package, and a decision not to devalue its currency, Thais contrasted China's sympathy with U.S. support for harsh IMF terms and perceived China as its true friend in a moment of crisis. To friendship was added gratitude, and a Thai decision to link itself more closely with the "rise of China" in Asia. In the next two years, about 1,500 exchanges took place between Thailand and China at all levels of government, and in February 1999 Beijing and Bangkok agreed on a "Plan of Action for the twenty-first century," outlining a road map of their expectations for deepening cooperation in the coming century.

The election of populist Sino-Thai billionaire businessman Thaksin Shinawatra in 2001 as Thailand's new president, largely on a pledge to rekindle Thailand's rapid economic growth, promised to maintain the momentum in Chinese-Thai relations. Indeed, Thaksin's foreign policy conflicts have largely been with the United States. Shortly after assuming office, Thaksin rushed twice to Beijing, armed with proposals for deeper cooperation. Beijing has backed Thaksin's initiative for a regional discussion forum entitled the "Asia Cooperation Dialogue" by hosting one of its annual meetings in 2004. It has supported Bangkok's efforts to improve relations with Myanmar in 2001, and break the internal Burmese deadlock through the "Bangkok process." Beijing has supported Thai efforts to promote multilateral cooperation to suppress drug smuggling. Thailand was the first ASEAN country Hu Jintao visited after becoming president. In January 2004, Thaksin told government officials that Thai diplomacy should emphasize China and India.[53] Bilateral trade has continued to grow rapidly, reaching nearly $22 billion in 2005 according to Chinese statistics, though Thailand runs a deficit. In response to the December 2004 Indian Ocean tsunami, China pledged modest government aid but also promised to help rebuild the Thai tourist industry by sending Chinese tourists as soon as the resorts were reconstructed. Distinguishing between Thaksin's personal connections to China, which he has visited eight times as prime minister, and other parts of the Thai elites' views of China, is difficult. Nonetheless, the Chinese Foreign Ministry rates Thailand, along with Indonesia, as one of Southeast Asia's two "strategic" countries.[54] In sum, there is no discernible pause in Thailand's rush into China's arms, and no indication that Beijing has let its attention to maintaining this relationship slip.

Taiwan

Taiwan hosts 130,000 Thai workers, who send home nearly half of all Thai remittances from abroad,[55] and retains substantial investments in Thailand (Taiwan was the fourth largest investor in 1999). But Taipei's political profile in Thailand has stagnated in the new century. Bangkok has adhered to the One China policy. As mentioned in Chapter 1, it even withdrew visas from Taiwanese legislators in January 2003 before a senior Chinese official arrived in Bangkok.[56]

Economics

Like other Southeast Asian states, Thai trade with China is expanding at a rapid clip. Exactly how rapidly depends, as always, on confusing statistics. It appears that Chinese-Thai bilateral trade reached a figure of about $17.3 billion in 2004, and probably $22 billion in 2005.[57] China is now Thailand's third largest market, after the United States and Japan. Thailand has long run a trade deficit with China. The manufactures trade deficit is particularly large, and is concentrated in electrical and electronic components. Anecdotal evidence suggests that Thai manufacturers of small appliances and electronics have been particularly hard hit by Chinese competition. A bilateral China-Thailand FTA for agricultural produce was designed to help implement the "early harvest" tariff reductions that Beijing offered as part of the negotiations leading to a China-ASEAN Free Trade Agreement (CAFTA), appears to have led to a massive increase in Thai fruit and vegetable exports to China since October 2003. On the other hand, some Thai farmers complain bitterly that Chinese agricultural products are available on the Thai market for less than Thai production costs.

Investment statistics are murky at best. Thai companies were often the first on the ground when China's doors began to open to investment and Beijing subsequently went out of its way to ask Thai companies to invest in construction and transportation projects in Southwestern China. According to Chinese statistics, by 2001 China had invested $233 million in Thailand, while Thai companies had directly invested $2 billion, or ten times as much, in China. But Chinese investment in Thailand and Thai investment in China remains miniscule compared to the investment by both the United States and Japan in both countries.

Bangkok and Beijing share an interest in large infrastructure projects designed to link Southeastern China to mainland Southeast Asia, and in the construction of a pipeline or other means to transport oil across the Kra isthmus, thus bypassing the Strait of Malacca. The amount of money already committed to this work in Thailand may be impossible to determine. The planned projects in which Thailand would participate include the Singapore-Kunming Rail Link, the Kunming-Bangkok Highway, and Greater Mekong Subregion development (addressed earlier in this chapter). The violence in southern Thailand between Muslim separatists and the government has already claimed more than a thousand lives, and will undoubtedly delay further consideration of a pipeline across the 160-mile Kra isthmus, which could have significant economic and geopolitical implications for both Thailand and China.

Beijing extended a $2 billion credit line to Bangkok as part of a regional currency swap facility to help countries facing troubles similar to those in the 1997–1998 economic crisis.[58] However, currency swap arrangements through the Chiang Mai initiative, led by Japan, appear to potentially provide Thailand with $80 billion to draw on in the event of a crisis. Viewed from that perspective, China's credit line is unimpressive.

Soft Power

Advocates of the impact of "soft power" in the relationships between China and Southeast Asian states usually hold up Thailand as their prime example. And, as addressed in Chapter 7, they have a point—to a point.

Thais and Chinese share many cultural similarities. Many of those in the 10–15 percent of the Thai population of ethnic Chinese origin have intermarried with ethnic Thais, and are thoroughly integrated into Thai society. Particularly influential is the Sino-Thai business elite, which brings cultural, familial, and business ties to China, and "exerts political influence in support of a positive relationship with China."[59] As mentioned previously, former Prime Minister Thaksin has trumpeted his Sino-Thai inheritance. Moreover, Chinese leaders have made a sustained and successful effort to build close relations with Thailand's highly respected monarchy. Senior Chinese visitors regularly meet the king and Princess Maha Chakri Sirindhorn, the king's daughter She has played a "special role in relations with China, having visited that country 16 times as of August 2003."[60]

In addition to business and governmental ties, about 800,000 Chinese tourists now visit Thailand annually, and an increasing number of Thai students are headed for China for their higher education. Mandarin schools and universities are opening rapidly in Thailand, particularly in the northern part of the country, and the Thai government now encourages the study of Chinese in state-run secondary schools. Finally, "China-chic" has certainly been fashionable for the past few years in Thailand.

Security

The Chinese-Thai security relationship is close, but the military-to-military component of this relationship is stalled by senior Thai military officers' preference for more sophisticated armaments than those now available from China.

The Thai Navy purchased Chinese military equipment, including frigates, before the Asian Financial Crisis, and in 2000 China provided Thailand with antiship cruise missiles. In 2002, Beijing offered $200 million in credits to both the Thai Army and Navy toward the purchase of Chinese arms,[61] and Thailand was negotiating to build patrol boats under license. The following year, China's defense ministry offered credits for $600 million worth of military equipment. However, the Thai reaction was restrained. By 2005, a knowledgeable observer agreed that the Thai Navy was "getting closer to China; they will conduct joint naval exercises,"[62] but the Thais do not appear to have agreed to acquire additional Chinese equipment.

During 2001, Defense Minister Chavalit proposed annual security meetings with his Chinese counterpart, and these have taken place since 2002. In addition, military-to-military exchanges, including those between the heads of the respective armed forces, are regular events. China's special relationship with Thailand eased the way for the first Chinese observer group to monitor a multilateral military exercise in Southeast Asia, the 2005 Cobra Gold exercise in Thailand with U.S. and Singaporean forces.

SUMMARY

Mainland Southeast Asia is China's backyard, also often called its "soft underbelly." In this part of Southeast Asia, China once sought deference. Now Beijing's political support for authoritarian regimes and economic assistance, as well as the pull of a booming economy and China's sheer looming presence as the giant to the north, give Beijing the most influential voice in mainland Southeast Asian capitals.

Nonetheless, deference is not domination. Thailand's former Prime Minister Taksin bent to the north wind, but he is no longer in office and his country is free to straighten up or bend in another direction. Vietnam has historically deferred to China but vigorously defends its independence. Only in the poverty-stricken, authoritarian states of Cambodia, Laos, and Myanmar do the governing regimes depend on Beijing (and in the case of Laos, Hanoi as well) for political support. This presence allows China to muffle potential local opposition to economic development that will benefit primarily Southwestern China, such as new dams and transportation routes. However, China's primary goal in this part of Southeast Asia appears to be modest: to promote stability on its periphery.

Further south in Southeast Asia, beyond China's periphery, is maritime Southeast Asia. Beijing's ties with this larger and much richer part of Southeast Asia are addressed in the next chapter.

CHAPTER 4

China and Maritime Southeast Asia

China's relationship with maritime Southeast Asia is based on trade. Trade with this island world dwarfs China's trade with mainland Southeast Asia.[1] China's investments in Southeast Asia are concentrated in oil and liquefied natural gas (LNG) projects in Indonesia. Through the Strait of Malacca, which separates Malaysia and Indonesia, flows 80 percent of China's oil imports, the most crucial component in the continued expansion of the Chinese economy.

This island world is not part of China's backyard. Beijing's expectations and relationships in maritime Southeast Asia do not include the security component found in its ties to the states of continental Southeast Asia. China has never played an important political role in maritime Southeast Asia.[2] The old Chinese "tributary" system has little historical resonance among the islands, where its practice was spasmodic and was snuffed out five hundred years ago with the arrival of the first European power. In maritime Southeast Asia, the United States has been the dominant security presence for more than half a century.

Islam and Christianity, not Buddhism, are the dominant religions in maritime Southeast Asia. Moreover, Beijing isn't the patron of any authoritarian or communist national elites. Instead, the countries in this part of Southeast Asia are democracies.[3] Until the recent addition of four mainland countries, ASEAN, though it included Thailand, was based in maritime Southeast Asia. Indonesia views itself, not China, as the "natural leader" of this Malay world. Chinese trade with Indonesia and the Philippines has only taken off within the past five years, and good bilateral relations with Beijing are a recent phenomenon.

The ethnic Chinese are a small minority, constituting about 5 percent of insular Southeast Asia's approximately 350 million people. The distinct, unassimilated ethnic Chinese communities in maritime Southeast Asia and their traditional commercial influence raise questions about Beijing's ties to these "Chinese," who once identified themselves as Chinese residing, often temporarily, overseas. But the world has changed in the last fifty years, and research suggests that these citizens of maritime Southeast Asian states, while proud of their Chinese heritage, are first and foremost citizens of the countries where they reside. "Home" is no longer China, but Singapore, Manila, or Medan. The outlook for China's "soft power" in maritime Southeast Asia is thus mixed. Ties between China and overseas ethnic Chinese may be seen as a way to promote trade, and overseas Chinese may look increasingly to China for cultural inspiration, but the re-orientation to China is a two-edged sword. Ethnic Chinese are distinct minorities (except in Singapore) and are historically resented for their commercial enterprise. If perceptions of China's role in the region turn sour or if hubris leads Beijing to overplay its hand, these minorities could pay a price.

While the divisions between mainland and maritime Southeast Asia are crucial to understanding Southeast Asia's reactions to China, the region as a whole shares a role in China's view of the world. ASEAN covers both parts of Southeast Asia, and night does not become day precisely on the Thai/Malaysian border.[4] The Thai and Malaysian relationships with China share many similarities. Neither sees China as a current threat. Both assume China's inevitable rise, both are middle-income economies looking for niches in the evolving Asian economic order, both are supporters of East Asian multilateralism, and both occasionally use deferential language and seek small roles as China's friend in the region. Neither is likely to resist Chinese pressure on its own, and both are likely to seek and assume a mediating role, such as Malaysia's when it helped broker a compromise between China and the Philippines over an ASEAN-China declaration on the South China Sea.

On the other hand, Malaysia has a territorial dispute with China; Thailand doesn't. Malaysia is two-thirds Muslim; Thailand is Buddhist. Malaysia has no history of deference to China; Thailand does. Malaysia's economy is more dependent on trade than Thailand's. Malaysia is more attuned to Indonesia than to China, and culturally more aligned with the Muslim world. Malaysia's "China policy" is the product of the fertile mind of one individual, former Prime Minister Mahathir, and an eventual review might suggest adjustments. Thai support for Bangkok's "China policy" is more broadly based on thirty years of cooperation.

Indonesia is China's greatest challenge in Southeast Asia. Almost the size of the United States, Indonesia remains geopolitically the only ASEAN country capable of offering an alternative to potential Chinese hegemony in Southeast Asia. In the short run, Indonesia's political elite hopes that China will overlook some of the country's deficiencies and pay a premium to invest in Indonesian energy resources, as well as accelerate Indonesia's economic recovery by providing a market for exports. In the next few years, however, as Indonesia gets back on its feet economically, Jakarta will be alert to signs that China is ignoring Southeast Asia's interests, trying to impose its will in the region, or insufficiently accommodating Indonesia's "natural leadership" in Southeast Asia. The evolving trade relationship is also bound to exacerbate tensions that will have to be carefully managed if Indonesian manufacturers prove to be uncompetitive in the China-ASEAN Free Trade Area (CAFTA). Finally, China's skyrocketing energy imports suggest that Beijing's eye, when it turns to Southeast Asia, will focus increasingly on maritime chokepoints, which pass through or next to Indonesia.

CHINA–MALAYSIA

Malaysia sees little point in attempting to resist the growth of Chinese influence in the region, and intends to find a role for itself in a China-centered Asian economic order that it now suspects is inevitable. Malaysia's former prime minister, Mahathir Mohamed, who dominated both foreign and domestic affairs for over twenty years (1981–2003), switched his search for an Asian model from Japan to China after Japan's economy began to sputter in the early 1990s. Under Prime Minister Abdullah Badawi, Malaysia's China policy is coasting along under similar assumptions about the inevitability of China's "rise. The small Malaysian policy elite does recognize China's potential to become overbearing in the future, and welcomes the continued presence and involvement of the United States and Japan in the region.[5] However, there is little evidence of caution where China is concerned and no publicly expressed desire to slow the pace of the current Chinese-Malaysian romance.[6]

Moreover, Thailand and Malaysia, comparatively wealthy states in Southeast Asia, are competing not only to find a niche in the presumed-to-be evolving Asian economic order, but also to serve as China's friend in the region. Under Thai Prime Minister Taksin, Bangkok was more eager to throw in its lot with China, while Kuala Lumpur has been comparatively better balanced. Although domestic factors play a small role in the current Malaysian approach to China, the ethnic divide in Malaysia places a natural brake on potential Chinese political influence in Malaysia.[7]

Economics, principally trade, are at the heart of the Malaysian-Chinese relationship, though some observers argue that Chinese "soft power" may soon buttress the already close bilateral relationship.[8] Though investment in each others' economies may be slowing, Malaysia became China's largest trade partner in the region in 2002. Kuala Lumpur will try to ride the China wave as long as possible, and hope for a soft landing.

Diplomacy

Mahathir Mohamed was the architect of Malaysia's China policy. Despite his addiction to anti-Western rhetoric, Mahathir's approach to relations with the United States and China was largely pragmatic, though he shared with Beijing grievances about the Western-dominated international political and economic order. Although enamored with Japan as a development model for Malaysia in the 1980's, he visited China in 1985. After the predominantly ethnic Chinese Communist Party of Malaya (CPM) finally laid down its arms in 1989, and the Japanese economy began to slow, Mahathir turned to China. By the early 1990s, Mahathir had begun to advocate the formation of an East Asian Economic Community, which would exclude the United States—an idea that Chinese Premier Li Peng supported "in principle."

To justify his outreach to China, Mahathir argued that China was not a "threat," that traditional "containment" was in any case impractical, and that China could and should be "engaged." This approach was deemed likely to elicit a reciprocal Chinese response as long as China's "vital interests" were respected.[9] With regard to the "China threat" theory, Mahathir consistently argued that China had no history of imperial expansion similar to that of the West. Moreover, he was concerned that the strengthening of U.S. security alliances in Asia in an attempt to contain China would provoke precisely the Chinese behavior that such alliances were designed to guard against. Malaysia had thus concluded that China must be drawn into a closer relationship with ASEAN and ASEAN-inspired processes. This required, in turn, clear support for the "One China" policy, and in 1999 Mahathir went so far as to recommend "Taiwan should accept the formula that applies to Hong Kong since it reverted to Chinese rule—one country, two systems."[10]

Thus Malaysia has welcomed and encouraged Chinese involvement in the ASEAN+3, the ASEAN Regional Forum (ARF), and the East Asian Summit (EAS). The latter can be considered inspired by the East Asia Economic Grouping that Mahathir advanced in 1994 (which met stiff U.S. opposition) and his subsequently "toned down" East Asian Economic Caucus (EAEC). These two proposed organizations would have excluded non-Asian members, theoretically to enable Asian countries to stand up to economic pressure from outside East Asia. Recently ASEAN insisted on remaining in the driver's seat in the process leading to the first EAS, which was marred by Chinese/Japanese tensions. Malaysia hosted this summit (absent the United States) in December 2005.

By the late 1990s the official view from Kuala Lumpur, echoed by officials and think tankers alike, was that China posed no threat to Malaysia and had become a responsible regional partner. China reciprocated, both substantively and symbolically. In April 2002, in a move widely interpreted as a signal that Beijing's priorities lay with Asia, then-Vice Premier Hu Jintao visited Malaysia and Singapore before traveling on to Washington after he had been tipped to succeed Jiang Zemin. Before leaving office in October 2003, Prime Minister Mahathir assured a business convention in Kuala Lumpur that "Asian nations need not fear China's growing military and economic power because it lacked a tradition of foreign conquest."[11] Prime Minister Abdullah Badawi has followed in his predecessor's footsteps, visiting China in September 2003, just before becoming prime minister, and again in September 2004, when both sides commemorated the 30th anniversary of diplomatic relations.

Taiwan

Malaysia was quick to exploit Beijing's harsh public scolding of Singapore when Singapore's Prime Minister-designate had the temerity to visit Taiwan in July 2004. Malaysia's Deputy Prime Minister Najib publicly "instructed" Malaysian cabinet Ministers to forgo official visits to Taiwan.[12] On the other hand, at the end of 2002, Taiwan's cumulative investment in Malaysia was estimated at $9.2 billion, and two-way trade that year stood at more than $7.2 billion, earning Taiwan a place as

Malaysia's fifth largest trading partner.[13] However, Taiwan, which once served as an outlet for the pent-up demand for higher education among Malaysia's ethnic Chinese, is a fading cultural influence. Perhaps the bottom line is that, as a Malaysian academic put it, "Taiwan will be blamed by Malaysians if there is trouble" with China.[14]

Economics

Trade between China and Malaysia has boomed for the past fifteen years. Malaysia overtook Singapore as China's largest trade partner in Southeast Asia in 2002, though it subsequently fell to second place in 2004. Trade statistics vary widely, depending on the source, but suffice it to say that trade with China in 2004 was about 11 percent of Malaysia's total trade and slightly less than 20 percent of its trade if Hong Kong is included in Malaysia's "China trade." China is Malaysia's fourth largest trading partner. Malaysia runs a substantial trade surplus. Its major exports to China are palm oil, and electrical and electronic products.[15] Trade with China appears to be more complementary than competitive,[16] but recent data suggest that China's electronic exports to Malaysia in 2005 were twice Malaysia's electronic exports to China. Some pundits are warning that the rapid growth in trade may soon slow, as China turns increasingly to more advanced economies for technology that was once provided by Malaysia. Nonetheless, in 2005 bilateral trade had reached $30.7 billion.

More particular to the China-Malaysia economic relationship has been close cooperation on exchange rates, though it is not clear whether Beijing tipped Kuala Lumpur before China's 2005 currency revaluation. The only Asian currencies then linked to the dollar were the Chinese RMB, the Hong Kong dollar, and the Malaysian ringgit. When Beijing moved away from the dollar to a basket of currencies, resulting in a minor revaluation of the RMB in July 2005, Malaysia responded immediately with a currency revaluation of its own.[17]

Ethnic Chinese businessmen in Malaysia were quick to invest in China after Prime Minister Mahathir led a trade delegation to China in 1993, but accurate figures on Malaysian investment are hard to come by, in part, because investment is often also channeled through Singapore. The "Malaysia-China Forum 2004" estimated Malaysian cumulative investment in China at $3.1 billion and Chinese investment in Malaysia at $1.1 billion. In 1999, Malaysia and China agreed to participate in the $2.5 billion Singapore-to-Kunming railway and Chinese companies took a 40 percent stake in a $1 billion paper pulp project in eastern Malaysia. Most observers believe that new Malaysian investment in China has tapered off in the new century. The most interesting aspect of Malaysian investment is the participation not just of ethnic Chinese but also of Malaysian government-linked corporations, which are Malay dominated—for example, Sime Darby and certain Malaysian banks. Both the Malaysian and Chinese governments have encouraged investment by "bumiputeras" (indigenous peoples, largely Malays). One Malaysian Chinese source stated: "The Chinese Embassy on its part urged Malaysian Chinese businessmen to partner Malay businessmen in order to reduce ethnic salience."[18]

Malaysians, with a per capita income about twice that of the Chinese and much higher labor costs, do worry about a diversion of foreign direct investment (FDI) to China. However, the impact that China's attraction for foreign investors has on FDI to Malaysia is a controversial subject. Malaysia, for example, does continue to slightly outrank China in some competitiveness rankings.[19] The key for Malaysia is to identify niches where it can remain competitive in a wider East Asian market.

Soft Power

Some observers argue that the China's relationship with Malaysia will be broadened and buttressed through Chinese "soft power," much like China's relationship with Thailand and several other Southeast Asian states geographically closer to China. Chinese cultural influence is clearly on the rise in Malaysia; the problem is determining the responsiveness of the larger "bumiputera" community, not just the 26 percent of Malaysia's population that is ethnic Chinese.

One of the most sensitive and complicated issues is ethnic Chinese identification with China. Although the evidence is largely anecdotal, the consensus of opinion is that this community is first and foremost Malaysian. One academic's research suggests that there is "no longer a cultural or political tie to China among Chinese minority in Southeast Asia. Less than 1% wants to emigrate from Malaysia to China. You see distinct national 'identity formation' among ethnic Chinese minorities, a cleavage that didn't exist 30–40 years ago."[20] That identity formation seems to include learning and conversing in Mandarin, rather than the various Chinese dialects that the Chinese minorities brought with them to Malaysia. The level of Mandarin proficiency has increased significantly among the younger generation. In addition, some observers argue that the Chinese "clan associations" in Malaysia have seen a decline in membership. Mandarin also seems to be stressed among some ethnic Chinese families as they seek to cover their bets by sending one child to China for higher education. Education may be a key to the "identity" of Malaysia's ethnic Chinese. Certainly, once the Malaysian government began permitting study in China in the 1980s, interest in education in Taiwan declined. In addition, for the first time, Malaysian ethnic Chinese can attend higher educational institutions (though these institutions are not called universities) that teach in Mandarin in Malaysia.[21] One interesting claim is that ethnic Chinese are also now more willing to express their views, whether through anti-Japanese demonstrations in Johor and Kuala Lumpur or through support for Beijing in response to Chen Shui-bian's perceived steps toward Taiwanese independence. One Malaysian ethnic-Chinese observer claimed, "If you had a survey, 65–70% of the Chinese would support China's use of force against Taiwan. It is gut feelings. It is support of Chinese unity."[22]

As to Chinese "soft power" among Malaysia's non-ethnic Chinese majority, observers point to a rapid expansion of contacts, through business, tourism, the exchange of students, and allegedly even the arrival of "Chinese girls," apparently for the sex trade.[23] Prime Minister Badawi said more than 500,000 Chinese tourists came to Malaysia in 2004 (see Chapter 6), and 10,000 Chinese students. CCTV in English provides international news from China's perspective, as does the *People's Daily*, and the Chinese government has expanded its "public diplomacy," particularly in connection with celebrations in 2005 of the 600th anniversary of Chinese Admiral Zheng He's visit to the Malay peninsula. Airlines now fly directly from Malaysia to a rapidly growing number of Chinese cities. In addition, since the United States launched its global war on terror, anti-Western sentiments among Muslims in Malaysia may be rebounding to China's favor. China is perceived as less hostile to Islam than the West.[24] As one seasoned Western observer put it, the bottom line is that, unlike their fathers and grandfathers, now "no one is worried about a special Chinese connection to the ethnic Chinese community."[25]

Security

In Malaysia, the one government institution that appears to harbor apprehension about China as a long-term threat to the nation's security is the Ministry of Defense. Several senior Malaysian officers and defense analyst have occasionally revealed that "fear of China as a potential threat has never gone away" in the Malaysian armed forces.[26] China has also been raised as a mid- to long-term threat at Malaysian think-tank conferences, and Malaysian academics and officials will privately admit that they are "wary" of China.[27] Moreover, Malaysia's modernization of its naval forces has been undertaken, in part, with an eye to protecting Malaysia's claims in the Spratly islands in the South China Sea (see Chapter 5).

However, in connection with this dispute, one security analyst, who wrote in 1991 that "no matter what twists and turns Malaysia-China relations may take, it can be argued that Malaysia has, and will in the foreseeable future regard China as its greatest threat in one form or another,"[28] had changed his tune by 1996, noting that "China is no longer regarded as a direct and immediate threat." Moreover, Malaysia often viewed China's "creeping aggression" in the South China Sea in the 1990s as directed against Vietnam. It has preferred to deal bilaterally with China on South China Sea issues, despite the consequences for some of Malaysia's ASEAN partners. Malaysian thinking appears to be that alignment with Beijing could encourage China to be "less adamant about its claims in the future vis-à-vis Malaysia."[29]

Malaysian apprehensions about China as a potential threat have been kept tightly under wraps for a decade, at least publicly. In fact, Malaysia's public line is to warn against the strengthening of the U.S.-Japan defense alliance. As far back as 1997, Mahathir expressed concern about the adoption of new "guidelines" for U.S.-Japanese security cooperation. He argued that they were aimed at China. In June 2005 at the Asia-Pacific Roundtable Conference, Prime Minister Abdullah Badawi sounded a similar theme when he criticized a recent statement about Taiwan by U.S. and Japanese defense ministers because, he said, "no rising military power (China) will soon threaten the military supremacy of the existing (American) hegemonic order."[30]

As for arms acquisitions, Kuala Lumpur is on a buying spree, and is acquiring military equipment from a variety of foreign sources. In principle, there is no ban against Chinese military equipment. In the past, Beijing's inability to crack the Malaysian market has been explained by Malaysia's preference for higher-quality Russian, Western European, and American equipment. However, in June 2004, Defense Minister Najib announced Malaysia's decision to purchase medium-range KS-1 A missiles from China. Reportedly, Beijing will also transfer technology related to short-range air defense between 2006 and 2009.[31]

In addition, in September 2005 China's and Malaysia's Defense Ministers signed an agreement on bilateral military-to-military cooperation that establishes a joint committee and provides a framework for military training and the exchange of visits, personnel, and information.[32] These small steps toward the establishment of military-to-military ties with China should, however, be set against Malaysia's mutually beneficial, if mostly "below the horizon," military-to-military relationship with the United States over the past three decades. The network of ties between Malaysian and American military personnel is dense and complemented by Malaysia's links to Australia through the old Five Power Defense Arrangements.

One of the more intriguing Malaysia–Chinese connections may involve security in the Strait of Malacca, about which Premier Wen Jiabao has publicly agonized. Unverifiable rumors suggest that Malaysia carried Chinese water in criticizing India's decision to assist in escorting high-value vessels through the Strait of Malacca during the U.S. invasion of Afghanistan to remove the Taliban and Al Qaeda following the September 11, 2001 terrorist attacks in the United States.[33] On the other hand, New Delhi claims that it first consulted Southeast Asian states before agreeing to escort these high-value vessels. Malaysia has also apparently argued within ASEAN circles that China, like Japan and other nonlittoral states, can play a role in improving security and safety in the Strait of Malacca.

CHINA–SINGAPORE

Singapore's sophisticated "hedging" combines simultaneous economic and political engagement with Beijing and the cultivation of closer security relations with the United States. China is secondary. Singapore's most serious security concerns do not center on China. Instead, "the presence of the world's most powerful state (the United States) serves as an effective deterrent to the danger that local powers might be tempted to flex their military muscles against the island-republic."[34] More recently, the United States has been seen as essential to help guard against the threat of international terrorism in Southeast Asia. As for China, it "may threaten Singapore's and Southeast Asia's security in 20 to 30 years, but in the meantime, economic integration with China offers opportunities that the ASEAN countries cannot afford to ignore."[35]

Moreover, Singapore argues that a successful China, engaged in the region and the world at large, best serves Southeast Asian interests. Singapore shares the ASEAN consensus that China should be entangled in a web of close economic, political, and cultural relations with its southern neighbors, and has responded enthusiastically to China's conciliatory diplomacy and rapidly expanding trade ties to the region. On the economic side of the house, Singapore has put its money where its mouth is through substantial investment in China.

A tiny, rich, predominantly ethnic Chinese island in a Malay sea, Singapore has punched above its weigh in shaping reactions to China's increasing influence in the region. At the same time, its articulate leaders, diplomats, and academics have tended to conflate Singapore's perceptions and priorities with those of the Southeast Asia as a whole. The result is a tendency to overemphasize the U.S. role in balancing China in the region, while the rivalry within East Asia between China and Japan receives less attention than it deserves.[36] That said, Singapore tries hard to be helpful to larger powers.[37]

Diplomacy

Singapore's diplomacy is remarkably sophisticated, blending an appreciation of the larger balance of power and influence in Asia with an understanding of its own core interests.

Acutely aware of its immediate neighbors' views, Singapore waited to follow in Indonesia's wake before it established formal relations with Beijing. It became the last ASEAN state to do so, in 1991. Acutely aware of the shared ethnicity of the majority of its citizens with China, Singapore has sought to abort or assuage neighbors' suspicions by engaging Beijing through multilateral Southeast Asian or Asian mechanisms, such as ASEAN. Within these constraints, its diplomatic activity to draw China into East Asia multilateral institutions and socialize China into the "ASEAN way" has been intense. Over the past decade and a half, Singapore's leaders have established close personal relations with their Chinese counterparts and have assiduously sold Singapore as a gateway and interlocutor. Chinese President Hu Jintao's visit to Malaysia and Singapore in April 2002 on his way to Washington was widely seen as an affirmation not only of China's priority on Asia, but also of China's regard for these two Southeast Asian states.

But Singapore has also been prepared to resist Beijing's pressure on issues of real significance to China's leadership. Singapore was the only Southeast Asian state to condemn the 1989 Tiananmen massacre in Beijing.[38] More recently, after Singapore's Prime Minister-designate visited Taiwan in June 2004, Singapore refused to be cowed by Beijing's "explosion of anger," subsequent cancellations of several visits, and postponement of the start of negotiations for a China-Singapore Free Trade Agreement. And it backed Tokyo, during a time of heightened tensions in the Chinese-Japanese relationship in 2005, by declaring that Singapore would support Japan's bid for a permanent seat on the United Nations' Security Council.[39]

Taiwan

Singapore had close political, military, and cultural links with Taiwan, but Taiwan's investment expansion within Southeast Asia in the 1990s did not include Singapore. Neither were Singapore and Taiwan major trading partners. The connections between leaders were important. Taiwan "head of state" Lee's first visit to a state with which Taiwan did not have diplomatic relations was to Singapore in 1989. In the heyday of Taiwan's "Go South" policy in the 1990s, Singapore consented to a bilateral investment protection agreement. Singapore's armed forces trained in Taiwan. Senior Minister Lee Kuan Yew visited Taipei in 2000 and 2002. However, Singapore's ties to Taiwan have atrophied since Chen Shui-bian assumed power in Taipei at the beginning of the new century.

Beijing's new sensitivity was dramatically demonstrated in its reaction to then prime minister designate Lee Hsien Loong's June 2004 visit to Taiwan. Singapore did not buckle under the pressure. Beijing and Singapore have since patched up their relations, but Singapore's assumption that it could be friends with both Taipei and Beijing and explain away visits to Taiwan as attempts to get a first-hand look at the situation, appears to be a thing of the past. Singapore has, however, maintained its arrangement to continue to use Taiwan for division-level military training.[40]

Economics

Trade

China is an important and rapidly growing trade partner. However, in 2004 it was still only Singapore's fifth most important export market, taking 8 percent of Singapore's exports. Singapore's share of China's expanding exports has remained at 2 percent for many years. However, "At the launch of the Singapore Chamber of Commerce & Industry in Beijing in 2002, Minister of Trade and Industry George Yeo pointed out that Singapore's trade with the Greater China region (Hong Kong, Taiwan, and China) had reached $19.4 billion, which surpassed Singapore's trade with the U.S."[41] It has only continued to grow rapidly over the past four years. In 2004, Singapore again captured the top spot as a trade partner in Southeast Asia for China, and in 2005 trade reached $33 billion. The announced goal for China-Singapore trade is $50 billion by 2010.

Investment

Singapore dominates Southeast Asian investment in China. In 1997, China became Singapore's top foreign investment destination. By the end of 2001, investment in China constituted 13 percent of Singapore's direct investment abroad.[42] With a cumulative contractual investment value of $44.7 billion (2003) in at least 12,000 projects, Singapore is China's seventh-largest investor.[43] The total amount actually invested in 2005 is about $28 billion.[44] Most of Singapore's investments are now primarily in manufacturing and real estate. As early as 1993, the Singapore Government built an industrial township in Suzhou, and private and government corporations have since broadened their investments. In particular, Singapore has been asked to invest in a large technology park in Xian.[45]

Soft Power

Singapore is the only predominantly ethnic Chinese state in Southeast Asia, and it is also the region's wealthiest and most cosmopolitan of cities. Three-quarters of Singaporeans are ethnic Chinese and often speak and read Mandarin. Many older ethnic Chinese Singaporeans complain that their children's English fluency has declined because they speak Mandarin among themselves and "Singlish" with other young Singaporeans of a different ethnic background.[46] The old problems of citizenship and formal identity were overcome decades ago, when Beijing acknowledged that ethnic Chinese Singaporeans are citizens of Singapore, not China. Chinese delegations have been routinely visiting Singapore on fact-finding missions for more than fifteen years,[47] and in 2005 Singapore celebrated the 600th Anniversary of Chinese Admiral Zheng He's visit to Singapore with elaborate ceremonies. China's considerable cultural connections range from the search for roots in China among some Singaporeans in the 1980s, to the million Chinese tourists expected to visit Singapore in 2005, and to the Chinese citizens who turn to Singapore for education, medical care, or jobs. And yet China's "soft power" appears to have little discernible influence on the Singapore elite's calculation of the city-state's core foreign policy and security interests.

Security

Singapore is one of the few Southeast Asian countries to have a sophisticated appreciation of China's growing military might. More hard-headed than some of its ASEAN colleagues about the declarations and pronouncements that characterize so much of ASEAN's product, it has been supportive of efforts to encourage Beijing to increased the transparency of its military plans. Bilaterally, Singapore has been cautious about establishing security or even military-to-military ties with China. Sophisticated military equipment is purchased from the United States or Western Europe. Singaporean defense and military officials who have traveled to China have been disappointed by the lack of transparency, but Singapore is considering sending an officer to China for advanced training. In 2004, Singapore politely declined Beijing's offer of training facilities for the Singaporean armed forces on Hainan (as a substitute for Taiwan),[48] commenting that Singapore was "always willing to listen, but any decision on Hainan could not impinge on its existing (training) relationships."[49]

CHINA–INDONESIA

Although improving relations with Indonesia is China's greatest challenge in Southeast Asia, "China is not looming large on anyone's scope in Indonesia."[50] Moreover, Indonesia will remain the most "persistently ambivalent"[51] Southeast Asian state in response to China's drive to enhance its influence in the region. Indonesia's size and location, its traditional role as primus inter pares within ASEAN, and tensions in its emerging economic relationship with China all but guarantee such ambivalence. In the past few years, however, Indonesia has been responsive to Chinese overtures for a closer relationship. Jakarta recognizes that China can provide FDI and an export market to help Indonesia overcome the lingering effects of the 1997–1998 Asian Financial Crisis. Moreover, some in the Indonesian foreign policy elite believe that China can be used as an indirect form of "soft balancing" against the United States or at least as leverage with Washington.[52]

Historically, Indonesia's China policy has been determined primarily by Indonesian domestic politics—both Presidents Sukarno and Suharto used China for their own domestic political purposes. Suharto used the "latent threat" of Communism to justify domestic repression for more than thirty years, and Jakarta refused to normalize relations between the two countries from 1967 to 1990. With Indonesia's turbulent but ultimately successful transition to democracy, the sectors of the elite that were traditionally most opposed to China have either lost influence (the military) or modified their views (Muslim leaders). Domestic political change has thus opened the door for rapid growth in Chinese-Indonesian economic relations, with the political cap of a declared "Strategic Partnership" between the two states. With the signing of this partnership in April 2005, Chinese President Hu Jintao declared a "new era" in Indonesian-Chinese relations.

That said, resentment over the structure of trade, with Indonesia providing raw materials while Chinese companies compete with domestic Indonesian manufacturers, and indigenous Indonesians' long history of resenting the economic role of the country's ethnic Chinese minority, could easily be conflated. Add to this China's growing dependence on imported energy and on the strategic maritime chokepoints within or next to Indonesia, as well as China's apparent claim to Indonesia's maritime domain within part of the South China Sea.[53] In addition, as Indonesia's economy recovers, Jakarta's elite will seek to reaffirm Indonesia's self-perception as the leader of ASEAN. Its push in 2003 for an ASEAN community and its opposition to Chinese-Malaysian domination of early planning for the 2005 EAS signaled Jakarta's renewed interest in assuming its old role in ASEAN.[54] In Southeast Asia, Beijing will face its greatest test in "neutralizing" Jakarta, which remains acutely sensitive to interference in Indonesia's domestic affairs. Beijing will need to avoid overplaying its hand and provoking an attempt by Indonesia to serve as the counterweight to China's influence in the region.

Hu Jintao's visit to Indonesia in April 2005, and the declaration of a "strategic partnership"[55] between the two states would appear to signal Jakarta's decision to bury a painful history of bilateral relations and finally join other Southeast Asian states in welcoming China's "peaceful rise" in the region. Certainly Jakarta hopes to turn atmospherics into concrete economic benefits and leverage with the United States, but as stated by one scholar,

> with regard to the Strategic Partnership, it is difficult to believe that the declaration of a strategic partnership and more coordinated economic activities can have a major immediate effect and help to overcome years of resentment and suspicion that have been part and parcel of Jakarta's relations with Beijing. It is equally difficult to believe that negative attitudes toward Indonesia's Chinese community will change any time soon.[56]

Instead, not foreign policy but trade and investment are likely to serve as the bedrock of the relationship, though China's economic competition poses a challenge to Indonesia's own economic growth and political stability.

Diplomacy

The fall of President Suharto in 1998 was not immediately followed by outreach to China, because Indonesians were focused on their democratic revolution and collapsing economy. The first elected president, Abdurrahman Wahid, chose Beijing for his first official trip abroad in 1999 and soon announced a "Look Towards Asia" policy, a proposal for political or trade blocks including China. This proposal had as much substance as several of Abdurrahman Wahid's other bizarre foreign policy pronouncements.[57] The two governments subsequently agreed to a "framework" statement on developing relations in the twenty-first century, renouncing the threat or use of force and pledging cooperation in trade and development. They affirmed a staple of Chinese-Indonesian relations—Indonesia would acknowledge the "One China" policy in return for Beijing's affirmation of Chinese support for the national unity and territorial integrity of Indonesia. Premier Zhu Rongji visited Jakarta in November 2001.

According to a senior Indonesian observer, after Abdurrahman Wahid's successor, President Megawati Sukarnoputri, assumed the presidency in 2001, China privately proposed that the two countries establish a new "special relationship."[58] Although a special relationship of sorts took several more years to develop, Megawati was more attuned than her predecessor to the Indonesian Foreign Ministry's traditional argument that Jakarta requires reasonably good relations with Beijing to maneuver on the regional and international stage.[59] She met President Jiang Zemin during the 2001 APEC meeting in Shanghai, and during her March 2002 state visit to China she was warmly received in Beijing, where Jiang Zemin recalled that her father (Indonesia's first President) had close ties with a previous generation of Chinese leaders. She sought unsuccessfully to convince China to select Indonesia as the source of Liquified Natural Gas for China's first LNG terminal in Guangdong. Li Peng, Chairman of China's National People's Congress, and Defense Minister Chi Haotian both visited Jakarta in September 2002. China was also particularly active at the Bali ASEAN Summit in October 2003, which led to the signing of a China-ASEAN "strategic partnership." On April 25, 2005, following a commemoration of the Bandung Non-Aligned Summit of 1955, Presidents Hu Jintao and Susilo Bambang Yudhoyono signed the "Strategic Partnership" agreement in Jakarta.[60] The signing of the agreement was then followed by a state visit by President Yudhoyono to Beijing in July 2005, in which five additional agreements were signed, and the two countries expressed the intention to more than double bilateral trade from $14 billion to $30 billion in a five-year period.[61]

Outside the economic realm, a key issue for China is Taiwan. In addition, observers are looking for other signs that China' influence has increased. These could be either evidence of Japan's diminished clout in Jakarta[62] or Indonesian attempts to "leverage" China against the United States.[63]

Though Jakarta's commitment to the "One China" policy is unquestioned, Indonesia appears to lag behind other Southeast Asian states in responding to Chinese pressure on Taiwan. Jakarta did reaffirm its "One China" policy when the Chinese National People's Congress passed its antisecession law in March 2004. However, according to the press, the most recent Southeast Asian cabinet minister to visit Taiwan was the Indonesian Minister of Manpower and Transmigration Fahmi Idris, who traveled to Taipei in May 2005. In May 2006, Taiwan's President Chen Shui-bian stopped over in Batam, the Indonesian island across from Singapore.[64] There seems to have been little reaction to this visit, in contrast to Taiwanese Vice President Annette Lu's (Lu Hsiu Lien's) 2002 "vacation" in Indonesia, which, as was mentioned earlier, compelled Jakarta to issue a statement that she had not visited in her "supposed capacity" as vice president of an "entity" known as the "Republic of China."[65] However, if Taiwanese sources are correct, the economic relationship remains robust. Taiwan's claimed investments in Indonesia in 2005—approximately $13 billion and apparently concentrated in textile manufacturing—far surpasses Chinese investment, which totals $2 to $3 billion. Indonesian-Taiwanese bilateral trade has reached the $6 billion mark.[66]

Economics

For Indonesia, trade and dreams of Chinese FDI to reverse the 1997–2004 decline in foreign investment and help accelerate Indonesia's economic growth rate are at the heart of the changing Indonesian-Chinese relationship.

Trade

Indonesia froze direct trade with China from 1967 to 1985. Indirect trade links were restored in 1985, and in the late 1980s, trade ran about $500 million per annum. By 2000, it had reached about $7.5 billion. By 2003, it may have reached more than $10 billion. Chinese imports from Indonesia have risen steadily, from $848 million in 1990 to $5.748 billion in 2003; while China's exports to Indonesia have also risen, from $400 million in 1990 to $4.482 billion in 2003.[67] In 2004, Chinese sources and IMF statistics show a trade volume of $13.48 million with Indonesia, almost matching the $13.5 million in Indonesian-U.S. trade. In August 2005, Indonesian Vice President Kalla was quoted as stating that, up to that month, China-Indonesia trade in 2005 had reached $10 billion. China had become Indonesia's fifth largest trading partner. When China's Wen Jiabao and Indonesia's Susilo Bambang Yudhoyono met in Kuala Lumpur for the EAS in December 2005, the Chinese premier proposed, "enhanced cooperation in economic and energy policies, so as to realize the goal of increasing bilateral trade to $20 billion by 2008 and $30 billion by 2010."[68] In 2005, bilateral trade totaled $16.7 billion.

Indonesia exports raw materials and semifinished products to China, including oil and gas, coal, crude palm oil, rubber, paper, and organic chemicals. China's exports to

Indonesia consist primarily of electrical machinery and equipment, electronic goods and household appliances, textiles, and motorcycles. Chinese competition has reportedly had a particularly destructive impact on Indonesia's large footwear industry, and could cut a swath through Indonesia's textile production. In addition, China is an important market for timber smuggled from Indonesia, and the Indonesian government, frustrated with the billions in lost revenue from illegal fishing in Indonesian waters, has threatened to halt fisheries cooperation with China by 2007 unless China's fishing fleets provide at least 70 percent of their fish catch from Indonesian waters to Indonesia.[69] China has also become a major importer of Indonesian coal.[70]

ODA

The visits of Hu Jintao to Indonesia and Susilo Bambang Yudhoyono to China in 2005 provoked much confused press coverage, but it appears that China has agreed to provide economic assistance of $3.63 million, new loans of $300 million to add to the previously pledged loans of $400 million (apparently for the Surabaya-Madura bridge, and extended in October 2003), and another $20 million for disaster assistance in response to the Indian Ocean tsunami of December 2004.[71] These new loans (apparently soft loans at 3% interest) will be used to double-track a railroad in Jakarta, and to build a power plant in Kalimantan and a dam in west Java. In July 2005, during Yuhoyono's visit to China, Beijing also agreed to provide Jakarta with $100 million in "preferential buyer's credits."

Investment

Investment figures are notoriously inaccurate, and are particularly complicated by the withdrawal of substantial investments from Indonesia in the wake of the 1998 antiethnic Chinese riots. No one knows how much of this money was invested in China, and how much was subsequently reinvested, often by Indonesians of Chinese ethnic background, back into Indonesia.

In 2003, China's investment, as distinct from Indonesian ethnic Chinese investment, in Indonesia may have totaled about $2 billion, perhaps double Indonesian investment in China.[72] By 2005, it may have increased to $3 billion. Indonesian figures paint a much more striking figure, but they appear to be for cumulative approved investments. That is why press reports sometimes claim that Chinese investment jumped from $282 million at the end of 1999 to about $6.8 billion by the end of July 2003, a twenty-five-fold increase in four years. For example, in 2004, the Indonesian Investment Board claimed total Chinese investment in Indonesia was $6.5 billion, while Chinese government data showed $2 billion. In a pattern reminiscent of the Chinese approach in other Southeast Asian countries, Hu Jintao offered to facilitate $10 billion in Chinese investment. The Indonesian press is also filled with statements such as Indonesian Coordinating Minister for the Economy Aburizal Bakrie's alleged claim that "a group of Chinese investors have committed to investing up to $8.6 billion in Indonesia's oil palm sector over the next years."[73]

Energy

China's demand for imported energy and its angst about the security of its energy supplies, may raise Indonesia 's priority in Beijing's eyes. Southeast Asia's limited supply of oil is not the prize, but Indonesia sits astride both substantial natural gas reserves and the oil transportation chokepoints between the Middle East and China.

China reportedly imported $1.17 billion worth of Indonesian oil and natural gas in 2004.[74] Thus far, China's investments in Indonesian energy resources have been modest, although they may make up the bulk of Chinese investments in Southeast Asia. A 2002 memorandum of understanding established the Indonesia-China Energy Forum. This was followed by Petro China's moves to secure oil fields in Indonesia in 2003. China's National Offshore Oil Corporation has also invested in Indonesia's energy sector. In 2004, Hu Jintao claimed that China's investment in Indonesian energy sector totaled more than $1.2 billion.

Indonesia lobbied hard to obtain an approximately $10 billion contract to supply 3 million tons of LNG to Guangdong province annually for twenty years. In return, Indonesia was to buy twenty Chinese oil tankers. Though Australia won this contract, Indonesia received a "consolation prize"—an $8.4 billion contract to supply 2.5 million tons of LNG annually to Fujian Province for twenty years. This deal was signed in September 2002 at the First Indonesia-China Energy Forum, held in Bali. Delivery is to begin in 2007. In December 2005, according to press reporting, China sought to amend the agreement to take 1 million tons of gas, instead of 2.6 million tons, annually.[75]

Soft Power

China's and ethnic Chinese Indonesians' "soft power" in Indonesia was tightly restricted for so long that the limited opening of the past few years appears to be revolutionary. Certainly few Indonesian authorities still conflate China, ethnic Chinese Indonesians, and Communism. However, internal political conflict brought on by another severe recession could tempt some politicians to encourage a repetition of the anti-Chinese riots of 1998.[76] Moreover, only 84,000 Chinese tourists visited Indonesia in 2004 (compared to over half a million to Malaysia), and while China's educational exchange with Indonesia increased 51 percent in one year, there were still only 2,563 Indonesians granted visas to study in China in 2003.[77] On the other hand, China does now have some links to Indonesian universities, a "sinology" department has been established at the prestigious University of Indonesia, and four Chinese language newspapers are now available in Indonesia. The paperwork signed during Yudhoyono's visit to China included agreement on arrangements for teaching Mandarin in Indonesia, and perhaps a Chinese supported-cultural center. Whether the Chinese Government's "Confucian Institute" to teach Mandarin that is set to open in Jakarta is the same "cultural center" is unclear.[78]

More relevant may be anecdotal evidence of a palpable sense of personal freedom among ethnic Chinese Indonesians, which was demonstrated during celebration of the Chinese New Year in 2005. Coverage in major Indonesian media (Kompas and Suara Pembaruan) was extensive. As one observer in Jakarta remarked, many ethnic Chinese feel "free, free at last."[79] However, the transformation of Sino-Indonesians into another of the many types of ethnically hyphenated Indonesians will probably have less to do with China's "soft power" than it does with Indonesia's success in transforming itself into a democracy after 1998.[80]

Security

For several decades, Indonesia's armed forces (TNI) viewed China as the primary external threat to Indonesia's security. As the military's influence in Indonesian politics fades, this antagonism appears to also be dissipating. Though pockets of residual suspicion remain and may have some continued influence on military planning, the TNI generally appears to be interested in improved military relations with China. Nonetheless, one careful observer argues that the Indonesian armed forces view relations with their Chinese counterparts as more of a "red flag to wave at the Americans"[81] (who had restricted most military sales and relations with Indonesia's armed forces over human rights concerns) than as a serious option for acquiring military equipment and expertise.

In September 2002, Chinese Defense Minister Chi Haotian traveled to Jakarta. According to press reports, he discussed arms purchases, closer military cooperation, and exchange visits for military students. Susilo Bambang Yudhoyono, who was then Indonesia's Coordinating Minister for Politics and Security and is now president, agreed that the two countries should strengthen military exchanges and dialogue, as a means of "maintaining peace and prosperity in the Asia-Pacific region." During Chi's visit, TNI Chief of Staff General Endriartono Sutarto announced that Indonesia was considering buying military equipment from China, and a senior representative of China's defense science and technology industry was in Jakarta in September 2003 for talks on Chinese-Indonesian cooperation in defense research and production. Speaking to the press, Sutarto contrasted the TNI's good defense relations with China with the U.S. "embargo" on sales and training for the TNI.[82] In 2004, Indonesia and China were reportedly discussing the possibility of exchanging some Chinese military equipment for Indonesian commodities, and reputedly the Indonesian air force contacted its Chinese counterpart to discuss aircraft maintenance.[83] In any event, the poor reputation of Chinese military equipment led the Megawati administration to turn to Russia for a few modern fighters and helicopters.

The election of Susilo Bambang Yudhoyono (who had received U.S. military training) as Indonesia's new president in October 2004 had little immediate impact on Indonesian-Chinese security relations. By April 2005, Indonesia and China appeared to be settling on Chinese assistance in developing rocket technology. In that month, Indonesia's Minister for Research and Technology was quoted in the press as claiming that cooperation would be "established" on the transfer of Chinese rocket technology to Indonesia, and subsequent press comment seemed to indicate that China would assist with Indonesia's development of short-range (15–30 kilometer) guided missiles.

The July 2005 China-Indonesia joint statement issued during President Yudhoyono's visit included a sentence that "the two countries will work together in developing each other's defense industries as well as in setting up a consultation mechanism for defense and security officials." The Indonesian Defense Ministry's director general for defense strategy stated that the agreement "specifies Chinese assistance in a broad range of military production, including aircraft and ships, small arms and ammunition as well as missiles . . . its everything. Whatever we would want to have from them, they would support."[84] In August, Defense Minister Sudarsono was quoted in the press as stating that Indonesia "will be cooperating with China to acquire a capability for missiles and rockets with ranges up to 150 kilometers."[85] In September, he said that Indonesia is "considering jointly producing short-range missiles with China after 2009," though he added that Indonesia was also looking to India as a possible source of military equipment. In the months since these statements were recorded in the press, U.S. restrictions on the sale of U.S. military equipment and on spare parts for equipment purchased in previous years have been lifted.

CHINA–PHILIPPINES

In 2005, China finally turned the corner in its relations with the Philippines, the last major Southeast Asian state to respond positively to China's "charm offensive" and the allure of its booming economy. The rapid expansion of bilateral trade and a tripartite agreement for Chinese/Vietnamese/Filipino seismic research in part of the contested South China Sea has finally pushed Manila's deep suspicion of Beijing at least temporarily into the background.[86] During his 2005 visit, Chinese President Hu Jintao announced the beginning of a "golden age of partnership" in Chinese-Philippine relations.[87]

However, the Philippine policy elite's views on China remain inconsistent, and its policy response ad hoc. There is no agreement on the implications of China's growing regional influence or, apparently, serious thought on how the Philippines might "hedge," instead of "balance," against Chinese economic and military power in the future. As in Indonesia, commercial considerations have prevailed. The Philippine armed forces, however, remain more apprehensive than their Indonesian counterparts. They continue to suspect that China's good behavior since the signing of the Declaration on the Conduct of the Parties in the South China Sea in November 2002 is tactical and temporary. As one expert noted, "The balance of views is fragile and another incident or development similar to Mischief Reef would easily tilt the perception of China in the Philippines towards the threat side."[88]

But trade, not security, is now the driver in the bilateral relationship. In 2005, bilateral trade reached the $17.5 billion mark. The rapid growth in trade, in which the Philippines enjoys a substantial surplus, and the beginnings of Chinese investment are "lifelines" for the Philippines' stumbling economy, which has attracted little FDI in recent years.

Diplomacy

As Beijing's outreach to Southeast Asia slowly gathered steam in the mid-1990s, its relations with Manila hit rock bottom. In 1995 Manila learned of China's occupation of Mischief Reef, within the Philippine's claimed area in the South China Sea.[89] This event created a firestorm among Manila politicians and media. News reports of continuing Chinese construction on disputed islands and the detention of Chinese fishermen in Manila's claimed waters continued to fan the flames until 2002, when these issues were largely sidelined through the Declaration on the Conduct of the Parties in the South China Sea.

Beijing never stopped trying to woo Manila, a campaign that has finally paid off. Jiang Zemin paid a state visit in 1996, and Premier Zhu Rongji traveled to Manila in 1999. In May 2000, Manila and Beijing concluded a framework of Bilateral Cooperation in the twenty-first century. But the ice started to break only with Philippine President Arroyo's visit to China in November 2001. When Wu Bangguo, Chairman of the China's NPC, was in Manila in August 2003, President Arroyo told him that her government considered China "a responsible power in the international arena." In September 2004, during President Arroyo's state visit to China, the two countries agreed to strengthen defense cooperation and to undertake "development projects" in the Philippines (which turned out to be Chinese loans—see below). But China's hard work appears to have paid off during Hu Jintao's visit in April 2005 to celebrate the thirtieth anniversary of the establishment of formal diplomatic relations between the two countries. Whether the partnership proves mutually profitable or not, Manila is unlikely to participate in arrangements that could be portrayed as "anti-Chinese."

Taiwan

The Philippines is committed to the "one China" policy but considerable pro-Taiwan sentiment, based on extensive business and personal networks, can be found in the Philippine Congress and business community. Particularly in the 1980s and early 1990s, Manila sanctioned a flow of unofficial travel by officials between Taiwan and the Philippines. However, Manila recently cancelled and then denied knowledge of an official visit by Taiwan's vice president and several cabinet ministers.[90] Nonetheless, old investment ties remain important, a pro-Taiwan lobby remains active, and about 120,000 Filipinos work in Taiwan legally.[91]

Economics

Trade

China is the Philippines third largest trade partner. According to Chinese and IMF statistics, trade reached $13.3 billion in 2004 and $17.5 billion in 2005.[92] During President Arroyo's visit to China in September 2004, China and the Philippines set a "target," to be reached within five years, of $20 billion in annual trade. That target was raised to $30 billion during Hu Jintao's 2005 visit to Manila.

The Philippines postponed its participation in the Chinese "early harvest" program under CAFTA, which was intended by Beijing to provide preferential access to the Chinese market for specific products from ASEAN countries. This was due to disagreement on the products to be included. The Philippines only agreed to participate in the program in November 2005.

Investment

According to Chinese figures, actual Philippine investment in China totaled $186 million in 2003 and $233 million in 2004, with "contracted investment" of $683 million. By the end of 2004, Chinese investment, according to Chinese figures, in the Philippines had reached $1.65 billion.[93] Major Filipino investors in China include the San Miguel group and Metro Bank. China is principally interested in extracting Philippine natural resources. In 2005 Shanghai Baosteel and the China Development Bank agreed to invest $950 million in Philnico Mining and Industrial to refurbish a mothballed nickel plant in the southern Philippines. Chinese firms have been invited to invest in several Filipino mining projects.[94]

In 2003, the Philippine National Oil Company and one of China's energy companies (CNOOC) agreed to joint exploration in Philippine waters off the island of Palawan. In 2005, CNOOC agreed to a "possible" $10 million investment on this project.[95]

The fear that China is "crowding out" FDI to the Philippines appears to be "overblown" since there is no "systemic diminution of the share of FDI to the Philippines in the midst of progressive expansion of FDI to China."[96] The Philippines often takes a more "opportunistic" view of Chinese investment than many of its ASEAN neighbors. According to one Filipino scholar, the "major reason for the difference in perspective is that the Philippines has already been losing out to its ASEAN neighbors in attracting foreign direct investment (FDI)."[97]

In September 2003, Beijing and Manila agreed to a currency swap deal in which Beijing agreed to provide as much as a $1 billion credit to the Philippines when necessary to overcome temporary balance of payments problems.

ODA

In 2005 the Chinese Export & Import Bank agreed to lend the Philippines $500 million, at 3 percent interest repayable over twenty years, to build a railway line north from Manila. In addition, China has offered another "loan" of $24 million to be used for unspecified purposes. According to the press, in August 2005 China's Export-Import bank offered $2 billion in loans annually for the next three years.[98]

Security

Conflicting claims in the Spratly Islands in the South China Sea are at the heart of tensions between China and the Philippines, and crippled Beijing's efforts to establish closer relations with Manila for a decade. Under these waters are often believed to lie substantial energy resources. In addition, China's fishing activities in the Philippines' claimed exclusive economic zone are a constant irritant.[99] As in Indonesia, most of fishing boats and crews apprehended by Philippine security forces come from China, with several hundred fishermen typically arrested each year. They are often fined and turned over to Chinese authorities within weeks, but China has demanded that the harassment end. The smuggling of narcotics from south China to the Philippines by boat through the South China Sea has been a major "soft security" issue for Manila, though there has also recently been highly touted cooperation against this smuggling.

As the weaker party, Manila has consistently sought to "multilateralize" its bilateral dispute through ASEAN, some of whose other Southeast Asian members also have conflicting claims with both China and the Philippines. The Philippines played a major role in concluding the Declaration on the Conduct of the Parties in the South China Sea in 2002, negotiated between ASEAN and China.

The regional media is fascinated with a deal among the national oil companies of China, Vietnam, and the Philippines to undertake joint marine seismic work in a disputed part of the South China Sea. Each company will contribute $1 million to this work. President Arroyo hailed this agreement as a "diplomatic breakthrough for peace and security in the region."[100]

Tensions over the South China Sea and the Philippine-U.S. security relationship dominated the bilateral relationship for years. In 1999, China admonished the Philippines not to hold combined military exercises aimed at China. This warning was brought about by new U.S.-Philippine agreement on a new legal framework under which bilateral U.S.-Philippines military exercises could resume. Manila ignored that warning. But improved U.S.-Chinese relations after 2001 dampened Chinese criticism of the rejuvenated U.S.-Philippine security relationship, including the dispatch of U.S. forces to train Philippine armed forces personnel in counterterrorism operations in the southern Philippines. Nonetheless, for their part, Philippine officials "believe that the country wields a powerful card in dealing with China through its military alliance with the U.S."[101]

During this time frame, Manila did react when China objected to a proposed purchase of F-5 fighter aircraft from Taiwan in March 2002. Manila then placed the purchase on indefinite hold.

As it is with other key Southeast Asian governments, China is attempting to interest Manila in Chinese military hardware. In September 2002 during a visit to Manila, Defense Minister Chi Haotian told his Philippine counterpart that China "is prepared to cooperate with the modernization of the Philippine armed forces." Manila did not respond to this overture. The Philippines did, however, agree in 2004 to the establishment of a "high-level security dialog," intelligence exchanges, and training exercises. It also agreed that Beijing and Manila would send cadets to each other's military academies. In October 2004, the China Maritime Administration and the Philippine Coast Guard conducted a "table-top" search and rescue exercise, and Beijing pledged $1.2 million in military assistance to the Philippines.[102] During Hu Jintao's visit, the two sides signed a "Memorandum on Defense Cooperation" and announced the launching of a defense and security consultation mechanism.[103]

These steps to build a security relationship should be kept in perspective. The Armed Forces of the Philippines (AFP) are almost exclusively oriented toward the country's many internal security challenges, and depend on the United States for external defense. Washington provides substantial military assistance (over $100 million in 2004), including surplus U.S. military equipment and training, and maintains a Mutual Defense Treaty with the Philippines.[104]

CHINA–BRUNEI

Chinese President Hu Jintao's visit to miniscule Brunei in April 2005 is indicative of the time and effort senior Chinese leaders are prepared to invest in cultivating relations with Southeast Asian states. Although the territorial claims of the two states overlap in the South China Sea, China's purchases of oil from the wealthy mini-state form the basis for the current relationship. In November 2000 the two governments signed an agreement for the sale of 10,000 barrels per day of high-quality crude, and China took 20,000 barrels by 2004, or 10 percent of Brunei's production. China has expressed interest in possible future investment in hydrocarbon production in Brunei, has promoted Chinese tourism to Brunei (20,000 per annum), and has encouraged business connections between China and the 10 percent of Brunei's population that is ethnic Chinese. Chinese leaders have also cultivated close relations with Brunei's royal family, whose members have traveled to China frequently since relations were normalized in 1991. Nonetheless, China remains a minor factor in Brunei's world, which is centered on its relations with Malaysia and Singapore, and security ties to the United States.[105]

CHINA–EAST TIMOR

China supported East Timor's declaration of independence in 1975 and was the first country to officially recognize East Timor in May 2002, when independence was finally achieved after four hundred years of Portuguese colonialism and twenty-four years of Indonesian occupation and repression. Despite old ties with Beijing during the struggle for independence, Indonesia and Australia, not China, are the dominant influences in East Timor.[106]

Beijing's current goals in East Timor have both a political and an economic component. As in many other Southeast Asian countries, Beijing seeks to ensure support for its "one China" principle. It also recognizes that East Timor, which has already joined some regional organizations, is likely to be admitted to ASEAN before 2010. East Timor also plays a role in China's search for energy resources—the oil and gas resources of the Timor Gap, which will be shared with Australia, may prove to be worth as much as $30 billion.

As in many other small Southeast Asian countries, China has mixed high-level diplomatic courtship, comparatively small but high-profile aid, and commercial interest in the exploitation of natural resources. Premier Wen Jiabao received East Timor's President Xanana Gusmao in September 2003. Beijing has provided

$3.7 million in grant aid, pledged an additional $6.2 million, and financed the construction of East Timor's presidential palace and foreign ministry building, giving China a place as the fifth largest donor in 2003–2004. China has also provided small-scale security assistance, including non-lethal equipment and places for six East Timorese military officers in Chinese training courses. PetroChina has conducted seismic studies and is expected to bid to develop a field in the south of the country.[107]

SUMMARY

China has never played a major political or security role in maritime Southeast Asia, where the United States continues to coast along as the dominant security partner, including in combating terrorism. Instead, its current relationships with this part of Southeast Asia are based on trade and China's search for natural resources, particularly oil and gas to fuel its continued emergence as the world's largest manufacturer. In addition, through this region flow 80 percent of China's oil imports, which are predicted to grow rapidly under the eye of the United States Navy.

Beijing has assiduously courted all the states of maritime Southeast Asia, dampening old concerns and achieving a particularly close relationship with Malaysia. Indonesia, approximately as large, populous, and wealthy as China's entire "backyard" in mainland Southeast Asia combined, considers itself the natural leader of ASEAN and is likely to seek to consolidate its role as it continues to recover from the economic and political crisis of the past several years. Jakarta's ambivalent response to China's rising influence in Southeast Asia will continue. Managing—and, if necessary, seeking to neutralize—Jakarta will be China's greatest challenge in Southeast Asia.

The next chapter will examine Beijing's embrace of regionalism and multilateralism with Southeast Asia as a whole, which has been effectively coordinated with bilateral ties in Beijing's smooth diplomatic campaign over the past decade.

CHAPTER 5

China's Political and Security Relations with Southeast Asia as a Region

Beijing's embrace of East Asian regionalism and of multilateralism with Southeast Asia is part of its broader decision to jettison China's old confrontational policy and style. Diplomacy counts in Southeast Asia, and China's turn to multilateral diplomacy to complement its intense bilateral diplomacy was timely. In the latter half of the 1990s, ASEAN had diluted its solidarity through the acceptance of new members, and had subsequently failed to respond to the Asia Financial Crisis and turmoil in East Timor, leading to predictions of ASEAN's quiet burial.[1] Beijing's sympathetic attention helped give ASEAN the appearance of new relevance.

In the ensuing years, multilateral diplomacy provided a two-way street for China and Southeast Asia. China proposed sweeping, if largely symbolic, measures to forge new bonds with Southeast Asian states in ASEAN and these states persuaded China to think less confrontationally about its relations with the region. One result is an expanding, often interlocking, network of multilateral organizations: ASEAN, ASEAN+1, the ASEAN Regional Forum (ARF), ASEAN+3,[2] and finally an emerging series of "East Asian Summits," which may or may not eventually lead to an "East Asian Community." This network is supposed to foster a sense of regionalism, though these mechanisms only provide a means to move forward at a pace comfortable to all participants.

China and the Southeast Asian states, working through multilateral approaches, can point to two successes involving traditional and nontraditional security issues. At the ASEAN Summit in 2002, Beijing and several Southeast Asian states with overlapping territorial claims in the South China Sea agreed to temporarily set aside this most sensitive issue in their relations. In 2003, after substantial criticism and initial hesitation, Beijing caught the spirit of cooperation and agreed with ASEAN states on the utility of transparency and cooperative measures to eradicate the Severe Acute

Respiratory Syndrome (SARS) epidemic. The combination of China's conversion, though belated, and the drastic measures on the part of Southeast Asian governments to contain the virus proved successful. And, should potentially more devastating avian bird flu start to evolve into a pandemic, the SARS experience may provide a guide for future cooperation.

While China's bilateral relations are the bedrock on which it builds influence, multilateral mechanisms not only complement bilateral ties but also provide a particularly efficient means to broadcast China's message. The themes China has pushed through multilateral diplomacy include free trade between China and ASEAN, more attention to such nontraditional security issues as diseases and drugs, and a "New Security Concept." These themes echo many that ASEAN has long articulated. China's multilateral activism also allows it to help "set the rules of the game" for the emerging East Asian regional architecture, particularly attractive to a state that had only a minor voice in the U.S.-dominated institutional building more than fifty years ago.

China's turn to multilateralism raises a number of questions about the costs and benefits to individual states. The classic Southeast Asian argument is that multilateralism amplifies their states' collective voice through ASEAN, and is a key component of their "Gulliver Strategy" of tying China down with a web of procedures and collective norms that moderate Chinese behavior. There is much to be said for this argument. It would, however, be more convincing if ASEAN was a more cohesive organization.

The record of the past several years would suggest that China and its neighbors to the south have both benefited from cooperation through multilateral mechanisms, a process often touted by Beijing as "win-win." However, common assumptions that ASEAN member states benefit more than their giant neighbor to the north may not hold true under careful examination.

The reasons are complicated. The benefits to China include the following:

- China's multilateral diplomacy provides a unifying element in its relations with Southeast Asia. It is the sheet that covers its varied interests in and approaches to individual states.
- China's multilateral component gives it an additional means to influence ASEAN states, both through its particularly close relations with several individual ASEAN member states and through its relationship with the organization as a whole.
- Close ASEAN-Chinese cooperation also increases China's leverage in the emerging East Asian-only regional multilateral network.
- Multilateralism thus provides a network of diplomatic channels in which the United States does not participate.
- It has a particularly significant impact on public perceptions, since the language of multilateralism fits well with the verbiage of ASEAN.
- It includes a Chinese-ASEAN Free Trade Agreement (CAFTA), which undermines ASEAN's historically slow and halting attempts to strengthen economic links among ASEAN member states.

ASEAN member states have reflexively turned to an ever-multiplying number of multilateral organizations and mechanisms as a means both to spread the pablum of the "ASEAN way" and to, allegedly, place ASEAN, rather than China or Japan, in the "driver's seat" in setting norms and procedures within a wider East Asian multilateral web. And it is true that ASEAN retained control of the inaugural East Asian Summit (EAS) in 2005, setting the terms for participation in the summit and declining a Chinese offer to host the next Summit, which will be held in the Philippines. It is also true that Manila successfully turned to ASEAN for support in the process that eventually led to the 2002 Code of Conduct for the South China Sea. More generally, ASEAN can be used as a means to embarrass China (and others) into better behavior, as it was in responding to the SARS epidemic. Finally, ASEAN does amplify Southeast Asian member states' collective image and voice at the United Nations, and in the United States, in Europe, and elsewhere.

China, however, is often inside the ASEAN tent. China is so influential with some ASEAN members that it is often, in effect, inside ASEAN's deliberations. The frustration that several ASEAN member states have faced as their special envoys have been rudely rebuffed by Myanmar can't be laid at China's door, but Beijing's support contributed to the military regime's intransigence. ASEAN has not been able to press Myanmar for even cosmetic changes to its violations of human rights, which in turn has embarrassed the organization and left an open, bleeding sore in ASEAN's relations with the United States and Europe.[3] For Beijing, the human rights situation in Myanmar poses a choice between its commitment to ASEAN and to its bilateral interests in stability. Division within ASEAN clouds the issue, but essentially Beijing has let ASEAN flounder.

Within ASEAN, the basic problem is that the priorities of individual ASEAN member states have usually trumped integration within ASEAN itself. Multilateral engagement not only has often let China play as an "insider" within ASEAN but may have also further diluted ASEAN's own resilience, as individual states maneuver under the cloak of multilateralism to secure their own, often short-term, interests with China. Beijing has also profited from Indonesia's disarray over the past several years, though Indonesia did attempt to again take the ASEAN helm through the proposed establishment of an "ASEAN Community" in 2003. In 2006, ASEAN also pledged to establish its own free trade zone and draft a charter, which will for the first time include mechanisms to enforce agreements among member states.

In short, China helped ASEAN when it was ineffective—that is, when the ASEAN emperor had no clothes—back in the late 1990s. But now China is almost within the ASEAN tent. Moreover, if ASEAN fails to strengthen its internal cohesion, its relevance may slowly fade as broader East Asian regionalism becomes increasingly centered on China. However, two major issues—overlapping territorial claims and the SARS outbreak—have been "managed" through multilateral mechanisms, and Beijing has asked Southeast Asian states to do little in a multilateral context that they would not have been inclined to do in any case.[4] On the other hand, China and ASEAN have failed to develop a common approach to Myanmar that would alleviate the embarrassment both suffer as a consequence of their inability to secure even a modest improvement in one the world's worst human rights records.

China's role in addressing other serious transnational issues—terrorism and the response to the devastating 2004 tsunami—has been limited. The United States has been the driving force in constructing ad hoc coalitions, bypassing the elaborate multilateral networks of the region, to address these issues. Traditional security issues continued to be addressed at the bilateral level, and ASEAN states have reacted warily to Chinese proposals through ARF and the China-ASEAN strategic partnership to include traditional security issues on the multilateral agenda.

CHINA'S MULTILATERAL DIPLOMACY

Beijing's embrace of Southeast Asian regional organizations in the wake of the Asian Financial Crisis was an astute decision. China had been testing the waters and edging toward supplementing its bilateral ties in Southeast Asia with a multilateral component for several years.

By 1997 China's attempted subversion in the region was a fading memory, but previous conflict in the South China Sea kept Beijing's long rejection of accepted international rules and institutions in the minds of many Southeast Asians. China's old distrust of multilateral organizations was well known, as was its old preference for bilateral "elephant and mouse" dialogues that were widely believed to give it an advantage in dealing with smaller Southeast Asian states. However, China's new emphasis on stability around its periphery as a prerequisite for continued economic growth through foreign investment, and Beijing's growing economic and political ties with Southeast Asian states, promised at least a mixed picture for the future of ASEAN-Chinese relations.

Distrust of multilateral diplomacy had a long history in China. Despite the victorious Communists' expulsion of Chang Kai Shek's nationalists in 1949, China had been excluded from the United Nations in favor of the Nationalist regime that found refuge on Taiwan. In the early 1950s, it had fought an international coalition of forces led by the United States, whose intervention in Korea had been called for by the United Nations.[5] After its normalization of relations with the United States and its assumption of China's seat in the United Nations, China remained a passive and wary observer of regional organizations such as ASEAN. In 1991, China's Foreign Minister accepted an invitation to observe an ASEAN ministerial meeting, but only in 1993 did China begin to participate in meetings of ASEAN senior officials. It started with science, technology, and trade meetings and participated in more sensitive political consultations the following year.

In 1994, ASEAN formed the ASEAN Regional Forum (ARF) to reduce tension and enhance confidence building on security issues, and to provide an alternative to Beijing's perceived tactic of playing off one Southeast Asian claimant to part of the South China Sea against another. Beijing feared that the ARF would be dominated by the United States, that it would be used by ASEAN to internationalize the South China Sea dispute, and that it would provide a forum in which awkward questions about Taiwan might be raised. Nonetheless, though suspicious that the forum was designed to limit its flexibility, China joined in order not to "run the risk of arousing ASEAN suspicions about China's intentions in the region" and to "ensure a favorable position in a fluid and complex security situation."[6] Beijing's initial approach was cautious and defensive. Chinese analysts argued that ARF should "remain a low-key dialogue forum, driven primarily by ASEAN and focused on ASEAN issues."[7] Only as Beijing slowly gained confidence that the ARF would indeed operate on ASEAN's principles of incremental consensus building, did it begin to propose initiatives in this organization.[8]

In 1996, China joined the United States, Japan, and several other non-ASEAN states as a full ASEAN "dialogue" partner, a status commensurate with its role in the region.

Later, in 1997, in the glow of its deeply appreciated response to the financial crisis, China decided to throw its own multilateral "coming out" party. It finally acted on the assumption that regional multilateral forums could be used effectively to promote its own foreign policy agenda. China held its first separate summit meeting with ASEAN leaders in December 1997 (ASEAN+1), a mechanism that would evolve into summits, ministerial meetings, and senior officials' meetings exclusively between China and ASEAN states. It confidently participated in the first "ASEAN+3" summit (with Japan and the Republic of Korea), which Beijing saw as a means to propose East Asian-only financial cooperation and to expand its political influence in the region.

At the 1997 summits, themes emerged that China would stress repeatedly in subsequent diplomacy with ASEAN:

- No threat or use of force to resolve differences.
- Mutual respect and equal treatment in relations with Southeast Asian states.
- Consensus, rather than coercion, in state-to-state relations.
- Shelving of differences in order to pursue common interests.
- Pursuit of economic development as the most important priority for Asian countries.[9]

Regular annual China-ASEAN summits followed the 1997 meeting. Premier Zhu Rongji expanded on these themes in 1999, and promised to increase China's participation in regional bodies. In 2000, Zhu floated the idea of a China-ASEAN Free Trade Agreement (CAFTA), an economic proposal of major political significance—not least because it forestalled an attempt by Taiwan to revive its pre-Asian Financial Crisis "economic diplomacy" in Southeast Asia. China has continued to stress economic "win-win" arrangements, and has sweetened CAFTA with an "early harvest" proposal, which magnifies China's image as a benevolent, responsible regional power. (CAFTA is addressed in detail in Chapter 6).

In addition, in 2001 China indicated that it was prepared to sign ASEAN's 1976 Treaty of Amity and Cooperation (TAC)[10] (which it did in 2003) and was also ready to sign the protocol of ASEAN's Southeast Asia Nuclear Weapon Free Zone treaty.

THE "NEW SECURITY CONCEPT"

The New Security Concept was first announced in 1996 with much fanfare by Beijing, as an alternative to traditional Western doctrines of deterrence and collective security through military alliances.[11] Then-Foreign Minister Qian Qichen stressed the similarities between the Chinese security concept and ASEAN's own statements on cooperative security in 1997. When Jiang Zemin and then-Vice President Hu Jintao addressed regional security with Southeast Asian audiences in 1999 and 2000, they contrasted China's new security concept to "gunboat policy" and "Cold War mentality and hegemonism."[12]

Following the collision of a Chinese fighter and an American surveillance plane in April 2001, Chinese leaders muted their anti-American rhetoric with ASEAN and, after September 11, 2001, they folded counterterrorism into their proposals,[13] as they continued to press ASEAN to adopt China's security concept.

The core of the concept is:

- Mutual Trust (huxin, or nonhostility and nonsuspicion sustained by regular, multi-track dialogue and communications)
- Mutual Benefit (huli, common security derived from economic integration)
- Equality (pingdeng, or equality of voice regardless of differences in wealth, size, and power, and respect for diversity of cultures and ideologies)
- Cooperation (xiezuo, or nonexclusion, nontargeting of third parties, tolerance of differences, peaceful and equal consultation to resolve disputes and prevent military conflicts, and gradualism).[14]

At the ARF meeting in Brunei in August 2002, Foreign Minister Tang Jiaxuan formally submitted a "New Security Concept" position paper, asserting that it met the demands of "people everywhere." Tang urged that ASEAN and China work together to build a regional security structure embodying these principles.

The Bali Summit

The joint declaration from the October 2003 Bali Summit consolidates the progress China has made since 1997 in portraying itself as a benevolent regional partner sharing the values and goals of the Southeast Asian states grouped in ASEAN.

- The two sides agreed to establish a "Strategic Partnership for Peace and Prosperity." This was the first time China had signed a document on establishing a "strategic partnership" with a regional organization. Although, as is common with the bilateral Strategic Partnerships signed by China, this document is not precise in defining goals, the Joint Declaration on Strategic Partnership for Peace and Prosperity does describe political, economic, and security, and regional and international affairs agreements that were already in the process of being implemented.[15]
- China promised to respect the sovereignty and territorial integrity of each Southeast Asian nation.

- Political and economic cooperation would be intensified through the proposed CAFTA. The announced goal of increasing two-way annual trade to $100 billion by 2005, was surpassed in 2004.
- China pledged to provide assistance to ASEAN in reducing the "development gap" between ASEAN's more affluent members and its less-developed ones.
- Security cooperation would increase, and would include, "when appropriate," an expanded security-related dialogue.[16]

Moreover, in a highly symbolic gesture, at the Bali Summit China became the first non-Southeast Asian nation to accede to ASEAN's 1976 Treaty of Amity and Cooperation (TAC). This document pledges its signers to renounce the threat or use of force, to respect the independence and sovereignty of all nations, not to interfere in the internal affairs of others, and to resolve disputes through peaceful means. Parties agree to consult regularly, and to form a High Council of ministers from all members of the treaty to "take cognizance" of disputes among parties to the treaty, assist in finding peaceful solutions, and—if all parties agree—play a direct role in settling potential conflicts. The High Council has never met.

ASEAN leaders welcomed this step as signifying "deeper political trust and a higher level of cooperation," and announced that they had agreed to cooperate with China in sustaining peace "while upholding the authority and central role of the UN." Premier Wen Jiabao, addressing business leaders at a parallel private sector summit in Bali, conveyed the same reassuring message about China's peaceful intentions, with the additional line that "we Asian countries" needed to strengthen solidarity in light of some negative global trends—the "new manifestation of power politics," and the "pressure brought about by the unfair and irrational international economic order."[17]

China's initiative has encouraged other major powers, including India, Russia, and Japan, to sign the TAC as well. Moreover, ASEAN decided to make accession to the treaty a prerequisite for extending an invitation to attend the first EAS in 2005, thus effectively excluding the United States.

Since the Bali Conference, the emphasis has been on filling in the details of the sweeping agreements of 2003. China has also sought to insert itself as, in functional if not formal terms, a regular participant in the Southeast Asian multilateral community.

China has repeatedly reaffirmed its interest in moving toward signature of the protocol to ASEAN's 1995 Southeast Asia Nuclear Weapons Free Zone Treaty, and in encouraging all nuclear weapons states to do so.

In 2004, President Hu Jintao substituted the term "Peaceful Development" for "Peaceful Rise" at the Bo'ao Form.[18]

At the 2004 ASEAN Summit, China and ASEAN agreed on the "Action Plan" to implement the "Strategic Partnership." This elaborate "action plan" includes specifics for political, security/military, and economic cooperation, including China's donations of $5 million for a ASEAN-China cooperation fund and $15 million for "the participation of relevant Chinese agencies in regional cooperation, especially that with ASEAN." The accompanying Chairman's Statement from the ASEAN-China Summit welcomes China's decision to "dispatch young volunteers to ASEAN countries" (the Chinese version of a Peace Corps) and recognizes important economic agreements, specifically the Agreement on Trade in Goods and the Agreement on Dispute Settlement Mechanisms of the CAFTA.

China is also likely to have played a significant behind-the-scenes role in Myanmar's decision, announced shortly before the ASEAN, ARF, and ASEAN+3 meetings in July 2005, to "relinquish" its turn to serve as the ASEAN chair for 2006, which had threatened to lead the U.S. and the European Union to boycott ASEAN on human rights grounds.

Another Chinese initiative with considerable appeal among Southeast Asian political and economic elites is the China-ASEAN Eminent Persons Group, launched in Qingdao in August 2005, and opened by former Chinese Foreign Minister Qian Qichen. As a Singaporean ambassador noted, Southeast Asians were impressed that a former Chinese foreign minister would personally draft a concept paper for this group.[19] As a senior Southeast Asian diplomat commented, the Chinese "came up with twenty-six proposals. Many were throwaways, but all lead to closer strategic and defense coordination."[20]

THE EMERGING "EAST ASIAN COMMUNITY"

Malaysia hosted the first "East Asian Summit" in December 2005. This summit was designed to reflect a "growing but still nascent sense of regionalism in East Asia."[21] The intellectual origins for such a summit include former Malaysian Prime Minister Mahathir Mohammed's proposed East Asian Economic Community and the idea of an Asian Monetary Fund, suggested by Tokyo but scotched by Washington in response to the Asian Financial Crisis. The original idea also was that the summit might replace the ASEAN+3 process, which has evolved over the past eight years. China had been an enthusiastic supporter of the summit, and had offered to host another summit in 2006. The summit was intended to initiate a process that would eventually evolve into a "community."

East Asia has no history of a common "community" and the precedent for an attempt to impose one is Japan's declared "co-prosperity sphere" of World War II. The purpose and goals of the summit were not defined, and neither was its planned relationship with the other elements of East Asia's multilateral architecture. Attention was, therefore, focused on the criteria to decide who would be invited to the summit. The behind-the-scenes arguments within ASEAN focused on criteria that would permit the United States to participate, with Singapore and Japan (with Indonesia also playing a role) pressing hard against considerable apathy and some opposition for a formula that would encourage America's inclusion.[22] In the event, acceptance of the TAC paved the way for the inclusion of India, finessed the charge of Asian anti-Western racism by including Australia and New Zealand, and excluded the United States. These three invitees to the summit participated in the Asian+3 Summit in Vientiane, Laos, in November 2004.

Washington has paid little attention to the ASEAN+3, and its response to the planned summit was low-key. Washington's blasé attitude was based, in part, on the assumption that American interests would be "looked after" by its allies and friends.[23] It also included concern that another multilateral organization would create further redundancy in East Asia organizations and compete in particular with APEC.[24] Finally, some American pundits noted that the U.S. Senate was unlikely to take up American signature of ASEAN's TAC, the proximate reason for U.S. exclusion, in a timely manner.

For China, participation in a high-profile "Asia-only" summit without the Americans was likely to have substantial advantages, though Sino-Japanese rivalry placed constraints on China's ability to exploit this gift. The key question was whether ASEAN could adopt a cohesive position on the outcome and remain in the driver's seat, or whether Beijing would be able to work effectively with individual ASEAN members to frame the agenda for follow-on efforts to institutionalize the East Asian community. According to one scholar, "In the end, two overarching issues were played out: ASEAN's insistence on being at the center of all regional efforts and competition between China and Japan over the summit's composition and role, a competition related to their broader rivalry for power and influence. The result was something of a muddle, but a muddle that everyone can live with for now."[25] In fact, China "worked assiduously—and ultimately successfully—to ensure not only the continued existence but the central guiding role of the ASEAN+3"[26] and the United States was satisfied because "for the U.S. the best outcome of the summit is that it does nothing."[27] As has so often been the case in Southeast Asia in recent years, many Southeast Asians tended to blame the muddle on Japan and its "refusal to move in a helpful way."[28]

The next part of this chapter will review how China and Southeast Asian states have employed multilateral mechanisms to address conflicting territorial claims in the South China Sea, as well as transnational regional issues.

A TRADITIONAL SECURITY ISSUE: CONFLICTING CLAIMS IN THE SOUTH CHINA SEA

Overlapping territorial claims in the South China Sea, whose seabed contains oil and substantial natural gas deposits, is the most sensitive traditional security issue between China (and thus Taiwan) and Vietnam, the Philippines, Malaysia, and Brunei, four of ASEAN's ten member states.[29] Additional security concerns in the South China Sea for these states include access to rich fishing grounds, potential control of sea-lanes,[30] and, given the extent of the Chinese claim in the South China Sea as indicated on maps released in 1992, the possibility that China will sit at the maritime doorstep of several Southeast Asian states in the future. However, by enlisting ASEAN and through the ARF process, Southeast Asian states were able to patiently bring Beijing around, over several years, to agree to temporarily shelve the dispute. China agreed to a nonbinding "Declaration on the Conduct of Parties in the South China Sea" at the ASEAN Summit in Phnom Penh, Cambodia, in November 2002. Beijing could not reconcile what critics of its policy characterized as "creeping aggression" in the South China Sea with its "New Security Concept."

The South China Sea dispute illustrates the evolution of China's approach to its southern neighbors on an issue of growing importance to a country and regime deeply concerned about its energy security. In this dispute, ASEAN claimants long saw China as a threat and an occasional military aggressor in the South China Sea. China used military force twice to push Vietnamese garrisons off islands and occupy them itself: once in 1974, against South Vietnamese forces in the Paracels in the northern part of the South China Sea; and again in 1988, against a united Vietnam's Communist government,[31] in a Spratly island cluster. More alarming to most ASEAN states was China's occupation, in 1995, of Mischief Reef, claimed by the Philippines. Beijing built structures on the island, and Philippine military intelligence sources periodically reported new Chinese construction and activities at Mischief Reef, particularly in 1998.

Early attempts to manage differences were largely bilateral, though ASEAN's 1992 "Manila Declaration on the South China Sea" called for restraint. Bilateral agreements included the 1995 Philippines-China and 1996 Philippines-Vietnam agreements on "principles for a code of conduct" and the delimitation of the Vietnamese-Chinese boundary in the Gulf of Tonkin in 2000. The 1997 ASEAN-China Summit, the coming out party for Chinese multilateralism, called on the two sides to continue to exercise restraint and "handle relevant differences in a cool and constructive manner."[32]

In 1999, following revelations of China's buildup on Mischief Reef, Manila took the initiative to propose a "Code of Conduct" for all parties in the dispute over island claims. ASEAN's drafts for such a code included commitments not to occupy new islands or reefs, not to resort to force, and to make serious efforts to resolve differences peacefully. However, ASEAN did not present a united front in rejecting China's South China Sea claims or condemning its actions—which is scarcely surprising since in late 1990s ASEAN claimants sometimes came close to armed confrontation among themselves over disputed islands.[33] Moreover, ASEAN was internally divided over the geographic scope of the proposed code. Vietnam, a new ASEAN member, sought to reopen the issue of the Paracel islands, all of which have been occupied by China since 1974, while other ASEAN states, most prominently Malaysia, sought to have the code cover only the Spratlys. Kuala Lumpur also seemed to be the most prepared of the ASEAN claimants to accommodate Beijing, leading to accusations that it hoped to eventually cut a bilateral deal. Nonetheless, China agreed to discuss the drafting of a code.

China finally agreed not to a code but to the nonbinding "Declaration on the Conduct of Parties in the South China Sea," at the ASEAN Summit in Phnom Penh, Cambodia, in November 2002. The commitments in this document fall short of what ASEAN sought, but it calls on the parties to refrain from the occupation of additional uninhabited islands and other features, to continue regular consultations on the "observance" of the declaration, and to agree to work towards an eventual binding code of conduct. Since the Declaration on Conduct was signed in Phnom Penh, Manila has charged that China has continued to plant markers on disputed islands and deploy naval units to Mischief Reef. Philippine Defense Secretary Angelo Reyes reported in May 2003 that new fortifications were being built in the islands, but several of the Southeast Asian claimants have also taken steps to strengthen their claims.

ASEAN is convinced that the declaration has restrained China and serves as a building block for the future.[34] In effect, an argument can be made that it moves from "confidence building to conflict prevention."[35] A Chinese expert argues that it:

- Provides ASEAN and China with a formal, even if not legal, framework for understanding and cooperation
- Serves, more or less, as a safety valve to prevent the relevant parties from taking further unilateral actions
- Provides the parties with a solid basis for the adoption of a formal regional code of conduct, if this is the desire of all the parties concerned.[36]

It is the first formal agreement entered into by China concerning the South China Sea, and is an agreement between China and ASEAN, rather than individual Southeast Asian states.

It also urges the parties to promote exploration and cooperation on marine environmental protection, scientific research, safety of navigation, search and rescue, and efforts aimed at combating transnational crime. The Philippines and Vietnam had held "joint oceanographic and marine scientific research expeditions in disputed areas."[37] In 2005, agreement was reached among China, Vietnam, and the Philippines to conduct joint seismic studies in contested waters.

NONTRADITIONAL SECURITY

In Southeast Asia, Asia's Severe Acute Respiratory Syndrome (SARS) epidemic of 2003 was seen not just as a medical issue but also as an economic challenge potentially as devastating as the 1997 Asian Financial Crisis and thus as a major threat to political stability and national security. Chinese cooperation with Southeast Asian states to manage this threat is viewed by some as one of the "three waves of monumental transformation since the late 1980s" in the East Asian "socio-economic evolutionary process."[38] Even a Chinese commentator ranks combating "transnational crimes, epidemics" as the fourth priority, after Taiwan, economic development, and energy security.[39]

The Joint Declaration on Non-Traditional Security Issues was signed between China and the ten ASEAN member governments at their Phnom Penh summit meeting in November 2002. It fits like a glove with several Southeast Asian elites' growing conviction that transnational challenges—from epidemics to terrorism—pose far more significant threats to economic growth, social stability, and regime continuance than such classic security problems of the cold war era as an armed attack or subversion. In this joint declaration, these eleven states agreed to enhance intelligence sharing, training, and other forms of cooperation in stemming "transnational crime," including trafficking in narcotics and people, maritime piracy, terrorism, weapons smuggling, money laundering, and economic crimes. The joint declaration has not contributed significantly to efforts to deal with terrorism and maritime piracy, which have been addressed through Southeast Asian ad hoc arrangements. However, where the problems either have their origin in China itself, or where it is clear from ASEAN's point of view that these problems can be managed effectively only with China's participation, the declaration has provided essential political legitimacy to joint efforts. China learned a lesson about the need for regional cooperation from its experience with SARS.

EPIDEMICS AND POTENTIAL PANDEMICS

Beijing's intense campaign to portray China as Southeast Asia's most reliable and responsible partner would have taken a severe beating if China had failed to respond to growing panic as the SARS disease spread from China to Southeast Asia in early 2003. From the initial appearance of the disease, Southeast Asian elites were appalled by the possibility that the epidemic would wreck havoc with their economies just as many of their countries were finally recovering from the Asian Financial Crisis. Apocalyptic forecasts predicted that SARS could cost as much as $50 billion.

Beijing initially failed to acknowledge the depth of its problem and refused to promptly cooperate with international health authorities. SARS spread to Vietnam and Singapore, as infection spread out from the first international SARS carriers in Hong Kong in early March. Both Southeast Asian countries imposed drastic mandatory quarantine measures for anyone suspected of exposure, with criminal penalties for violation. Vietnam imposed controls on its border with China and quarantined more than 2,000 students returning from China in May. Malaysia, Thailand, and Indonesia, which had few SARS cases, adopted less stringent procedures, but shared in the sense of panic.

Despite the fear and anger, Southeast Asian countries realized that China's cooperation would be essential in dealing with the disease, and that they had little leverage to bring to bear on Beijing, which would probably react defensively to open criticism. The Southeast Asian response was to work through ASEAN to quietly persuade China's leadership that multilateral cooperation was necessary to deal with the disease. Singapore and Thailand, China's "best friend," invited China to an ASEAN summit in Bangkok at the end of April to agree on measures to combat the disease. Wen Jiabao participated in his first international meeting since taking office as China's premier. Wen, who subsequently became China's point man on Southeast Asia, indirectly apologized for China's initial lack of cooperation, telling a Bangkok press conference Beijing had already learned its lesson. The summit declaration announced agreed measures to combat SARS. These included prompt international reporting and full cooperation in sharing information on the disease. China's initial failure to do so could have had a devastating impact in Southeast Asia.

As it turned out, all Southeast Asian countries suffered sharp drops in tourism, a key sector for the region's economies, and saw serious declines in trade. Travel by overseas workers, important for the Philippines, Thailand and Indonesia, was temporarily halted. The Asian Development Bank (ADB) calculated in early May that if the SARS epidemic lasted six months, the cost in reduced GDP would be 2.3 percent for Singapore, and close to 1.5 percent each for Malaysia, Thailand, and Indonesia.[40] In the event, Southeast Asia's economies recovered rapidly.

With either the zeal of the newly converted or the zeal of the highly embarrassed, Chinese leaders donned the mantle of leadership in calling for international transparency and cooperation. In June, China's vice health minister took the opportunity of a Beijing SARS symposium to call on Asian governments to enhance the sharing of information about the disease, while ASEAN health ministers declared their region free of SARS. In July, senior ASEAN officials agreed on an initiative by China on the management of public health emergencies.

One author claims that cooperation to eradicate SARS was the third of the "socio-economic changes that have helped cement East Asian regionalism and 'concretize' the ASEAN+3 framework."[41] While this and the idea that "SARS has indeed helped create a new East Asian bonding and awareness" is an exaggeration, SARS was a pointed lesson in the vulnerability of Asian states to acute threats that originate as internal affairs, but escalate rapidly to sweep across borders and threaten regional economies and societies.

The current avian flu epidemic, now provoking cautionary measures at considerable expense around the world, continues to challenge the authorities in Southeast Asian states. China's reaction to this threat has drawn mixed reviews, but has been more impressive than Indonesia's. The latest major scandal concerning avian flu in Southeast Asia is Indonesia's decision to cover up the spread of the disease among poultry for up to two years, only revealed in October 2005 after a growing number of human deaths from the disease.

THE LIMITS OF MULTILATERALISM: REGIONAL AND TRANSNATIONAL ISSUES

Myanmar (Burma)

ASEAN admitted Myanmar in 1997, hoping that inclusion would gradually soften the military regime and nudge it toward national reconciliation with the Burmese National League for Democracy, led by Nobel prize recipient Aung San Suu Kyi. ASEAN's gamble has proven to be an embarrassing failure. China has seldom been willing to bring pressure on the generals in Myanmar to help a divided ASEAN save face; competition for influence in Myanmar from New Delhi and Bangkok presents Beijing with even more of a dilemma.

The military regime's conviction that only it can prevent the disintegration of the state, its violation of the human rights of ethnic minorities and of democratic activists in pursuit of national unity, and its intransigence in the face of both Western sanctions and the pleas to follow ASEAN states, leaves outsiders with little effective leverage. In 2005, behind the scenes pressure from ASEAN members (and perhaps from China) did convince the regime to skip its turn to assume the rotating chairmanship of ASEAN, but that proved to be the limit of the regime's responsiveness. Myanmar's participation in ASEAN and other ASEAN-inspired multilateral institutions has not rubbed off at home, and the rejection of the Malaysian foreign minister's pleas in 2005 was particularly crude and infuriating. Indonesia did a bit better with an offer to provide lessons learned from its own experience under a military regime before 1998, but to no discernible effect. ASEAN has rejected suspending Myanmar's membership as counterproductive and routinely denounced Western sanctions as ineffective. Beijing, meanwhile, is not going to put its stake in its neighbor at risk in an attempt to promote a regional Chinese-ASEAN solution to the Myanmar problem.

Terrorism

China has played a barely noticeable role in combating terrorism in Southeast Asia. There the United States, with a significant Australian contribution, has backed a coalition of threatened Southeast Asian states working through a series of bilateral arrangements and understandings to arrest and detain over 300 terrorists, and to suppress international and regional terrorist organizations operating in Southeast Asia. China has played no public role, except as an anxious observer, in efforts by the littoral states of the Strait of Malacca, pressured and supported principally by the United States and Japan, to protect shipping from pirates, and potentially terrorists, in the Strait.[42]

China has been supportive of counterterrorist initiatives by others in Asian multilateral forums, a position that has played a significant role in the improvement of China's relations with the United States since the 9/11 attacks in the United States. In ASEAN, ARF, and APEC meetings, Beijing has approved consensus statements, such as ASEAN's statement on countering terrorism at the 2002 ASEAN Summit, and pledged to cooperate in combating terrorism.[43]

Beijing's primary concern has been to secure Southeast Asian support for its repression of Turkic revolutionaries in Xinjiang province, some of whom have terrorist connections. In addition, though there is as yet no evidence of links between Southeast Asian terrorists associated with Jema'ah Islamiyah and Muslim insurgents in western China, China has sought to establish close links with ASEAN governments in intelligence sharing, financial networks, and related areas. Beijing is concerned about the possibility that international terrorists will link up with Turkic Islamic radicals or that the wealthy coastal provinces of China, with extensive trade and transportation links into Southeast Asia, will become targets.

The 2004 Tsunami

The Indian Ocean tsunami, the result of a magnitude 9.0 undersea earthquake off the coast of Sumatra, killed about 200,000 people in Southeast Asia, and devastated the lives of many more. The massive international response included a major role for the United States, including the U.S. Navy. Millions of Americans contributed more than $1 billion to that relief effort, the U.S. government's contribution totaled nearly that amount, and the U.S. Navy played the most prominent role of any external military in providing desperately needed assistance in the immediate aftermath of the disaster.

China's limited assistance of $83 million in government donations and $18 million in private donations, which used up most of its international disaster relief budget,[44] was very much appreciated, as much for its symbolism and for its effectiveness. As a Singaporean official commented, it showed that "China is a responsible regional player."[45]

Narcotics

China has addressed narcotics primarily through bilateral diplomacy with its Southeast Asian neighbors. Narcotics, including heroin and methamphetamines, flow directly from the infamous Thailand-Laos-Burma "Golden Triangle" across China's often loosely controlled borders, and are widely available in neighboring Yunnan province. In 2003, Beijing acknowledges 1.05 million officially registered drug addicts in China.[46] Intravenous heroin users account for over 70 percent of the rising number of confirmed HIV/AIDS cases in the country. Since the early 1990s Beijing has become alarmed, and has placed a high priority on suppressing the narcotics trade. The development of new transportation links to support the economic development of the relatively poor Southwest Chinese provinces, both to the wealthy Chinese coast and through mainland Southeast Asia, has complicated Chinese efforts to clamp down on the narcotics trade.

As with terrorism for the United States, suppressing narcotics is too important for China to wait on multilateral mechanisms. Beijing has, however, put its diplomatic efforts into the ASEAN+1, ASEAN+3, and GMS frameworks, and several subregional arrangements, such as a 1993 Memorandum of Understanding on drug control with the states of mainland Southeast Asia. China has also pressed counter-narcotics in the Upper Mekong Committee, a forum including Burma, China, India, Laos, and Thailand, and the Thai-sponsored "Asia Cooperation Dialogue" begun in 2002. Most of China's counter-narcotics efforts have gone into bilateral arrangements with Burma, Laos, Vietnam, Thailand, and due to smuggling from coastal China, the Philippines. These efforts have included initiatives to establish programs in intelligence sharing, combined police operations and arrests, training of law enforcement officers, crop substitution, and improved border control.

TRADITIONAL SECURITY

ASEAN member states have insisted since the organizations' founding in 1967 that traditional security issues should not be addressed through ASEAN, but between individual sovereign states on a bilateral basis. Security cooperation is almost always, even among ASEAN members, conducted on such a basis.[47]

An attempt by China to gain access in Southeast Asia that would permit it to sustain even small naval forces in the region would set off alarm bells and contradict

China's efforts over the past decade to argue that Southeast Asian states' traditional security arrangements, for example with the United States, are no longer required in view of China's New Security Concept. China has not, to the best of the author's knowledge, proposed combined military exercises with more than one Southeast Asian state, though it did conduct multilateral antiterrorist exercises in Central Asia under the auspices of the Shanghai Cooperation Council.

Nonetheless, at the ASEAN Summit in Bali in October 2003, China's foreign minister again proposed that the ARF sponsor a "security policy conference" of military and civilian officials.[48] ASEAN ministers agreed that a concept paper, written by China, could be circulated in due course to ARF participants, and in November 2004, Beijing hosted the first security policy conference of the ARF. At this conference, ASEAN states politely demurred on some of China's more ambitious suggestions but this conference complemented the initiation of new, albeit low-level, military-to-military ties between China and individual Southeast Asian states. In December 2004, the ASEAN-China plan of action to implement the strategic partnership apparently encouraged dialogue on security issues, cooperation on military training, joint exercises, and peacekeeping operations between China and ASEAN states. In May 2005, the second ARF conference was held in at Vientiane, Laos.

China's military and traditional security relationships with individual Southeast Asian states were addressed in Chapters 3 and 4, and traditional security issues are a major element in U.S. relations with several Southeast Asian states, addressed in Chapter 7.

SUMMARY

China's decision to supplement bilateral diplomacy with high-profile East Asian regionalism and multilateralism has been particularly welcomed in Southeast Asia, where it resonates with ASEAN norms and practices, and contributes to popular perceptions of China as a benign neighbor. China has proposed sweeping, if often largely symbolic initiatives, highlighting perceived American unilateralism. Although Southeast Asian states have reflexively turned to multilateralism as a means to "socialize" China in their procedures and norms, ASEAN's internal cohesiveness may have suffered.

China and its Southeast Asian neighbors have used multilateral mechanisms to sideline their most serious dispute, over conflicting claims in the South China Sea, and to address such threatening nontraditional issues as the SARs epidemic of 2003. Both have failed to nudge Myanmar toward sufficient national reconciliation to take the human rights situation in that country off the international agenda. Where the United States has taken the lead, ad hoc coalitions have been formed to bypass unresponsive multilateral mechanisms to build an antiterrorism coalition and respond to the devastating tsunami of 2004. ASEAN states tend to argue that multilateralism is a goal in and of itself, though the disappointing outcome of the EAS may dampen enthusiasm for an East Asian community.

The next chapter addresses what many observers believe to be the heart of China's relationships with Southeast Asia—the impact of China's booming economy on the economic growth and thus the political stability of many Southeast Asian countries.

CHAPTER 6

CHINA'S ECONOMIC RELATIONS WITH SOUTHEAST ASIA

China is widely expected to become Southeast Asia's most important trade partner in 2006. In 2004, China's trade with Southeast Asia topped $103 billion, or about 10 percent of ASEAN's total trade. In 2005, it had reached about $130 billion. Moreover, the rapid growth in China-ASEAN trade shows no signs of slowing.[1] The China-ASEAN Free Trade Agreement (CAFTA) may help maintain the momentum.

With the emergence of China as the world's new manufacturing hub, ASEAN countries became deeply concerned with the possibility that competition with China would crowd out their export-driven growth. These fears have subsided as their trade with China accelerated, though trade with the rest of the world stagnated for many years after the Asian Financial Crisis of 1997. Indeed, the reality of trade with China is now often conflated with anticipation of the future of that trade, creating a heady brew of anticipated domestic political stability based on continued economic growth and integration into a larger East Asian economic community.

The relative benefits of this expansion of trade are not yet clear, both between trade partners and for specific industries. The consensus of opinion is that both partners benefit as a whole, though trade with ASEAN may accelerate China's GDP growth more rapidly than that of the ASEAN states. The data suggests increasing intra-industry interdependence in ASEAN and China as both become more integrated parts of regional production networks for multinational firms. On the whole Southeast Asian exports appear to have lost out to China's in global markets and relatively cheap Chinese manufactured products are underselling local products in several Southeast Asian markets.

Many Southeast Asian elites feared that China was diverting FDI from Southeast Asia. In 2004, China was estimated to attract over 55 percent of FDI inflows to East Asia, compared to less than 20 percent for Southeast Asia, but FDI flows to Southeast

Asia rebounded in 2005.[2] Much of Southeast Asian angst was misplaced because there is no evidence that China and ASEAN are engaged in zero-sum competition for FDI. Nonetheless, Southeast Asian elites hope that the developing trade relationship and the CAFTA will encourage more foreign direct investment (FDI), including investment from China. Thus far, though Chinese leaders have pledged to encourage Chinese investment in Southeast Asia, FDI flows to the ASEAN countries continue to be dominated by the European Union, the United States, and Japan.[3] Moreover, Southeast Asian investment in China, which probably totals an FDI stock of $40 billion, continues to be about ten times larger than China's investment in Southeast Asia. The emergence of a clearer "China plus Southeast Asia" investment strategy on the part of multinational firms could help to shift relative FDI flows from China to Southeast Asia.[4]

China does not dominate most Southeast Asian states' economies. There is little evidence that Beijing has sought to leverage its growing trade relationships to lobby on specific commercial issues, though anticipation that China is the "wave of the future" may influence Southeast Asian elite decision making.[5] China has become one of Southeast Asia's major trading partners, but the negotiations between China and individual Southeast Asian countries over the details of implementing the CAFTA and its associated "early harvest" provisions suggest that some industries and agricultural interests in Southeast Asian states are wary of Chinese competition and prepared to seek protection. In addition, the United States, Japan, and the European Union continue to dominate as providers of FDI. China is only a comparatively significant source of aid and investment in Southeast Asia's least developed mainland states of Laos, Cambodia, and Myanmar.[6]

China's search for reliable energy supplies will play a less significant role in its relations with Southeast Asia as a whole than trade. Nonetheless, boundary disputes in the South China Sea and the security of energy supply lines through Southeast Asian maritime chokepoints are potential "high-politics" national security issues, and thus likely sources of tension. Moreover, these issues touch directly on the security concerns of not only several Southeast Asian states and China, but also on those of the United States, Japan, and India.

Access to Southeast Asian energy resources is important to China, but not critical. Southeast Asia is a net oil importer, but a significant source of natural gas. Indonesia hopes that China will pay a premium to invest in long-term LNG contracts. A pipeline through Myanmar, should it be constructed, may strengthen Beijing's bilateral relations with Myanmar and Thailand. Intervention by the U.S. Congress to discourage a Chinese oil company's acquisition of the U.S.-based Unocal company, which had substantial energy reserves in Southeast Asia, probably again reminded Beijing of its dependence on the United States and Southeast Asian governments for the security of China's energy supply lines.

In short, trade and energy issues are likely to remain at the heart of many Southeast Asian countries' relationships with China, but both issues carry considerable political baggage. From a Southeast Asian perspective, trade's value is enhanced by the political aura that surrounds the word, with its implications for continued economic growth and thus regime stability. Energy, on the other hand, implies the possibility of eventual tension if outsiders seek to intervene in Southeast Asia in the name of energy security.

This chapter examines the China-Southeast Asian economic relationship in terms of trade, investment, development assistance, and energy.

TRADE

In Southeast Asia, "trade" is not only an economic fact measured by the exchange of goods and services. Instead, the term "trade" is often associated with growing prosperity and political stability. Many of the coalitions that form Southeast Asian governing elites base their legitimacy in large part on economic growth.[7] Moreover, despite considerable speculation about the potential role of domestic demand,[8] both economic reality and the dominant economic model remain export-driven growth. Thus, private business considerations often compete with national strategic considerations in elite decision making.[9] The combination of extraordinary real growth in trade, anticipation of future growth, talk of economic "bandwagoning" with China in a larger East Asian economic community, and the impact of trade on domestic political legitimacy, contribute to the prominent role of trade in Southeast Asian relations with China.

The "China trade" is the bright spot in an otherwise lackluster export performance by Southeast Asian states in the new century. ASEAN international trade had been in a slump; Southeast Asian countries had good reasons to fear that competition from China would crowd out their exports. With the modest accomplishments of ASEAN's own free trade area[10] and slow growth in domestic demand in most Southeast Asian countries, increasing trade with China proved a key to Southeast Asian states' recovery from the 1997 debacle.

China-Southeast Asia trade statistics vary widely depending on the source.[11] Moreover, there is no consensus on when trade between "Hong Kong, China" and Southeast Asia should be included as part of China's trade with Southeast Asia.[12] In addition, anecdotal evidence suggests that an unusually high percentage of Southeast Asian-Chinese trade is "processing" trade, which leads to double counting as components cross several borders. One estimate is that "processed (imported) components contribute between 60 and 80% of the value of all Chinese exports."[13] This skews and exaggerates the significance of the emerging trade relationship.

Whatever statistics are employed, it is clear that the ASEAN countries' trade with most of the world has grown slowly for the past nine years even in nominal terms, and rapidly with China. Most observers believe that 2006 statistics, when they are compiled and released, will show that China-ASEAN trade has surpassed ASEAN's trade with its traditionally larger trade partners of the United States, Japan, and the European Union. In 2004, U.S.-ASEAN trade was $136 billion,[14] compared to $103 billion for China-ASEAN trade.[15]

Working from IMF statistics, bilateral trade with the ASEAN states reached an astonishing growth of over 45 percent in 2000 and nearly 43 percent in 2003. China's share of ASEAN trade more than quadrupled from 2.3 percent in 1990 to nearly 10

Table 6.1
China-Mainland and China-Hong Kong Trade with ASEAN States ($ million)[16]

	China Mainland			China Hong Kong		
	1999	2004	2005	1999	2004	2005
Brunei	8	299	261	41	59	33
Cambodia	160	482	563	161	460	507
Indonesia	4,830	13,481	16,799	2,308	2,861	3,194
Laos	32	114	131	10	7	8
Malaysia	5,280	26,261	30,726	5,287	8,978	9,744
Myanmar	508	1,146	1,209	101	84	84
Philippines	2,287	13,328	17,559	3,333	6,888	7,531
Singapore	8,563	26,684	33,247	11,921	19,859	23,398
Thailand	4,216	17,344	21,813	4,497	7,523	8,827
Vietnam	1,318	6,743	8,188	651	1,673	1,784

percent by 2004, and it doubled from 2000 to 2004 alone. The trade balance has been in ASEAN's favor.

Since China's economy is over two and a half times as large as the economies of all the Southeast Asian countries combined, ASEAN is more dependent on exports to China than vice versa. Southeast Asian countries are primarily suppliers of raw materials and intermediate inputs to China. The top items of ASEAN exports to and imports from China are electrical and electronic products, parts and components. The original ASEAN members, Indonesia, Malaysia, the Philippines, Singapore, and Thailand, account for 90 percent of Southeast Asia's trade with China. The maritime Southeast Asian states, that are not part of China's traditional "backyard," account for 77 percent of Southeast Asia's trade with China. Table 6.1 shows the value of the trade, expressed in millions of dollars, between China and individual Southeast Asian states and between Hong Kong and individual Southeast Asian states, for the years 1999, 2004, and 2005.

If 10 percent or more of trade is considered to make one economy dependent on another, then several ASEAN countries were becoming "dependent" on China even by 2003. In 2004, if this 10 percent figure is used, Myanmar, Indonesia, Malaysia, the Philippines, and Vietnam had already become "dependent" on their China trade. If "China, Hong Kong" trade is added to the figures for "China, Mainland," 16 percent of ASEAN's trade was with "China" in 2004.

However, we need to be cautious about the meaning of "dependence." There is little evidence that trade alone provides Beijing with leverage on Southeast Asian governments, though it may do so with some Southeast Asian companies or other companies invested in Southeast Asia. Japan's repeatedly demonstrated inability (or unwillingness) over the past thirty years to leverage its companies, and economic ministries, clout in Southeast Asia to exercise influence beyond narrow economic issues suggests that potential economic leverage can be difficult to translate into demonstrable effects.

The China-ASEAN Free Trade Agreement (CAFTA)

The China-ASEAN Free Trade Agreement (CAFTA) is more than an economic arrangement.[17] Beijing recognized that ASEAN states had legitimate concerns about direct competition with China in developed markets, particularly after China's accession to the World Trade Organization (WTO). Rather than deny the impact of China's "rise," Beijing made a political decision to acknowledge ASEAN concerns, and to propose economic policies designed to address these concerns. Southeast Asian states, in turn, made a political decision not to "circle the wagons" in their own ASEAN Free Trade Area (AFTA)[18] but to respond positively to China's overtures. ASEAN states thus expressed their acceptance of China's claimed benign intentions.

As Southeast Asia slowly recovered from the Asian Financial Crisis and began to focus on how to adjust to China's accession to the WTO, Chinese Premier Zhu Rongji stepped forward at the 2000 ASEAN Summit to propose the idea of comprehensive economic cooperation, including a China-ASEAN Free Trade Agreement. Though surprised, and initially wary, at the ASEAN+3 Summit the following year, ASEAN states agreed in principle to a free trade agreement.

At the next ASEAN+3 Summit in November 2002, ASEAN and China signed the Framework for Comprehensive Economic Cooperation Agreement that established the CAFTA. If implemented as proposed, ASEAN states will have preferential access to the Chinese market. Both ASEAN and China agreed to a framework agreement with special treatment and flexibility for the newer and poorer ASEAN members, where China has long exerted a predominant influence. Tariffs should be phased out for the wealthier, original ASEAN members of Brunei, Indonesia, Malaysia, the Philippines, Singapore, and Thailand by 2010, and by 2015 for the poorer ASEAN members of Cambodia, Laos, Myanmar (Burma), and Vietnam (the CLMV members of ASEAN). The framework agreement also provides for an "early harvest" in which the list of products and services to be liberalized will be determined by separate bilateral agreements to be negotiated between ASEAN member states and China. This "early harvest" provision was designed to provide ASEAN states with early access to China's market as well as lower tariffs for agricultural items.[19]

The joint China-ASEAN Declaration on Strategic Partnership for Peace and Prosperity was the centerpiece at the October 2003 ASEAN Summit in Bali, but economic ties were not forgotten. Chinese Premier Wen Jiabao lauded the growth of Chinese-ASEAN trade before a receptive audience, including the heads of state of the ASEAN countries. ASEAN Secretary General Ong Keng Yong praised Chinese growth as an opportunity for the region, noting that "When China grows, there are a lot of potentials and opportunities for all of us."[20] Within the declaration, CAFTA was identified as the pillar for ASEAN-China economic cooperation.

At the 2004 Summit, ASEAN and China adopted a sweeping plan of action for economic cooperation, which included the signing of the Agreement on Trade in Goods and the Agreement on Dispute Settlement Mechanisms. The two agreements went into force on January 1, 2005. Tariffs were to be reduced for approximately 7000 categories of industrial goods beginning in July 2005. Procedures for tariff reduction and elimination under the normal track and "sensitive track," as well as rules of origin for CAFTA, were also put in place. Tariffs for general products should come down to zero in 2010 and tariffs on "sensitive" goods by 2015.[21]

Who Will Benefit?

Protectionist pressures will complicate negotiations for trade liberalization. ASEAN's experience with its own ASEAN Free Trade Area (AFTA), which has often suffered from individual states' responsiveness to domestic protectionist pressures, and China's continuing and expanding trade deficit with ASEAN, suggest that implementing CAFTA will require determination on the part of both China's and Southeast Asia's political leadership. The difficulties of negotiating "early harvest" agreements between individual Southeast Asian states and China also suggest that implementation will not be a smooth process.

Particularly difficult to administer may be trade between the poorer CMLV countries and the Chinese provinces of Yunnan and Guangxi. From China's standpoint, CAFTA was designed, in part, to promote development in the Southwest provinces as a way of resolving an important domestic development gap with wealthier coastal provinces. Chinese influence predominates in these CMLV countries, but China has run an official trade surplus with them for the past fifteen years. CAFTA provides these states with an additional five years to adjust to its provisions. They may face relatively higher adjustment costs and must also deal with endemic corruption and smuggling across their borders, including with China.

CAFTA is designed to liberalize tariff and nontariff barriers. For the original, wealthier ASEAN-5 members, average tariff rates on Chinese products are already low at around 2.3 percent, compared to Chinese tariff rates on ASEAN products at around 9.4 percent.[22] Nontariff barriers imposed by China against ASEAN are also much higher than reciprocal nontariff barriers. Although trade barriers are higher in China, ASEAN states may face greater adjustment costs due to the difference in size between economies.

Predicting CAFTA's Consequences

In October 2001, the ASEAN-China Expert Group on Economic Cooperation published the results of its simulations, which predicted that CAFTA will increase ASEAN exports to China by 48 percent and China's exports to ASEAN by 55 percent, raising China's GDP by 0.3 percent and ASEAN's by 0.9 percent.[23]

A 2003 World Bank report[24] predicts CAFTA will increase China-ASEAN trade by at least $10 billion. According to the World Bank report, the major implications include:

- The acceleration of international production sharing will characterize China-ASEAN trade, with China increasingly a central player in production networks. Multinational firms will further rationalize their production by relocating segments of their production process from China to other countries in the region. China's demand for intermediate inputs will spur export growth from its neighbors.
- Liberalization of trade and investment will increase efficiency. This means, however, that ASEAN countries will have to undergo painful restructuring.

Agriculture sector liberalization will lead to gains in ASEAN exports. China's WTO accession will prevent it from increasing measures to protect domestic agriculture. Accession will also increase China's market for land-intensive products such as rice and for specialty, high-quality products from almost all countries. Reduction in protectionist measures for agriculture sets the stage for China's interests to coincide with those of countries that want to increase labor-intensive agricultural exports, such as the poorer ASEAN members.

- Demand will increase for natural resources such as wood and energy products.
- Opportunities for ASEAN telecom exports to China will increase. China is expected to be the largest market for telecoms in the world by 2010, and some ASEAN telecoms firms are highly competitive.

A third economic modeling exercise on the impact of CAFTA suggests that if CAFTA leads to the elimination of tariff and nontariff barriers, Chinese production will benefit especially in at least three sectors: textiles and apparel, motor vehicles and parts, and electronic equipment.

The only negative impact on China's trade balance would be its imports of ASEAN's agricultural products, which would cause a decline in domestic output. Countries well placed to benefit are the Philippines, Thailand, and Vietnam for rice, sugar, seafood, and poultry, and Malaysia for vegetable oils.

ASEAN countries estimate that their primary benefits will arise from market access to China for their quality food exports. They are predicted to also gain in exports of primary commodities, especially chemicals, rubber and plastic products, textile fibers, vehicles and parts, and electronic components and parts. For example, a 19 percent tariff cut in chemicals, rubber and plastic products will cause a rise of 77.6 percent in ASEAN exports to China. For vehicles and parts, ASEAN exports to China could grow by 473.5 percent as a result of a 20.1 percent tariff cut.

The overall result from the modeling exercise shows trade gains for both ASEAN and China in implementing CAFTA. China will increase its imports from ASEAN by 53.3 percent while China's exports to ASEAN will rise by 23.1 percent.

For ASEAN, trade among its members could decline significantly as a result, and ASEAN exports to third markets would face a decline of 1.4 percent for Japan, 0.8 percent for the United States and 1 percent for the European Union.

Overall, the real macroeconomic impact will be a real GDP increase by 0.36 percent for China and by 0.38 percent for ASEAN, with differences among its members (compared to the 2001 experts predictions of an increase in China's GDP by 0.3 percent and ASEAN's by 0.9 percent). Private investment is expected to increase by 0.7 percent for China and 0.8 percent for ASEAN. Private consumption and savings will rise by 0.4 percent and 0.2 percent respectively for China and by 0.5 percent and 0.8 percent respectively for ASEAN.

Beyond econometric modeling lies continued debate about the distribution of benefits from CAFTA. Moreover, to further complicate predictions of the relative benefits, the impact of the CAFTA would need to be integrated with predictions as to the impact of ASEAN's current negotiations for free trade agreements with several other countries, including Japan and India, as well as individual bilateral free trade negotiations with the United States, Japan, and others.

Moreover, it is not yet clear who has benefited most from the rapid growth in trade between Southeast Asia and China over the past several years. Until the data has been compiled and studies have been completed on Standard International Trade Classification (SITC) sectors, the ability of ASEAN countries to compete with China to retain market share in developed markets will not be known. The most we can say is that ASEAN states are participating in a new Asian division of labor as a supplier of components to the Chinese manufacturing hub. It appears, with regard to product categories, that:[25]

Manufactures

By 2003, about 40 percent of ASEAN exports to China consisted of machinery and electrical equipment.[26] A large percentage of these exports are integrated into finished products which are then re-exported from China. By 2004, China's exports of electrical equipment to Malaysia and Thailand had doubled the exports of these two states to China within the same category.

Primary Resources

The export of mineral products continues to increase. China has made significant investments in Southeast Asian mines and petroleum resources. In the long run, a declining percentage of China's oil will be derived from Southeast Asia (East Asia and the Pacific's percentage of China's energy imports fell from 2003 to 2004), but the region may eventually supply 40 percent of China's LNG imports.[27]

Agricultural Products

Chinese demand for agricultural products should favor ASEAN agricultural exports, but ASEAN exports of prepared foodstuffs appeared to drop in 2002 and the growth in ASEAN agricultural exports to China as a result of trade liberalization may not be as large as anticipated. Anecdotal information suggests that some Chinese agricultural products have been marketed in Thailand at levels below Thai production costs.[28]

Textiles, Apparel, and Footwear

Termination of the Multi-Fiber Agreement (MFA) in 2005 was expected to gut the textile producers of Southeast Asia, including Cambodia, Indonesia, the Philippines, and Vietnam, who are less competitive than China.[29] China has already undersold the Indonesian footwear industry.

Finally, CAFTA implementation will depend on individual countries, many of which will go through wrenching economic adjustments if it is ever fully implemented. The agreement will force individual ASEAN members to identify market niches and target consumer demand that reflect, in theory, comparative advantages.

It is widely believed that CAFTA could provide the more developed countries of Singapore, Malaysia, and Thailand with opportunities to produce some of the sophisticated manufactures that are now imported from countries outside a Chinese-ASEAN economic market. On the other hand, pundits have also predicted that China will turn directly to developed countries, bypassing Southeast Asia's more sophisticated manufactures. There is also considerable speculation about the potential for these ASEAN countries to provide for rising Chinese demand for such services as high-quality tourism, education, and healthcare. Certainly the flow of Chinese tourists is increasing rapidly (see Chapter 7).

ASEAN states and, in some cases, China are concerned about cushioning the impact of CAFTA on the projected losers in the process. Mainland Southeast Asian countries with common borders with China have been given more time to adjust, but are already flooded with cheap Chinese consumer products.

More controversial will be how to respond to increasing competition from Chinese goods in Indonesia, the Philippines, and Thailand, both in agriculture and manufacturing.

The World Bank report predicted that, under CAFTA, Thailand's "land-intensive" products would do well, and that it could expand its manufacturing base if it shifted into electronics, metals, and petrochemical products. In Thailand, complaints about Chinese dumping of both cheap manufactures and agricultural products accompanied the initiation of its 2004–2006 "early harvest" phase, and Bangkok has called for remedies. Thailand also expects enhanced tourism from China; though the flow of tourists from China has been flat at about 800,000 for several years. Nonetheless, Thailand included 242 "sensitive" products for which tariff rates will be not be cut to 20 percent until 2012 and another 100 "very sensitive" products for which tariffs will not be reduced by 50 percent until 2015, including coffee, tea, certain types of rice, soy oil, palm oil, sugar, raw silk, marble, ceramics, cars, motorcycles, paints, automobile types, steel, compressors, refrigerators, air conditioners, and toys.[30]

Although the World Bank report argued that the Philippines could increase production of food and feed grains, cottons, sugar, vegetables and fruits for export to China, the Philippines was the last ASEAN state to negotiate an "early harvest" provision, a reflection of growing pressures to protect its own agricultural industry. Organized farmers' groups complained that smuggled Chinese goods had adversely affected producers of dozens of agricultural commodities.

Indonesia has more economic sectors that compete with China than any other ASEAN state. The World Bank report predicted that Indonesian palm oil, rubber, timber, and processed oil would gain, but that footwear with leather soles and video recording apparatus, which together account for 12 percent of Indonesian exports to United States, would not be competitive. China has been primarily interested in tapping into Indonesia's oil and gas, minerals, and forestry products (wood and wood panel, pulp and paper.) Indonesia has reduced tariffs on some 600 products as part of its "early harvest" program since early 2004. However, Indonesia listed nearly 400 categories of sensitive and highly sensitive goods to be excluded from the CAFTA, including rice, sugar, soybeans, corn, electronics and automobiles, and selected branches of the textile and chemical industries.

FOREIGN DIRECT INVESTMENT (FDI)

As with trade, statistics on investment can suggest a misleading specificity. The general trend in the flow of foreign direct investment (FDI) to China and to Southeast Asia is clear. Actual annual flows of new FDI and investments from FDI stocks are less so. Even less reliable is the information on Southeast Asian investment in China and especially Chinese investment in Southeast Asia, which can be and are routed through a variety of third parties. China's possible role in diverting FDI from Southeast Asia is a subject of considerable debate, but it is not clear that China's ability to attract FDI is linked to the amount of FDI flowing to Southeast Asian states, or to decisions about the reinvestment of profits from already invested FDI.[31]

FDI Flows and Stock

As shown in Table 6.2, FDI flows into China reached $60.630 billion in 2004, while outward flows were calculated at $1.805 billion. Inward flows to "Hong-Kong, China" were $34.035 billion, while outward flows were calculated at $39.753 billion.[32] "Round-tripping" of investments out of China and then back again for tax and other advantages make calculations of investment in China problematic.

Up to the mid-1990s, as much as 60 percent of Chinese FDI stocks came from overseas Chinese,[33] many of whom lived in Southeast Asia. The overseas

Table 6.2
Total Global FDI into and from China and Southeast Asia ($ million)[35]

FDI Flows–China	2001 Total	2004 Total
Inward	46,846	60,630
Outward	6,884	1,850
FDI Flows–ASEAN	**2001 Total**	**2004 Total**
Inward	15,209	25,662
Outward	23,305	13,620

Table 6.3
Total FDI Flows into ASEAN States ($ million)[36]

	1996	2001	2004
Brunei	653	526	103
Cambodia	294	148	131
Indonesia	6,194	−3,279	1,023
Laos	128	24	17
Malaysia	7,297	554	4,624
Burma (Myanmar)	581	192	556
Philippines	1,618	982	469
Singapore	8,608	10,949	16,060
Thailand	2,270	3,813	1,064
Vietnam	1,803	1,300	1,610
ASEAN Total	29,447	15,209	25,662

Table 6.4
Percentage of FDI Inflows into Developing Asia-Pacific Absorbed by China and the Wealthier ASEAN-5 States[38]

	ASEAN-5	China
1996	27.5	42.8
2000	14.5	27.8
2001	15.5	41.9
2002	12.6	55.8
2003	14.4	49.9

Chinese share has since declined rapidly as a percentage of FDI flowing into China. Table 6.2 also shows Chinese outward FDI. According to UNCTAD statistics, China's outward FDI stocks in 2004, at $38.825 billion, had increased more than $10 billion since 2000. But Chinese outward direct investment is underestimated; one estimate is that illegal capital outflows from China totaled $53 billion just between 1997 and 1999.[34] On the other hand, how much of this $53 billion was reinvested in China is impossible to determine.

For comparison purposes, according to UNCTAD statistics, Southeast Asia's outward FDI stocks were $120.369 billion in 2004, or more than three times China's.[35] Tables 6.2 and 6.3 also show total FDI flows into ASEAN, a small percentage of China's total.

Table 6.4 shows the percentage of FDI inflows.[37]

In 2004, after Southeast Asian economies had begun to recover, ASEAN states attracted 40 percent as much FDI as China.

Southeast Asians worry that the rise in foreign investment in China comes at the expense of their economies in Southeast Asia. As shown in Table 6.3, there was sharp decline in FDI in the region from 1996 to 2001 (at $15 billion about half the 1996 total). Indonesia was hit the hardest, and suffered disinvestment through 2003. Singapore, which attracted about two-thirds of 2001 and 2004 investment in Southeast Asia, significantly increased its FDI flows. Thus the drop affected the rest of ASEAN disproportionately. Laos and Cambodia attract minuscule amounts of investment, while FDI into Myanmar only recovered its 1996 level in 2004. FDI flows to Malaysia, the Philippines, Thailand, and Vietnam declined significantly. The rapid rise in FDI into China coincided with its rapid decline into ASEAN, which only recovered when Indonesia stopped experiencing disinvestment.

Causality is more difficult to prove. Several factors may encourage investors to favor China over the ASEAN countries. The first is that investors follow other investors. The second is perceptions of political stability. China may not, in fact, have a comparative advantage over ASEAN countries in terms of political stability, particularly over ASEAN's relatively developed democracies, but Indonesia appeared unpredictable during its transition to a stable democracy. Once a leading destination for FDI, with stocks of over $60 billion as late as 2000, Indonesia suffered capital outflow until its election of a new President in 2004. Third, labor costs in China provide a considerable advantage over the middle-income ASEAN countries. Average Chinese labor costs are one-third of those in the Philippines, one-fourth of those in Malaysia, and less than one-tenth of those in Singapore.[39] Only those ASEAN countries that are much poorer than China, that is Vietnam, Laos,[40] Cambodia, and Myanmar, have labor costs comparable to those in China. Fourth, China's huge domestic market is a key reason that investors choose China, though the proposed CAFTA should alter this calculation. Finally, China's currency may be undervalued, though this too is controversial. Rates of return on investment are not a factor, since the average rate of return on FDI for China during the three years 1999–2001 was 5.9 percent, compared to 5.5 percent for Indonesia and 12.3 percent for Malaysia.[41]

Experts doubt ASEAN's suffering is linked to FDI flows to China. They tend to point to disincentives to investment that prevail in ASEAN countries, with the notable exception of Singapore.[42] Others note that an UNCTAD index of the ratio of the ASEAN share of global inward FDI to its share of global GDP is greater than one, meaning that its share of FDI is greater than that of the average economy in the rest of the world, and that this ratio for ASEAN is higher than that for China.[43] According to this measure, China receives proportionately less inward FDI than several ASEAN countries. In 2004 the ASEAN states' economies were about 40 percent the size of China's and received about 40 percent as much FDI as did China.[44]

Investment in the Other's Economies

Southeast Asia's ethnic Chinese were among the first investors in China in the early 1990s, and Beijing encouraged both private and government-linked Southeast Asian businesses to follow in their ethnic Chinese communities' footsteps. According to the Chinese Ministry of Commerce, cumulative ASEAN investment in China at the end of 2002 had a committed value of $58 billion, and an actual value of $29 billion. ASEAN investment totaled some 7 percent of total investment in China during the 1990s, but declined to 5 percent in the early years of this century.[45]

The largest ASEAN investor in China is Singapore, which began investing in China as soon as it opened up to foreign investment. Ethnic Chinese ancestral ties led initially to investment in small businesses in Guangdong and Fujian provinces, but Singapore, including government-linked companies, has since branched out into ambitious projects in other provinces. By the end of 2001 Singapore was the fifth largest investor in China, with a cumulative total realized investment of $18.6 billion.[46] By 2004, some estimates credited Singapore with $30 billion in investments.[47] Others suggest cumulative Singaporean investment of $28 billion in 2005. Another often cited figure gives Southeast Asians an aggregate of $40 billion over time, largely in the manufacturing and service sectors, with some 70 percent of that figure either from or circulated through Singapore. Malaysia and Thailand have also been significant investors in China, particularly in China's southwest, with some estimates suggesting investments of several billion each.[48] No one knows what percentage of the investments withdrawn from Indonesia after the Asian Financial Crisis ended up in China. The best guess is that Southeast Asian states' aggregate investment (FDI stocks) in China may total as much as $40 billion.

China's investment in Southeast Asian countries is comparatively small, but appears to be suddenly growing rapidly. Chinese cumulative total investment until 2003 may have been less than 1 percent of cumulative total investment in the ASEAN states. The various figures cited for Chinese investment range from a cumulative total of $821[49] million to less than $2 billion in 2001, accounting for 7.7 percent of China's overseas investments.[50] ASEAN Secretariat data shows such FDI inflows from China to ASEAN at $147.3 million in 2001, $80.9 million in 2002, $188.7 million in 2003, and $225.9 million in 2004.[51] Other sources suggest that China invested $151 million in ASEAN in 2001,[52] or 1 percent of the global flow of FDI into ASEAN that year. Many of these numbers, however, make little sense. For example, the alleged cumulative total of Chinese investment in ASEAN of $821.4 million in 2001 included Chinese investment in Myanmar of $8.9 million, which is too low. The best guess is Chinese cumulative investment of about $2 billion in ASEAN countries by 2002.

Malaysia and more recently Indonesia appear to have attracted a substantial share of Chinese investment in Southeast Asia. Chinese investments in Thailand went into manufacturing, garments, food processing, power generation, pharmaceuticals, and the trade and real estate sectors. Chinese investments in Singapore have gone mainly into insurance, banking, finance, shipping, and trade. China's investments in the Philippines were mainly in mining. China's investments in Indonesia are directed to the oil and the chemical, household electric appliances and motorcycle manufacturing sectors. Chinese companies are now the largest offshore oil producers in Indonesia.

Chinese investments—mostly from state-owned enterprises—have also targeted the newer ASEAN members. China's investments in Cambodia may have totaled $240 million by 2002, and China became Cambodia's largest investor by 2004. In Laos, ethnic Chinese may have become the country's largest private investors. In Myanmar, which hosts perhaps one million Chinese immigrants, Chinese investment has gone into the exploitation of timber, energy, and mineral resources. Finally, China has invested in Vietnam's forestry, fishery, agricultural, light industry, aluminum, infrastructure, and tourism.

Despite the reality of China's comparatively limited role as an investor in Southeast Asia, accelerating investment contributes to the impression of China as a potentially important future investor in Southeast Asia. The "Malaysia-China Forum" estimated Chinese investment in Malaysia at $1.1 billion in 2004. Vietnamese sources list Chinese cumulative investment at $540 million in 2004. In 2004, the Indonesian investment board listed $6.5 billion in Chinese investment in Indonesia, while Chinese government data showed $2 billion. According to Chinese figures, by the end of 2004, Chinese investment in the Philippines totaled $1.65 billion.

The current Chinese search for secure oil and natural gas will play a major role in Chinese investment in the region, and has already led Chinese companies to expend over $1 billion on several major acquisitions in Indonesia. In addition, Wen Jiabao discussed possible future Liquified Natural Gas purchases with Indonesian leaders during the October 2003 ASEAN Summit at Bali. In 2005, Chinese leaders pledged to encourage investment of as much as $10 billion in Indonesia in the next few years.

In short, Southeast Asian investment in China is probably about ten times Chinese investment in Southeast Asia, but the latter may be growing rapidly. The Asian Financial Crisis of 1997 led to a decline in FDI flows to Southeast Asia at the same time that FDI flows to China accelerated rapidly, but the relationship between the two phenomena is complex and causality is difficult to prove. Moreover, several Southeast Asian countries are beginning to attract renewed interest on the part of foreign investors and hope that CAFTA will lure an increasing share of foreign investment back to Southeast Asia.

DEVELOPMENT ASSISTANCE

China has successfully conveyed an impression of itself as a grander and more generous donor to the poorer states of Southeast Asia than the numbers warrant. The Chinese package often includes a high-level visit, pledges that aid comes without political strings, loans described as aid, loans forgiven, and promises to facilitate trade. The amounts are usually small, but the political impact is large.

Beijing is also particularly adept in responding to natural disasters. It has a good record in extending small amounts of emergency medical and food aid, as well as small reconstruction assistance, in the wake of earthquakes and other calamities in Southeast Asia in recent years. Its contribution of approximately $83 million in the wake of the Indian Ocean tsunami of 2004 was miniscule compared to the outpouring of aid from the international community as a whole.[53] But it received more than its fair share of the credit, in part because the Chinese style is to accompany aid with effusive high-level condolences and the suggestion that it deserves special thanks because China too is a fellow developing country prepared to share its limited resources with others.

For the mainland Southeast Asian countries falling within China's "backyard," aid has been quite small. For example, Cambodia received timely, if largely symbolic, military aid in the wake of Premier Hun Sen's internal coup, and $3.6 million for a military training center. The total amount of Chinese economic aid was reportedly only $68.8 million over a ten-year period ending in 2002, with a high point of $16.3 million in 2001,[54] but it is not clear whether this amount includes another $18.3 million in "foreign assistance guarantees" in 2002. Beijing also pledged to help finance a small section of the Singapore-Kunming railroad that will pass through Cambodia. In another typical gesture, Beijing announced that Cambodia's debts to China were cancelled as of 2002. In 2006, Cambodia announced that China had extended a "no strings attached" loan of $600 million to build roads and bridges and other infrastructure projects.

Perhaps better than any other recipient of Chinese aid, Vietnam demonstrates China's ability to use small amounts of aid to wring almost obsequious expressions of gratitude from its neighbors. In recent years, the trickle of economic assistance, mainly to sustain Chinese projects started during the war years, has included a $36 million soft loan to upgrade the Thai Nguyen steel complex in 1999, assistance for the Ha Bac Nitrogenous Fertilizer Plant, which was completed in November 2001,[55] and $40 million for a copper mine project. In 2002, Beijing extended a soft loan of $120 million, and in 2003 touted its offer to write off part of Vietnam's debt.

Myanmar appears to be the major recipient of Chinese largesse in Southeast Asia. China is often said to have provided up to $3 billion in aid to the military regime over the past fifteen years, of which between $1.6 and $2 billion is labeled military aid. But the only economic aid that can actually be identified seems to be two offers of either "preferential" or "soft" loans of $200 million, one in the wake of the house arrest of Myanmar's leading dissident in 2003.

With the relatively wealthy maritime Southeast Asian states, where China expects to reap trade or investment benefits, Chinese "aid" can be more generous. For example, during President Hu Jintao's 2005 visit to Indonesia, China extended $3.63 in aid, added $300 million in new "soft" loans to $400 million already pledged, and then confirmed $100 million in "preferential buyer's credits" during the Indonesian President's subsequent reciprocal visit to China. During Hu Jintao's 2005 visit to the Philippines, Beijing sweetened the visit with a $500 million loan at 3 percent interest for a railway and another "loan" for $24 million. In 2006, Beijing reportedly offered Manila $2 billion in loans annually through its export-import bank.

In short, China does not make the OECD lists of the top ten donors of ODA to Southeast Asian countries, and its aid is small compared to that provided by Japan or the United States. Nonetheless, by bundling tiny amounts of aid, substantial preferential loans at below market rates, and promises to facilitate trade, Beijing has conveyed an impression of Chinese generosity toward its smaller southern neighbors.

ENERGY

China's rapidly growing dependence on imported energy to fuel its continued economic growth is driving Beijing's campaign to secure oil and gas supplies across the globe. Southeast Asia does not have sufficient proven energy resources to make a significant dent in alleviating China's energy security angst. Instead, Chinese priorities are access to potential energy resources in disputed parts of the South China Sea and, above all else, energy transport routes through the region.

China is the world's second largest consumer of energy. It is the third largest importer of oil, behind the United States and Japan, now importing more than 40 percent of its oil, a figure that is expected to rise to 75 percent of its oil requirements within twenty years.[56] However, China imported only 11.5 percent of its crude oil from the Asia-Pacific region in 2004, down from 15.2 percent in 2003, and Southeast Asia as a whole is a net oil importer.[57] Chinese companies have aggressively pursued the acquisition of existing oil fields and exploration rights from other companies in Indonesia's oil patches.[58] Petro China Co. acquired Devon Energy-Indonesia Oil in 2002, valued at between $215 and $262 million, and the China National Offshore Oil Corporation (CNOOC) acquired nine subsidiaries of Repson-YPF SA in five Indonesian oil and gas fields in 2003, valued at $585 million.[59] Chinese companies also have interests in oil exploration in Myanmar and Thailand, and have discussed the possibility of a joint venture with the Indonesian national oil company to build large refineries in Indonesia.[60] Although Jakarta has finally resolved a dispute with ExxonMobil over the extension of a major contract, much of the Indonesian elite hopes Chinese oil companies will be prepared to accept higher associated costs and thus lower potential returns on their investments to exploit Indonesia's oil resources.

But natural gas, not oil, is the primary driver in China's search for secure energy in Southeast Asia. The Department of Energy (DOE) forecasts that imports will account for 40 percent of China's gas needs by 2025, much of which will be supplied in the form of liquefied natural gas (LNG) from Southeast Asia, including Indonesia, Malaysia, Brunei, Myanmar, and potentially the South China Sea.[61] Much to Indonesia's disappointment, Australia won the first contract to supply approximately $1 billion worth of LNG annually to China over the next twenty-five years, starting in 2006. However, for China's second LNG terminal, CNOOC signed a supply contract with Indonesia for LNG from Tangguh in 2007, and in the process used its leverage to purchase a 12.5 percent equity stake in the project for $275 million. Since LNG involves long-term, fixed contracts, governments play a critical role in LNG contract negotiations. Beijing's diplomacy and growing trade relations with Southeast Asian states can be leveraged to forge a long-term natural gas-based partnership with Indonesia. On the other hand, LNG contracts also provide the supplier with leverage over the recipient since the enormous investment in liquefaction and regasification plants make it expensive for either party to abrogate these contracts.[62]

A bid by the CNOOC to acquire the California-based Unocal became a political issue in the United States in 2005, but the public debate in America never focused on the fact that 70 percent of UNOCAL oil and gas reserves were in Asia, mostly under long-term contract to Asian nations like Thailand and Indonesia. Although both Southeast Asian and Chinese officials were discrete in public,[63] CNOOC's ultimately unsuccessful bid was a significant setback for China's campaign to acquire energy resources in Southeast Asia. Unocal's oil production in Southeast Asia of 76,000 barrels per day would have more than doubled China's oil production in the region, and it supplied one-quarter of Thailand's total gas consumption.

By acquiring Unocal, China would also have gained control of Myanmar's offshore Yadana gas exports by pipeline to Thailand, further enhancing its role as an energy supplier to China's "best friend." Finally, China would have acquired offshore gas fields that will provide a growing share of the gas feed to the large Bontang LNG project in Kalimantan, Indonesia.[64] In short, CNOOC's acquisition of Unocal would have strengthened China's strategic position as a major producer of oil and gas in Southeast Asia.

Conflicting boundary claims in the South China Sea have been addressed in the previous chapter as an example of successful Chinese-Southeast Asian efforts to temporarily shelve sovereignty issues through multilateral diplomacy. Here we will focus on the economic resources that may lie under the conflicting claims. Oil discoveries have been modest, but natural gas appears to be abundant around the edge of the sea. Chinese geologists, however, had consistently estimated that considerably higher potential oil and gas resources lie under the South China Sea than their western colleagues. "For example, published Chinese estimates for total oil resources in the South China Sea range from roughly 100 to 200 billion barrels, compared to a 1993–1994 U.S. Geologic Survey estimate of 28 billion barrels."[65] In addition, China's official maps include a vague dotted line in the South China Sea that could be interpreted to include a Chinese claim to Indonesia's extensive natural gas fields off the shores of the Natuna Islands separating the two parts of Malaysia. The November 2002 ASEAN-Chinese "Declaration on the Conduct of the Parties in the South China Sea" and a recent agreement for joint seismic study among China and two Southeast Asian countries suggests that, for the foreseeable future, Beijing is placing greater emphasis on developing the energy resources that lie under the sea than on sovereignty issues.

An even more difficult issue for Beijing than the South China Sea, however, is Southeast Asia's role as the critical transportation route for current and future Chinese oil and LNG supplies. Premier Wen Jiabao has publicly lamented China's "Malacca dilemma," as well he may. Formally, Beijing relies on littoral Southeast Asian states to provide security for energy supplies transiting the straits and other chokepoints. In fact, China relies on the United States, which will not surrender its domination of Southeast Asian waters for the foreseeable future. To ameliorate if not to solve this dilemma, China has considered alternative oil transport routes bypassing the Strait of Malacca and the South China Sea. At one point, China showed some interest in proposals to revive a two thousand year old trade route by building an oil pipeline across the Kra peninsula, but the Islamic revolt in southern Thailand finally drove the nail into that impractical idea. More attractive to Beijing, but with its own set of problems, would be a large oil pipeline from the coast of Myanmar to southwestern China, an area Beijing has stressed as a major development target.

China's basic problem is simple; there is no solution to China's growing dependence on energy resources from the Middle East and Africa, which must pass through Southeast Asia.

SUMMARY

The Chinese market has helped several Southeast Asian countries export their way back to economic growth, but China and Southeast Asia are economic competitors in developed markets such as Japan, Europe, and the United States. They are not zero-sum competitors for FDI from developed economies. It is not yet clear whether the export of components from ASEAN states to China, which has become East Asia's major assembly plant, compensates for lost markets for Southeast Asia's finished products in Japan, Europe, and the United States. Wealthier ASEAN countries hope to fill niches in an increasingly integrated East Asian economy but the emerging regional division of labor suggests they may often fail to compete, and poorer countries should be worried that Chinese economic competition will confine them to producers of raw materials to feed China's voracious manufacturing base.

Recognizing Southeast Asian concerns, China took the initiative to propose and then push a China-ASEAN Free Trade Agreement, which has temporarily assuaged most Southeast Asian concerns. Despite fantastic rates of growth in trade, China is only one of Southeast Asia's three major trade partners and does not yet dominate Southeast Asian economies. There is no evidence that China has successfully sought to leverage its growing economic clout.

Within the next twenty years, an estimated two-thirds of China's petroleum imports, which will have quadrupled, will flow from the Middle East through Southeast Asian waters. Moreover, China and four Southeast Asian countries claim parts of the natural gas rich South China Sea. China has already built dams on the Mekong, and plans more, which have had a negative impact downriver in Southeast Asia. China's energy angst, already acute, could become a source of friction in China's relationships with several of its neighbors to the South.[66]

The next chapter will consider the controversial issue of China's alleged "soft power" in Southeast Asia.

CHAPTER 7

"Soft Power"

"Soft Power" is a popular new mantra in Southeast Asia. This common term is used by so many different people to describe so many different things that it conveys little more than vague impressions. It has little explanatory value in and of itself. Academics praise or dismiss it, journalists use the term with abandon, and politicians fill speeches with references to soft power. Debate, even discussion, of Chinese soft power in Southeast Asia is largely hot air (or hot ink) until the term is defined.

Definitions of "soft power" range from all power or influence that does not involve coercion by armed force to the appeal of Chinese culture to ethnic Chinese minorities in the region. If the former—all nonmilitary power and influence—then the term has little value. China does not now pose a military threat to Southeast Asia; it has sought to redefine the concept of "security" in Southeast Asian terms; its comprehensive strategy for the region has a minimal traditional security component. In short, if soft power encompasses all but military issues it must include almost all the elements of Chinese influence in Southeast Asia. If the latter, the term dissolves into a study of an influential but small ethnic minority in the region.

Moreover, an American-centric version of soft power is more misleading than helpful. Soft power's primary intellectual advocate defines soft power as "the ability to get what you want through attraction rather than coercion or payments . . . Its sources include the attractiveness of a country's culture, political ideals, and policies."[1] Naturally, therefore, those who look through an American lens tend to dismiss China's soft power because the American version of soft power stresses the appeal of American political ideals such as a rights-based democratic political system and individuals' human rights.

Southeast Asians, however, don't look through an American lens. In their eyes, the soft power soup can include economic benefits, shared norms and values, cooperation on nontraditional issues, infatuation with the new China, the mutual benefits of tourism and education, diplomacy and style, and networking and reciprocal obligations within ethnic Chinese communities. In Southeast Asia, moreover, it is not the soup that matters as much as it is the attractiveness of specific ingredients in the soup to specific segments of Southeast Asian societies.

So what is soft power?

Because it is so difficult to define and then measure, one approach to soft power is to rely on polling and the commercial popularity of films, books, or other cultural artifacts as measures of this power. Putting aside for the moment the actual power of public opinion as revealed by polling, these measurements are both less available and reliable in Southeast Asia than they are in Japan, Europe, or the United States.

A second approach is to string together facts that attempt to convey the attractiveness of the values, culture, or products of a particular country. Thus the rapid growth in the flow of Chinese tourists to many Southeast Asian countries is thrown together with comments on Chinese consumer products, mixed with trade statistics, and supplemented with statements about the appeal to Southeast Asian youth of "Chinese" cultural exports. The result is a hodgepodge of impressions.

A third approach to soft power is to recommend government policies to enhance a state's soft power. The measures advocated often hark back to U.S. public diplomacy programs of the cold war era. They tell us little about Chinese soft power in Southeast Asia.

One critique argues that the traditional view of soft power confuses "attention, attractiveness, and persuasiveness."[2] The essential argument is that persuasion is the bottom line of "soft power," while attention and attractiveness are no more than prerequisites. Persuasion requires a confidence on the part of the party to be persuaded that the persuader is "articulating common goals in a framework of mutual respect." The critique goes on to argue that the United States has confused "attentiveness" on the part of others to American power with Washington's ability to "persuade," primarily because the current American leadership has failed to ""pursue common goals in a manner that does not threaten the autonomy of others." Whether this critique applies to the United States or not, it is useful because it stresses the mutual benefits and common goals aspect to soft power in Southeast Asia.

But what is the relative importance of "attraction" or "persuasion" in Chinese-Southeast Asian soft power relationships? China is attractive to some Southeast Asians but proof that it has yet "persuaded" Southeast Asian elites to act against their own interests is difficult to come by.[3] In addition, as in any relationship, another question is who is exercising soft power over whom? Almost all published material on soft power involving Chinese-Southeast Asian relationships starts with the assumption that China is exercising soft power in Southeast Asia. However, it is China that has often adjusted to Southeast Asian norms, not vice versa, which is another reminder of the interactive nature of soft power in this relationship.

A radically different take is to attempt not to measure or string together impressions of soft power, and not to distinguish attraction from persuasion, but to define soft power's components. Once the components are identified, it is possible to ask who is attentive to and attracted by Chinese soft power and what components of soft power are particularly appealing to which Southeast Asians? In other words, which components of the soft power soup appeal to which segments of Southeast Asian societies?

Chinese soft power weighs little more than a feather in large swaths of Southeast Asia. The Javanese peasant, whose great-grandfather bitterly resented the local ethnic Chinese merchant in his day, is probably impervious to Chinese "soft power." Muslims, who constitute almost half of Southeast Asia's population, look abroad to the wider Islamic community, not to China, for values and inspiration. Ethnic Chinese, who constitute about 5 percent of Southeast Asia's population, naturally respond positively to China's reemergence as a respected state. However, they are acutely conscious of their status as minorities.[4] In addition, the expulsion of much of Vietnam's ethnic Chinese minority after 1975 and Vietnam's experience with Chinese culture over the last thousand years appears to have inoculated Vietnamese against China's new soft power, or at least dampened its impact.

Chinese soft power appears to have more appeal in Myanmar, Laos, Cambodia, and Thailand, each with their own historical dynamic in relation to China. The substantial ethnic Chinese minorities in Myanmar, Laos, and Cambodia, which include many new Chinese immigrants to these countries, appear to still be relatively closely tied to the motherland. Thailand's success in integrating its Sino-Thai minority, and that minority's allegiance to the Thai state, appears to have smoothed the way for Chinese soft power. Although Beijing is enthusiastically promoting Chinese language studies, culture, and education throughout Southeast Asia, examples of growing interest are found among ethnic Chinese minorities and, among the indigenous populations of the region, mostly in mainland Southeast Asia. Thus Chinese soft power is not broadly based among the population of much of Southeast Asia. The parts of Southeast Asian society most influenced by Chinese soft power appear to be first the political and economic elites, second the ethnic Chinese minorities, and third and more broadly, mainland Southeast Asian societies with the exception of Vietnam. Why?

In Southeast Asia, soft power does not include the appeal of the "city on the Hill" or of values, as in the American version. Instead, by soft power we mean awe with the pace of economic development in the giant neighbor to the north and the elites' desire to strengthen their political hold on power by latching on to China's economic engine. National elites also appreciate the attention Chinese officials pay them in contrast to the American tendency to lecture, and feel comfortable with the language of soft power and multilateralism, which mirrors the language employed by Southeast Asian politicians and officials for the past several decades. Thus, even while they may retain doubts about the efficacy of soft power, Southeast Asian elites and intellectuals find reassurance and practical benefits in advocating the relevance of the term. Moreover, soft power is interactive. China's soft power derives from Beijing's courtship and what regional neighbors perceive as mutual benefits. As a result, China has accumulated soft power capital, and Southeast Asian governments naturally are now more inclined than they were in the past to anticipate and consider Chinese views when formulating national policies.[5]

Finally, China's soft power may be structurally different than, for example, that of the United States or Japan. Soft power traditionally includes both governmental and private actors, with much of the emphasis on the appeal of culture and products produced by the private sector. But in China's case, the bulk of China's soft power, or at least the appeal of that soft power to Southeast Asian elites, is associated with the state. Thus Chinese soft power may be more contingent of the behavior of China's government than traditional American-centric notions of soft power would predict. Moreover, the current infatuation that is part of China's "attraction," though real, will inevitably wear off as Southeast Asians and Chinese come into even greater contact with each other.

The body of this Chapter considers elements of China's "soft power" in Southeast Asia.

DIPLOMACY AND STYLE

Earlier chapters have provided ample evidence of the success of China's attentive diplomacy in Southeast Asia over the past decade. There is little value to be gained in again reviewing the role of this diplomacy, from the top Chinese leaders down through several layers of officials, in assuring Southeast Asians of China's benign intentions. There is also no doubt that this diplomatic campaign has been among the most important reasons for China's success in accumulating "soft power" in Southeast Asia.[6]

The impact of the "style" of China's diplomacy is highlighted by comparisons to that of the United States and Japan. In stark contrast to the warmth of Chinese relations with many Southeast Asians are reactions to the diplomatic style of the current American and Japanese administration. For example, with regard to the United States, as a prominent Thai academic noted, "When Hu visited an Asia-Pacific summit in October 2003, he pressed the flesh and used the soothing language of co-operation. By contrast, George Bush came in with heavy security and the old traditional style of the superpower demanding its way."[7]

Another example is provided by an American commentator, who wrote, "Such concerns were reinforced at a June 2004 security conference for Asia defense ministers, in which U.S. Secretary of Defense Rumsfeld reiterated White House demands that Asian countries improve their effort to counter terror.[8] Several Asian defense ministers and scholars responded that a new U.S. approach employing soft power such as education and development assistance in the region would better serve American interests in engaging Asian publics in the fight against terrorism. Or as Singapore analyst Simon Tay has argued, "if the United States lives up to its own values—'championing aspirations of human dignity,' 'igniting a new era of economic growth,' and 'expanding the circle of development by opening societies and building the infrastructure of democracy,' US leadership would be much more acceptable to the people of the region."[9] Moreover, as one Southeast Asian diplomat noted, China's diplomacy is skillful "particularly in comparison with the Japanese. Japanese consensus decision-making means that consensus is usually arrived at too late . . . expectations are key and the Japanese are not leveraging their contribution."[10]

NORMS AND VALUES

In the original sense in which "soft power" was first articulated in the United States, the enduring appeal of certain "political ideals" was considered an important component of soft power. This element of soft power does not help to explain China's growing influence in the region. Few Southeast Asians find the values of the Chinese Communist Party in the least appealing.

But this does not mean that Southeast Asians share the American assumption that Chinese competition with the United States' in terms of morality or norms and values is inconceivable. The democratic component of "values" is seldom stressed publicly in Southeast Asia, and appears to often be given little attention in discussions of soft power.[11] Of all the Southeast Asian states, only Singapore condemned the Tiananmen massacre in Beijing in 1989. Even former Singapore Prime Minister Lee Kuan Yew seemed to play down communist authoritarianism when he recently noted that the "communist party is a very broad church."[12] And the American reputation as a "shining beacon" of individual freedom and democracy has been compromised by recent unilateralism and, particularly in the Muslim half of Southeast Asia, an often-portrayed image in the media of America's aggressive occupation of Muslim states and torture of prisoners in the name of countering terrorism.

Southeast Asian ambivalence in promoting political rights, even in their own region, has been repeatedly shown by the ASEAN states' approach to flagrant violation of these rights in Myanmar. Some Southeast Asian leaders have modified their traditional reluctance to interfere in the domestic affairs of other countries and condemned the regime's detention of the pro-democracy leader Aung San Suu Kyi and attacks on her supporters, but ASEAN has resisted American (and European) resort to sanctions or other coercive means to promote democracy and human rights. In terms of the rule of law and human rights, China's reputation in the West and among some Southeast Asian advocacy groups is compromised by its support for Myanmar's military regime. However, this component in the soft power soup, which should spoil the soup to Western taste buds, appears to have little impact on China's soft power in Southeast Asia. In short, individual human rights are not as prominent in the Southeast Asian version of soft power as they are in the West.

If the Southeast Asian version of soft power places a different priority on individuals' human rights, is there an Asian value system that links China and Southeast Asia? The argument for the appeal of allegedly uniquely Asian values and norms suffers from the same problems that bedeviled the use of the term "Asian values" by more authoritarian Southeast Asian leaders in the 1990s, when it was used to fend off American pressure in support of universal human rights. In that decade China joined in the efforts of many ASEAN leaders to promote "Asian values," but the term suffers not only from its imprecision, but also from its use by such leaders as Malaysia's former Prime Minister Mahathir in stridently anti-Western speeches for domestic political reasons.

Nonetheless, references to "Asian values" do appear to reflect an unease with American society's individualism, and an insistence that the "the family, the extended family, the clan and the state . . . not the individual" are the building blocks of society.[13] Its resonance may also now be supplemented by a growing, though unmeasurable, perception that the United States and its citizens should not be considered to be part of "Asia," despite the assumption to the contrary implicit in the American use of the term "Asia-Pacific."

Within Southeast Asian circles, the argument has been made that the pattern of reciprocal ties and understandings, often referred to as the "ASEAN way," has created a network of personal and institutional connections and expectations that dampen conflict among ASEAN's ten member states. An international relations school of thought has advanced the argument that a uniquely ASEAN international relations "culture" has emerged which encourages cooperation. The underlying assumption is that the process is as important as the product. The argument is that China is in the process of "socialization" into this "culture," or at least has agreed to respect its norms and values.

The problem with this argument is the difficulty of measuring how the social milieu inside institutions, much less an institution as weakly structured as ASEAN, foster "cultures." The "effects of familiarity, consensus building, consultation, non-coercive argumentation, the avoidance of legalistic solutions to distributive problems, etc.,—the process itself" is supposed to be critical to explaining the outcome. Unfortunately, the outcome is a mixed bag.[14] Within Southeast Asia itself ASEAN's thousands of meetings each year do build personal networks, which individual politicians and officials draw on to moderate conflicts or reach agreement on how to deal with or sideline a wide variety of issues, when they perceive that doing so is in their interests. Chinese leaders have copied this mechanism to build personal connections through hundreds of meetings with their Southeast Asian counterparts.[15] But ASEAN has also regularly failed to address the big issues—such as the ASEAN financial crisis of 1997, the violence following East Timor's vote for independence in 1999, and countering international terrorism. In addition, Southeast Asian attempts to export the "ASEAN way," through such East Asian institutions as the ASEAN+1, ASEAN+3, and ASEAN Regional Forum (ARF), and thus draw China into similar patterns and networks, have also had mixed results.

In sum, Chinese and many Southeast Asian leaders do appear to share a distrust of the Western focus on the individual. Moreover, the Chinese vision of a world in which one country rarely intervenes in another's domestic affairs appeals to many elites that resent U.S. criticism and demands. China does not lecture them on democracy or human rights. Thus Southeast Asian and Chinese elites share an interest in de-emphasizing the individual "political" and "rights" components of "soft power." However, the broader idea that uniquely "Confucian values" or even "Asian values" inherently bind China and Southeast Asia, particularly Muslim Southeast Asia, does not appear to be supported by convincing evidence. Instead, China has brilliantly adjusted the style of its diplomacy to accommodate the fears and aspirations of

Southeast Asian elites, and to construct a network of contacts to sideline or resolve differences.

RESPONSIBLE LEADERSHIP

"If China is to emerge as a real leader within Southeast Asia, it will also need to assume more of the social and political burden that leadership entails."[16] Despite the hortatory nature of this statement, its author does raise often-neglected nontraditional issues, which Beijing has recognized as an important part of its public image and relationships with Southeast Asia.

The Chinese leadership, which often visits Southeast Asia to put its ears to the ground, has begun to understand the value of transparency on such issues as environmental protection, public health, and drug trafficking. Its initially secretive response to the SARS epidemic and Chinese provincial officials continued reluctance to share information on avian bird flu with their cross-border Southeast Asian counterparts, had undercut China's reputation.

But Beijing now tries to work more openly and cooperatively with its neighbors. Beijing signaled its intention to address these concerns in May 2002, when it issued a position paper at the ARF outlining the necessity of improving cooperation on nontraditional security issues. And Beijing's decision to acknowledge its mistakes and follow-up, after much initial hesitation in connection with the SARS crisis, set a pattern of responsible behavior. China has made a major issue of HIV/AIDs, particularly in its relations with mainland Southeast Asian countries that export the drugs that contribute to this scourge in China. Beijing has also trumpeted its efforts to work with Southeast Asian countries to deal with the threat that avian bird flu could mutate into a form transmitted between humans, thus setting the stage for a pandemic, and has stressed its massive campaign in late 2005 to inoculate domestic fowl.[17] It has been most recalcitrant in refusing to fully recognize the impact of its extensive program to dam the Mekong River, which has had a severe impact on the livelihood of people living downriver in Laos, Cambodia, and southern Vietnam. But even here, Beijing's national level leaders are now pledging to take downriver concerns into account.

Finally, China's turn to leadership advances China's influence in comparison with the United States. Washington often cites its "concrete assistance" and stresses its "functional" approach to problems, by implication suggesting that China (and others) provide sympathy but little real help. The United States certainly improved its tattered image through its massive and effective response to the devastating Indian Ocean tsunami of December 2004, in which approximately a quarter million Asians died. U.S. assistance, both immediate through the U.S. Navy and long-term through outpourings of both public and private aid, dwarfs China's contribution.[18] Nonetheless, the Southeast Asian response was not to compare China negatively with the U.S. China also received credit in Southeast Asia for its limited assistance, which consumed half of China's budget for disaster relief abroad.

THE TRADITIONAL INSTRUMENTS OF SOFT POWER: PUBLIC DIPLOMACY, TOURISM, EDUCATION

"Chinese culture belongs not only to the Chinese but also to the whole world," said President Hu in Australia. "We stand ready to step up cultural exchanges with the rest of the world in a joint promotion of cultural prosperity."[19]

Often cited as evidence of China's new "soft power" in Southeast Asian are the rapid increase in tourist flowing to and from China, an upsurge in Southeast Asians attending Chinese institutions of higher learning and vice versa, and the growing number of students studying Mandarin in Southeast Asia, often in Chinese-supported language centers and schools.[20] These facts and figures are supplemented by statements about the high quality of China's diplomatic representation and public diplomacy in the region and sometimes less credible assertions about the appeal of popular Chinese culture, particularly among Southeast Asia youth. However, the impact of these scattered examples of Chinese "soft power" must be disentangled to account for ethnicity and location in Southeast Asia if the net effect of China's soft power is to be gauged.

In recent years there has been a massive increase in personal contacts between Chinese and Southeast Asians, usually through Chinese and Southeast Asian tourism. By 2002, over 10 million Chinese tourists were traveling abroad each year, spending an estimated $10.6 billion.[21] By 2020 China expects to send more tourists abroad than any other nation,[22] though the World Tourism Association predicts that China will become the fourth-largest source of overseas tourists by that date.[23] The Chinese Ministry of Foreign Affairs designates foreign countries as officially approved tourist destinations, and all ASEAN countries are now on the list. Chinese citizens may not visit these Southeast Asian countries any time they choose to do so, but approved tourist agencies can arrange group tours without further authorization.[24]

The overall growth in Chinese tourism to Southeast Asia has been impressive. In 1995, 795,000 Chinese visited the ASEAN countries. By 2004 that figure reached 3,163,642.[25] Chinese tourist arrivals in the individual ASEAN countries are shown in Table 7.1.[26]

Table 7.1
Chinese Tourist Arrivals in ASEAN (1999–2004)[26]

Country	1999	2004
Brunei	1,044	7,586
Cambodia	26,805	46,325
Indonesia	14,742	30,331
Laos	20,269	33,019
Malaysia	190,851	550,241
Myanmar	12,148	17,890
Philippines	21,220	39,581
Singapore	372,881	880,188
Thailand	775,626	780,050
Vietnam	484,102	778,431

The results show that Singapore, Thailand, Vietnam, and Malaysia are the most important destinations for Chinese tourists, though the flow of Chinese tourists to Thailand has remained static. Vietnam has increased its attractiveness considerably. Singapore publicly announced that it expects 1 million Chinese tourists in 2005, as did Thailand for 2006.[27] At the other end of the spectrum, very few Chinese tourists have visited Brunei, Myanmar, Indonesia, and the Philippines.[28]

The flow of Chinese tourists has an economic as well as a cultural impact. Several Southeast Asian commentators have tagged tourism as an economic niche that the region is particularly well placed to exploit. China has also started to attract more tourists from Southeast Asia, as well as businessmen, and in the last century encouraged "roots travel" as a way to bring ethnic Chinese back to the mainland. Chinese statistics[29] show "Foreign Visitor Arrivals" for 2004 as:

Indonesia	349,832
Malaysia	741,909
Philippines	549,390
Singapore	636,826
Thailand	464,179
Other Asians	516,000 (of which only a percentage would be Southeast Asians)

Thus at least 2,740,000 Southeast Asians visits took place to China. According to Chinese statistics, moreover, most of these visits took place for "sightseeing/leisure" rather than "business" or "visiting friends/relatives."

However, some journalists have reported that Chinese tourists are widely regarded as Asia's new "ugly Americans."[30] Anecdotal evidence suggests that Chinese tourists, usually organized through packaged group tours, tend to fill the lower-end, less profitable sector of the tourism market.[31] On the other hand, Wang Gungwu, director of the East Asia Institute at the National University in Singapore, was quoted as stating, "As the new Chinese tourists from the rapidly expanding middle class travel, they carry with them an image of a vastly different and more inviting China than even a few years ago, richer, more confident and more influential."[32]

The problem is that we have no means to measure the impact of this personal, cross-cultural contact as a factor in China's influence in Southeast Asia. The presumption from general polling of attitudes toward China in Southeast Asia would suggest that it is positive, but Japan stills sends more tourists to Southeast Asia than any other country and there is little empirical evidence that these personal contacts have increased Japanese "soft power" in the region.

Students

Southeast Asians are increasingly prepared to consider study in China as a means to secure a higher education. Moreover, anecdotal evidence suggests that Chinese are also increasingly interested in studying in Southeast Asia, particularly in Singapore, Malaysia, and Thailand. Southeast Asian students who received visas to study in China jumped more than 50 percent from 2002 to 2004, from 9,437 to 15,123.[33]

Particularly impressive is the fact that Indonesia sent 3,750 students to China in 2004. Moreover, "while the Singapore government still sends a handful of students on scholarships to the top universities in the United States and Britain, it has introduced a parallel program to send equal numbers of its best students to China and India."[34]

However, "as this data does not tell us what the students studied, the quality of the institution, and whether or not the students were overseas Chinese, it is difficult to draw specific conclusions about China's growing influence."[35] Moreover, until we have research that demonstrates whether this increase reflects more than a shift from Taiwan to the mainland on the part of ethnic Chinese Southeast Asian students searching for a higher education, we have little from which to judge the "soft power" impact.[36] In addition, the experience of Malaysian students in the United States, who often developed an allegiance to the Islamic opposition party while abroad, suggests that study in a foreign country does not necessarily enhance the "soft power" of the host nation.

Flowing in the opposite direction are Chinese students in Southeast Asia. At Assumption University in Bangkok, Chinese enrollment has jumped from 50 to 800 students, according to press reporting. In the summer of 2004, 51 Chinese officials graduated with a degree from the Master of Science program at Nanyang Technological University.

Chinese Language and Cultural Centers

Beijing supports the establishment of Chinese language and cultural centers in Southeast Asia. However, the worldwide budget for "Confucius Institutes" is only $12 million, often stretched by using ethnic Chinese in Southeast Asia to teach Mandarin.[37]

Beijing is careful to include a cultural and educational component in its agreements with Southeast Asian states. For example, the China-Indonesia Joint Statement issued during President Hu Jintao's July 2005 visit states that the "two leaders also exchanged views on the possibility of establishing a center for Chinese culture and teaching the Chinese language in Indonesia," and a subsequent statement appeared to confirm agreement to do so. Moreover, as mentioned previously, the study of Mandarin has skyrocketed, four Chinese newspapers have appeared, and the prestigious University of Indonesia has established a department of Sinology.

The Chinese have been even more active closer to China, particularly in Thailand and Cambodia. In the Thai case, Chinese provincial governments and universities appear to be involved as well. In northern Thailand, Chang Mai University has agreed to "reciprocal study" with a university in Kunming, and the Sirindhorn Chinese Language and Culture Center has been established with much fanfare at Mae Fah Luang University in Chang Rai.[38] Even ASEAN is getting in the act, and has established an ASEAN Center of Contemporary Chinese Studies in Hanoi.

The Media

Further research on the impact of China's media penetration beyond the ethnic Chinese communities of Southeast Asia is required, but China has increased its TV and radio broadcasts to Southeast Asia and the official media in many Southeast Asian countries is increasingly prepared to use Chinese sources for its news and other programs. In addition, the People's Daily newspaper is now readily available in Malaysia, and perhaps in other Southeast Asian countries. A content analysis of Southeast Asian newspapers in Chinese may well reveal more information sourced from China (instead of Hong Kong or Taiwan), but these papers are only read by ethnic Chinese Southeast Asians.

Public Diplomacy

Among Southeast Asian diplomats, one hears repeated references to a sharp improvement in the quality of China's Ambassadors and other diplomats, who are regionalists and speak Southeast Asian languages. In addition, the public reaction in maritime Southeast Asia suggest that one clear success in Chinese cultural diplomacy has been the 600th anniversary celebrations in Singapore and Malaysia of Muslim Chinese Admiral Zheng He's first mission in 1405 to explore Southeast Asia and the Indian Ocean.[39] In an echo of America's cold war public diplomacy, Beijing has proposed that it send the Chinese version of "Peace Corps" volunteers to several of the poorer Southeast Asia countries.[40]

Popular Responses

In addition, the most enthusiastic proponent in print of China's cultural impact in Southeast Asia writes, "Fascination for popular Chinese culture among ASEAN youth in films, pop music, and television has been noticeable, even though such popular culture may in fact have emanated from Hong Kong (its films, actors, actresses and Canto-pop) or Taiwan (like Meteor Garden television series), and not necessarily from China. Joint 'Chinese' film production, such as 'Hero' or 'Crouching Tiger, Hidden Dragon' have hit international box offices and given popular Chinese culture a big boost. Chinese cinema idols, like Zhang Yimou and Gong Li, are beginning to command a following. Furthermore, mainland Chinese consumer brand-names (like Hai-er, TCL, or Huawei) have spread and become popular in ASEAN societies."[41] "Chinese culture, cuisine, curios, art, acupuncture, herbal medicine, and fashion have all emerged in regional (Southeast Asian) culture."[42]

Other analysts are a bit more cautious when they note that "Fashion conscious, business-driven young Asians view warp-speed Shanghai as the new version of Manhattan . . . Overall, China's stepped up endeavors in cultural suasion remain modest compared to those of the United States, and American popular culture, from Hollywood movies to MTV, is still vastly more exportable and accessible, all agree. . . . But the trend is clear, educators and diplomats here say: the Americans are losing influence."[43]

THE ROLE OF ETHNIC CHINESE

"In ways not seen previously, the Chinese leadership is tapping into the overseas Chinese community throughout Asia to play an important role diplomatically and economically in furthering the mainland's interest."[44] Perhaps this applies to other parts of Asia, but the evidence from Southeast Asia provides a more complex, nuanced picture.[45]

It is true that Beijing has sought to network with ethnic Chinese organizations and called upon their ethnic kinsmen in Southeast Asia to contribute to China's effort to improve relations with individual countries.[46] It is also true that China relied in the 1980s and early 1990s on Southeast Asian ethnic Chinese minorities, who often have a disproportionate role in Southeast Asian commerce,[47] to lead the way as foreign investors in China. Many did so, and apparently red tape in China often continues to be waived for Southeast Asian ethnic Chinese business tycoons who have invested billions of dollars in the mainland. In October 2003, during Hu Jintao's visit to Bangkok for the APEC Summit, he spoke at a luncheon for more than 1,000 Chinese and Sino-Thai businessmen.

On the other hand, Beijing has also been careful to encourage semigovernment entities, often dominated by indigenous Southeast Asians, to participate in investment in and trade with China. President Hu Jintao also addressed an enthusiastic group of officials and businessmen, most of whom were not ethnic Chinese, during his 2005 visit to Indonesia. Moreover, we have no data on the percentage of Southeast Asian investment owned by ethnic Chinese or the number of ethnic Chinese Southeast Asians who have traveled to China to work either for ethnic Chinese Southeast Asian firms or for Chinese companies. All we can say with confidence is that Beijing promotes China's economic interests both among ethnic Chinese and indigenous Southeast Asians.

In addition, ethnic Chinese in Southeast Asia know that Beijing has repeatedly demonstrated its reluctance to intervene on their behalf if such intervention would compromise China's broader foreign policy goals.[48] And Southeast Asia's ethnic Chinese minorities, except in Singapore where the ethnic Chinese are the majority, seldom have a demonstrable influence on their states' foreign policies or diplomacy, with the possible exception of trade and investment issues.

Ethnic Chinese constitute only about 5 percent of Southeast Asia's 550 million people.[49] In contrast with the situation before World War II, where ethnic Chinese viewed themselves as "overseas Chinese" who lived in various parts of Southeast Asia, ethnic Chinese are now citizens of their own Southeast Asian countries. Thus they are first and foremost Indonesian, Malaysian, Filipino, Singaporean, or Thai. The exception to this pattern may be the stream of recent Chinese immigrants to Myanmar, Cambodia, and Laos, who may better fit the earlier pattern of "overseas" Chinese, though information on the status and loyalties of these Chinese is poor.[50]

In addition, in the other Southeast Asian states there is a small population of recent migrants from China, mixed with the wave of more than 3 million Chinese tourists and some students, about whom there are more rumors than information.[51] The vast majority of ethnic Chinese are nationals of Southeast Asian states, for whom China is no longer home.

That said, Southeast Asia's ethnic Chinese minorities have been confronted with extraordinarily complex calls on their identity and loyalty. As scholars on this issue have written, ethnic Chinese minorities in Southeast Asia were first inheritors of a deeply rooted cultural identification and then called upon to become Chinese nationalists even while they lived in colonial states or Thailand. After Southeast Asian countries became independent they were asked to shed their previous orientation and loyalties, substituting identification with a particular nation-state. More recently, they have been called on to adjust to globalization, not just in terms of economics but also to "defend their minority or ethnic interests in the larger nation-states that they belong to."[52]

China has recognized and contributed to these changing allegiances by revising its own citizenship law in 1980[53] and exercising restraint in the face of anti-Chinese discrimination or violence in Southeast Asian states.[54] However, there is some evidence that Beijing, as its image in Southeast Asia has improved, has become less wary about appealing to ethnic Chinese citizens in mainland Southeast Asia. The Chinese government organized a "Global Get-together of Overseas Chinese and People of Chinese Origin in Vietnam, Cambodia and Laos" in Guangzhou in 2003, which reportedly attracted close to 1000 guests. Senior Chinese leaders told them that Beijing would provide better service to overseas Chinese wishing to participate in economic, cultural, and scientific exchanges.[55] China has also reportedly sought to attract talented ethnic Chinese from abroad to staff China's science and technology centers.

Beijing's restraint has contributed to a marked decline in antiethnic Chinese sentiment in Southeast Asia. During the early part of the chaotic transition to democracy in Indonesia, demonstrations often spilled over into violence against ethnic Chinese Indonesian citizens. Beijing declined to protest or intervene in what it viewed as an Indonesian domestic issue, with the Foreign Ministry stating, "we believe that the Indonesian government can control the situation, maintain social stability and racial harmony."[56] When contenders for power fanned the flames of anti-Chinese sentiment in May 1998, leading to the worst anti-Chinese riots since Indonesia's independence, Beijing declined to publicly "express concern" until several months later. Only in August did the People's Daily newspaper urge Indonesia to take "strong steps to punish the lawless and to protect the personal safety and property of the ethnic Chinese, and treat them fairly."[57] Beijing was cautious and careful because there was no indication that these riots, whose victims were ethnic Chinese Indonesian citizens, were directed against China. In short, Beijing refused to complicate China's diplomatic plans for the region by confusing ethnicity with nationality.

Jakarta has, at least temporarily, "rehabilitated" the Indonesian ethnic Chinese community. Beijing's restraint and growing ties between China and "business associates" of former Indonesian President Megawati Sukarnoputri, paved the way for the lunar New Year or "Imlek" to be designated an official Indonesian holiday in 2003.[58] However, while Sino-Indonesian politicians may be "coming out" and playing a more visible role,[59] it is doubtful that democracy has increased ethnic Chinese influence in the face of an increasingly Islamic atmosphere. The Suharto regime was particularly noted for the close relationship the political leadership maintained with wealthy Chinese businessmen.

In Malaysia, according to one commentator, "Chinese tycoons are playing an increasingly prominent role both domestically and externally, especially in leading economic recovery and the current reforms in Malaysia 'against' its Bumiputera policy." This may exaggerate the Chinese "tycoons" role, as well as that played by the ethnic Chinese community. Malaysia's political compact has, since 1969, led to the replacement of old loyalties to dialect groups, and the emergence of a pan-Malaysian "Chinese" identity, forged primarily through Chinese language schools that teach through the medium of Mandarin. Peranakan Chinese (locally born Chinese who speak Malay at home) are integrating back into the broader Chinese community.[60] Malaysian Chinese have retained their sense of distinct ethnic identity due to religious barriers to intermarriage with Muslims, the Chinese language education system, which is now extended to the higher-education level,[61] and affirmative action programs designed to reduce interethnic disparities in education and employment. It is the success of these affirmative action-programs and Malaysia's continued development over the past thirty years, rather than China's rise or Chinese tycoons that set the stage for declining concern among Malays that Malaysia's ethnic Chinese citizens would place their ethnicity before their nationality. Nonetheless, some commentators believe that Malaysia's ethnic Chinese, as a minority primarily educated in Mandarin, identify more with China and Chinese culture than their English-educated counterparts in wealthier, ethnic Chinese dominated Singapore.[62]

In the Philippines, Filipino-Chinese movies captured the top prizes in the Metro-Manila Film Festival for the past two years. There are more "chinovelas" (Chinese serials) on local television in the afternoon and the Taiwanese boy band, F-4, is currently the Philippines biggest craze.[63] It's not, however, clear what this might mean in terms of China's influence among the assimilated Chinese minority of the Philippines. On the other hand, the thoroughly integrated Sino-Thai had added political influence to their commercial base through the ruling Thai Rak Thai Party. Former Prime Minister Thaksin Shinawatra had touted his Chinese heritage and claimed a personal ability to bridge differences between Bangkok and Beijing.

Despite an extensive literature on Southeast Asia's ethnic Chinese minority, there is little empirical research on the sensitive issue of links between the identity of ethnic Chinese communities in Southeast Asia and ties between Beijing and these communities. There is anecdotal evidence suggesting that younger ethnic Chinese, unlike their parents whose communities were often centered on dialect and clan organizations, usually now view themselves as part of a broader ethnic Chinese, Mandarin-speaking minority in a particular Southeast Asian country. Moreover, at least in the wealthier parts of Southeast Asia and particularly among the English-speaking ethnic Chinese, the Chinese community is remarkably cosmopolitan. It may be fair to say that throughout the region once scorned ethnic Chinese communities are celebrating their success, but they are celebrating primarily their ethnic Chinese backgrounds and networks, not ties, much less allegiance, to Beijing.

The most significant aspect of Beijing's new influence in Southeast Asia may be its growing dominance, for the ethnic Chinese communities of Southeast Asia, as the Chinese source of cultural contact, education, and economic links. "The most significant change in Southeast Asia has perhaps been in the attitude of these ethnic Chinese, who have become less biased, less anti-communist, and less anti-Beijing in their thinking."[64] As explained in Chapter 2, Taiwan, with whom Southeast Asian ethnic Chinese often had close links through the 1990s, is fading as an alternative center of "Chineseness."

The fate of Southeast Asia's ethnic Chinese still depends, to some extent, on Beijing's behavior and perceptions of China's success. One vision is that "the ethnic Chinese may be able to serve as a golden bridge between China and ASEAN states, provided that China will not reverse its policy and that ethnic Chinese continue to integrate with local societies."[65] But no one is likely to soon forget the long history of anti-Chinese sentiment in Southeast Asia, which suggests that assertiveness on Beijing's part could still lead to outbreaks of antiethnic Chinese violence in parts of the region.

MEASURING SUCCESS: PUBLIC AND ELITE PERCEPTIONS

Many Southeast Asians are awed by the pace of economic growth among the 1.3 billion people who inhabit their neighbor to the north. In addition, the attention that Chinese leaders and officials lavish on China's southern neighbors is flattering. In contrast, American attention is composed "of the rather haphazard byproducts of our domestic politics, the activities of interest groups, and applications of generic concern."[66]

This infatuation is reminiscent of reactions in many parts of Southeast Asia to the rise of Japan thirty years ago, though the Southeast Asian infatuation with Japan was primarily with Japan's economic growth and Japanese commercial products. Even in its heyday in the 1980s Japan suffered from lingering resentment of its occupation of the region during World War II, its cultural insularity, the absence of substantial Japanese ethnic communities to supplement its economic juggernaut, and the perception that Japanese companies were reluctant to share knowledge with local firms. The current infatuation with China is broader and better balanced, and thus likely to be more enduring.

Thus at least in parts of Southeast Asia, not only leaders but also ordinary people increasingly see China as a benign, positive force, a reputation that once belonged to the United States and, to a lesser extent, Japan. In Thailand, polls taken in late 2003 showed that 76 percent of respondents considered China to be Thailand's closest friend. Only 9 percent picked the United States, and only 8 percent named Thailand's traditional top trading and investment partner, Japan. Polling in the

Philippines and Indonesia showed that 70 percent of the former and 68 percent of the latter had "positive views" of China.[67] Polling in August and September 2005, showed a "favorable opinion of the U.S., China" with 91 percent of Malaysians having a "favorable view" (46 percent for the United States), 83 percent of Thais (73 percent for the United States), 81 percent of Filipinos (95 percent for the United States), and 66 percent of Indonesians (42 percent for the United States). Equally interesting are the summaries in the report that addresses this and other polling data, which characterize Thailand as "Positive Images Predominate," Malaysia as "A Love Affair (Especially for the Ethnic Chinese)," the Philippines as "China is Fine, but all Eyes Are On the U.S." and Indonesia as "China as a Remote, Benign Presence."[68] A Pew "Global Attitudes Survey" showed Indonesian favorable opinion of the United States ranging over time, from 75 percent favorable in 1999/2000, to 15 percent in 2003, and back 38 percent in 2005.[69]

These polls, however, tell us very little except that China is widely seen as benign. Polling results do not distinguish between popular antipathy to current American policies and more basic anti-Americanism, none of which, moreover, has a demonstrable connection with perceptions of China. Finally, anecdotal evidence suggests that elite and popular perceptions in Southeast Asia may vary widely. Thus inevitably, in the absence of data that measures responses from the same participants to the same questions over time, polling is less informative than it might be, for example, in the United States, Japan, or Europe.

Moreover, familiarity can breed disappointment as well as admiration. Southeast Asian investments, including Singapore's multibillion investment in Suzhou, have not been as profitable as many boosters expected. Chinese products, particularly small manufactures, are competing with their local equivalents in many Southeast Asian markets. Complaints are now heard about demanding Chinese tourists that sound remarkably similar to complaints about Japanese tourists thirty years ago.[70] In addition, anecdotal evidence suggests that Southeast Asian ethnic Chinese are often offended when Chinese assume that they want to return to China, or that their ethnicity is more important than their nationality.[71] Moreover, as Southeast Asians and Chinese come into greater contact with each other, perceptions are likely to be colored more by individuals' behavior than China's current benign reputation.

SUMMARY

Claims about China's soft power in Southeast Asia should be treated with caution. In the days before the term soft power became prominent, the terms cultural and diplomatic influence would have been employed to describe the same phenomena. China has successfully conducted a sophisticated, reassuring diplomatic campaign and projected a benign image. This campaign, combined with growing economic ties, has provided Beijing with greater influence.

China's soft power has increased not because Southeast Asians are attracted to Chinese values. Rather, China's attraction has grown primarily because ties with China benefit, and thus appeal, to national elites and the small but often influential ethnic Chinese minorities in Southeast Asia. This "power" is enhanced by anticipation of further benefits for Southeast Asians as ties with China deepen. The romance, based in part on placing contentious issues to the side, may fade as the partners in the relationship come to know each other better.

The next chapter assesses American interests and policies in Southeast Asia.

CHAPTER 8

The United States and Southeast Asia: Neglect or Sensible Caution?

The United States, which reached across the Pacific to acquire the Philippines in the late nineteenth century and shielded and dominated Southeast Asia from the close of World War II until the collapse of the Soviet Union in 1989, has usually seen the region primarily through the prism of broader interests, from the containment of communism to the eradication of international terrorism. The tendency to treat Southeast Asia as an appendage of East Asia as a whole, within which the United States focuses on China and Japan, adds another filter between Washington and reality on the ground. Thus U.S. policy has often been derivative of extra regional concerns and divorced from U.S. interests specific to Southeast Asia.

The result is episodes of deep intervention, such as U.S. intervention in Vietnam until 1975, alternating with long stretches of neglect, which are punctuated by ad hoc responses to short-term crises.[1] This pattern is not due to a conscious decision to ignore the region. The United States did not withdraw after the Cold War, as some Southeast Asians claimed to have feared. But neither has it devoted sustained attention to the area. Instead, issues specific to Southeast Asia seldom require the involvement of a global power's often distracted senior foreign policy officials.[2] Thus, there has been little internal pressure to overcome mid-level American policymakers' reluctance to limit their options by first defining America's limited interests in the region, and second, devoting sustained attention to advancing these interests. Moreover, in a complex region with several influential states, U.S. policymakers correctly assess that they are not now involved in a zero-sum or bipolar contest for influence.

Southeast Asia is often referred to as strategically important to the United States. Much of it is not, but parts of it are and will continue to be. There are two vital concerns for the United States. First, the United States has a permanent strategic interest in the ability to control sea-lanes and maritime chokepoints that connect the Indian and Pacific Oceans. Through these flow not only U.S. armed forces but also the energy resources from the Middle East essential to power the economies of China and Japan. Thus U.S. security concerns are focused on maritime Southeast Asia, not on China's backyard.[3] In the absence of a clear threat to these jugulars of international trade, the United States is likely to pay little attention unless China demonstrates the ability to project and sustain naval power into maritime Southeast Asia. At this time, China can dispatch a small naval force to the region, but it can't maintain that force. Now and for the foreseeable future there is no Chinese threat to America's most fundamental security interest in Southeast Asia. Second, the United States continues to pursue its long-standing economic goals of open markets and equal commercial access. In 2004, the ASEAN region continued to be the destination for more U.S. exports than China. In 2003, U.S. foreign direct investment (FDI) in ASEAN totaled more than seven times U.S. investment in China.[4] Moreover, the pattern of American investment includes a diversification from the old concentration on oil, gas, and other natural resources. The China-ASEAN Free Trade Agreement, if and when it is implemented, could eventually lead to trade diversion inimical to U.S. interests. Protection of these fundamental security and economic interests also contributes to the success or failure of the third permanent interest, the advancement of global U.S. foreign policy concerns in Southeast Asia. These include the promotion of democracy and human rights, the eradication of international terrorism, and, potentially, international cooperation against pandemics.

For the United States, Myanmar, of marginal strategic significance, is primarily useful as a symbol of America's global commitment to democracy and human rights.[5] The refusal of the government of the United States to compromise its support for human rights by attempting to compete for influence with the oppressive Myanmar regime, so often recommended by ASEAN under the term "engagement," helps affirm America's human rights credentials. Some critics argue that the United States is allowing the Myanmar tail to wag the ASEAN dog—that is complicating relations with ASEAN in pursuit of human rights goals that are unattainable in Myanmar. However, in this case, global concerns trump regional interest in improving relations with ASEAN. Moreover, the expansion of ASEAN in the later half of the 1990s complicated U.S. policy options. The United States would find an attractive partner in an ASEAN composed of the original ASEAN 5 states,[6] which are democracies of some strategic importance, but ASEAN's expansion led to the inclusion of states with authoritarian domestic political regimes often beholden to China. Nonetheless, in a bow to Southeast Asian sensitivities and to answer the accusation of excessive American "bilateralism," Washington has now designed its own version of a "partnership" with ASEAN.

Washington labeled Southeast Asia the "second front" in the Global War On Terror (GWOT) in 2002. More high-level attention, albeit exclusively in the context of counterterrorism, has been devoted to Southeast Asia in the past few years than since the American withdrawal from Vietnam in 1973. Regional elites have often complained that American counterterrorism "policy is a blanket which fails to cover significant portions of Southeast Asia and bifurcates U.S. policy in the region as a result."[7] In fact, it simply recognizes reality, both in terms of U.S. interests and the demonstrated inability of ASEAN, as distinct from a few of its members, to serve as an effective partner against international terrorism. To meet the challenge, the United States designed an effective plan based on cooperation with and assistance to relevant Southeast Asian states. Though it worked well, many Southeast Asian Muslims remain dubious about American intentions as a consequence not of U.S. policy or programs in Southeast Asia, but of the United States-led intervention in Iraq. In deference to Southeast Asian sensitivities, in public the State Department has begun to de-emphasize counterterrorism as the driving force in U.S. regional policy. In 2006, with its attention focused on Iraq and the threat of terrorism fading in Southeast Asia, Washington has paid less attention to the region. It has also recognized that the East Asian agenda is different from its own, and accommodated Southeast Asia preferences by focusing increasingly on trade issues.

Finally, Southeast Asia is open to many external influences. Current tensions in the U.S.-Chinese bilateral relationship—largely focused on bilateral economic issues and Taiwan—have seldom spilled over into Southeast Asia. Nonetheless, in 2005 senior U.S. Defense Department officials began to again voice concern about the "rise of China,"[8] though the Department of State's Deputy Secretary was quoted as commenting, "the theme is not U.S. versus China in Southeast Asia."[9] If domestic political and economic constituencies in the United States coalesce to portray China as a threat, the United States could shoot itself in the foot in Southeast Asia. The last thing Southeast Asian states want is to be compelled to choose between the United States and China. Thus an American attempt to turn Southeast Asia into a battleground in a larger zero-sum conflict with China would elicit little support for the United States in the region.

SECURITY

The United States has been described as the security "guarantor" for Southeast Asia. This label may have been accurate during the Cold War, but its relevance slowly declined through the 1990s and the first years of the twenty-first century as the threat of subversion or military attack by a foreign state, or a resort to force in the South China Sea dispute, was perceived to dissipate.

The Bush administration came to office critical of its predecessor's alleged tilt toward China, which it viewed as a "strategic competitor,"[10] and determined to refurbish American alliances. In the post-9/11 environment in Washington, terrorism replaced China as the primary threat and the purpose of revitalizing alliances in East Asia became confused. In Northeast Asia, revitalization of the crucial alliance with Japan was aimed at distinguishing an ally, Japan, from a perceived potential threat, China. In Southeast Asia, the Bush administration's new focus on "treaty allies" included aid for the Philippines to combat terrorism and a pointless extension of major non-NATO ally status to Thailand, China's "best friend" in the region.[11] This is part of the larger problem faced by the United States with its traditional East Asian "hub and spokes" security model. The military forces it deploys to deal with East Asian Cold War legacies such as North Korea and Taiwan are seldom relevant to the campaign to combat the modern threat of terrorism in Southeast Asia.

In Southeast Asia, the pressing security issue for the United States is terrorism. In the future, should either Chinese policy undergo a radical transformation or should U.S.-Chinese relations deteriorate, a more traditional security concern may reemerge. In either case, U.S. security interests would remain focused on part of Southeast Asia. As General Sherman said during the American Civil War, when encouraged to turn back North to deal with rebels threatening his supply lines after the capture of Atlanta, if General Hood "will go to the Ohio river, I will give him rations. My business is down South."[12] For the United States in Southeast Asia, America's business is also down south. Whether based on countering terrorism or strategic competition, American security interests are centered on the Strait of Malacca and Indonesia.

Traditional Security Relationships

Traditional U.S. security relationships in Southeast Asia reflect the legacy of the Cold War. In the absence of a convincing conventional security threat, the United States has sought to strengthen its security relationships with old allies and friends and to restore military-to-military ties with Indonesia. Much of the instinct to do so, however, may be based on a misperception that states such as Singapore, the Philippines, and Thailand will be available, if necessary, to help balance China. The rationale for this assumption, particularly if the United States and China were to confront each other over Taiwan, is not clear.

The Philippines did sign a Visiting Forces Agreement (VFA) in 1999, and U.S. military assistance has increased from $1.9 million in 1999 to $136 million in 2005 to combat terrorism.[13] The "inaugural feature of U.S. counter-terrorism policy in Southeast Asia after September 11 was a military mission, albeit a modest one, the U.S.-Philippine joint 'training exercise,' to help Manila eradicate the Abu Sayyaf Group."[14] Washington has rejected the suggestions of some Filipino politicians that the VFA enhances the security of Philippine claims in the South China Sea.

In 2001, Singapore constructed a facility designed to accommodate a U.S aircraft carrier. U.S. air force planes have access to Singaporean airbases. In addition, the United States and Singapore have negotiated a new "Framework Agreement for the Promotion of Strategic Partnership in Defense and Security." Singapore has also been Washington's closest ally in combating terrorism in the region, including in the neighboring Strait of Malacca. But Singapore, as mentioned previously, is only secondarily balancing against the potential of Chinese military power, which Singaporean officials have publicly acknowledged will not pose a threat to them for several decades.

Thais acknowledge that they view their old alliance relationship with the United States as a form of "insurance," while they strengthen their entente with China. The extension of major non-NATO ally status (MNNA) to Thailand by the United States in 2003 was a gesture of little significance, though Thailand did allow the United

States to use Utapao airbase to help coordinate the humanitarian response to the December 2004 Indian Ocean tsunami.

The Bush administration has lifted Congressional restrictions on military-to-military cooperation with Indonesia's armed forces, imposed after human rights violations by members of the Indonesian armed forces in East Timor in the last century. After Indonesia's democratic transformation, these restrictions were antiquated and no longer served a purpose.

In addition to strengthening bilateral security relationships with allies and friends, the United States has accelerated the tempo of its military exercise programs with the armed forces of some Southeast Asian states. The most prominent of these exercises are Balikatan with the Philippines and Cobra Gold with Thailand. The large annual Cobra Gold exercise has become increasingly multilateral, with China as one of the observers at the 2005 exercise. In addition, the United States is slowly strengthening military to military training and other ties with such non-alliance partners in the region as Vietnam, which has agreed to a U.S. international military education and training (IMET) program.

If nothing else, the renewed emphasis on traditional security ties with allies and friends strengthens regional states' perceptions of the U.S. commitment to the area, although the purpose of that "security" commitment is not always clear.

Terrorism

As the shock of the 9/11, 2001, terrorist attacks in the United States reverberated through the United States government, few officials thought immediately of the consequences for American policy in East Asia. Only a few months earlier, President Bush had vowed to defend Taiwan with "whatever it takes," which itself followed on the tense atmosphere after a Chinese fighter jet's collision with an American surveillance air plane in April 2001. Washington's East Asia policy continued to reflect assumptions trumpeted during the 2000 Presidential campaign, specifically the Bush administration's characterization of China as a "strategic competitor" of the United States in Asia.

However, in the aftermath of the 9/11 attacks few in America questioned that terrorism was the greatest threat to the United States since the end of the Cold War. The subsequent "discovery" of terrorists networks in Southeast Asia in December 2001, and the fear that al Qaeda had extended its tentacles into Southeast Asia, dramatically altered U.S. priorities in East Asia and the nature of the region's relations with Washington. Southeast Asia, long the object of "benign neglect," suddenly became the "second front" in a global war on terror.

The consequences threatened to be revolutionary for traditional U.S. East Asia policy. China became no longer a "strategic competitor," but a potential ally in the campaign against terrorism. Moreover, the global war against terrorism "simultaneously increased attention to Southeast Asia (or the East Asian littoral) while diminishing the overall importance of Asia as the war on terrorism has gone global."[15] The subsequent history of U.S. East Asia policy reflects the success of the traditional "old guard" of East Asian experts in reaffirming North Korea and China as the primary American security concerns in Asia.[16] The ambivalent response of many Southeast Asian elites to Washington's sudden embrace in the name of counterterrorism also contributed to the gradual reassertion of these traditional American priorities in Asia. Even more important, as the Washington policy elite has focused on Iraq, the terrorist threat in Southeast Asia has simultaneously diminished. In the meantime, combating terrorism had temporarily raised Southeast Asia's profile in Washington to new heights not achieved for thirty years. Terrorism made Southeast Asia again central to U.S. strategy, but only temporarily.

In Southeast Asia, the United States designed a cost-effective counterterrorism campaign based on cooperation with and assistance to relevant Southeast Asian states, specifically Indonesia, Malaysia, the Philippines, Singapore, and Thailand. This strategy combined close intelligence liaison,[17] the personal involvement of President Bush through his October 2003 trip to the region and visits by Southeast Asian leaders to Washington, a rare resort to multilateralism both with ASEAN and APEC, substantial training and technical assistance, and a limited military role in the Philippines. The result was the apprehension of several al Qaeda members, including the only Southeast Asian member of the al Qaeda shura (council), and the arrest or detention of hundreds of terrorists tied to the regional Jema'ah Islamiyah terrorist network. Terrorist networks in the region have been severely degraded, though the Jemaah Islamiyah has not been suppressed in Indonesia and terrorists continue to find refuge in the southern Philippines. Most impressive, however, was Washington's attentiveness to the domestic political constraints under which Southeast Asian political leaders labored, and the recognition that uninvited direct action to capture individual terrorists would prove counterproductive in the larger war against terrorism.

The trumpeting of post-9/11 U.S. doctrines of unilateral preemption had alarmed leaders in Southeast Asian capitals. The United States pressed for an ASEAN statement condemning terrorism at the 2002 Summit in Brunei, which provided useful political cover for Southeast Asian governments' cooperation against terrorists. The United States also successfully insisted on linking terrorism and trade at the 2003 Bangkok APEC Summit, though America's emphasis on security collaboration was often contrasted unfavorably with China's focus on the more traditional APEC topic of trade liberalization. In connection with his attendance at this Summit, President Bush preached the message of counterterrorism during bilateral visits to the Philippines, Thailand, Singapore and Indonesia.

Indonesian and Thai leaders, in particular, were initially reluctant to acknowledge the terrorist threat in their midst. Southeast Asia elites only became fully engaged after the Bali attack drove home the consequences of ignoring the threat. Above all, Southeast Asian Muslims remain dubious about American intentions. These doubts were primarily a consequence not of U.S. policies or programs in Southeast Asia, but of the United States-led invasions first of Afghanistan and then Iraq. Particularly important in feeding suspicion of U.S. motives has been the continued insurgency in the latter. Even U.S. allies Thailand and the Philippines, which were persuaded to dispatch token military forces to Iraq, quickly withdrew them.

In short, "return to Southeast Asia" the United States strengthened relations with the governments of Australia, and the Philippines, Singapore, Malaysia, and eventually Indonesia, but the Iraq fiasco has led to a sharp decline in positive public attitudes toward the United States, despite American sensitivity to delicate domestic factors in Southeast Asian states. Equally significant, in conjunction with the American-led campaign against terrorism, U.S.-China relations have become less confrontational. In contrast with the cold war and the tensions of early 2001, China is on the side of the United States in fighting terror, and the administrations' early attention to China ebbed as the demands of counterterrorism took precedence. China appears comfortable with America's return to Southeast Asia to combat terrorism as long as this return is not transformed into an attempt to contain China.[18]

ECONOMICS

The United States remains Southeast Asia's most important economic partner. Only Japan competes as a balanced economic power through trade, foreign direct investment (FDI), and official aid. China may have moved to the top as a trade partner for the ASEAN states in 2006, but both cumulative Japanese and American investment and both countries' annual official aid outstrips China's, and will continue to do so for the foreseeable future.

The extraordinarily rapid growth of Southeast Asian–Chinese trade is often cited as the key example of China's growing influence in Southeast Asia, and the greatest challenge to American predominance in the region. In 2004, U.S. trade with the ASEAN states of approximately $136 billion continued to outstrip Japan's at $119 billion and China's at $103 billion.[19] However, U.S.-ASEAN trade only recovered its 2000 level, in nominal terms, in 2004. Southeast Asian exports to the U.S. market have grown only slightly since 2000 and declined in real terms adjusted for inflation, as have imports from the United States. Moreover, the percentage of ASEAN states' exports destined for the United States has declined with China's rise as a market.

The trajectory of China-Southeast Asian trade compared to relatively stable U.S.-Southeast Asian trade, has led some to ask whether emerging trade patterns represent a gravitational pull toward an Asian economic community that will eventually diminish the role of the United States. When the data becomes available, it is likely to show that Southeast Asia has lost out to China in exporting finished products to the U.S. market. But Southeast Asia continues to be a more significant market for U.S. exports than China ($47.91 billion compared to $34.721 billion respectively in 2004) and U.S. business leaders have not alleged direct competition between Chinese and U.S. exports to Southeast Asian markets.[20] Moreover, statistics on trade between Southeast Asia and China may include an unusually large dose of double counting, as China processes Southeast Asian products into manufactures for export to developed countries or as firms ship components between China and Southeast Asia whose finished product is then exported to the developed world. A recent modeling exercise shows trade gains for both ASEAN and China if and when they fully implement the

CAFTA by 2015. This agreement is projected to create a slight trade diversion, but CAFTA is already pockmarked with exceptions.[21]

China's predicted replacement of the United States as Southeast Asia's largest trade partner is not mirrored in statistics on investment. In 2003, cumulative U.S. investment in ASEAN stood at slightly more than $88 billion, compared to cumulative U.S. investment in China of nearly $12 billion.[22] China's cumulative investment in Southeast Asia is miniscule in comparison, though rising rapidly. There is no evidence of Chinese firms competing directly with U.S. companies in Southeast Asia, or of Chinese government attempts to lobby either on behalf of Chinese firms that would compete with U.S. companies or to complicate U.S. negotiations on Free Trade Agreements with Singapore and Thailand. China's anxious search for energy supplies has led to speculation that China would be prepared to pay higher prices for oil and LNG than U.S.-based energy companies. This speculation was reinforced by an unsuccessful bid in 2005 by the China National Offshore Oil Company (CNOOC) to acquire UNOCAL, which held 70 percent of its reserves in Southeast Asia. However, there has been no suggestion that China paid above market prices for its acquisition of oil blocks in Indonesia. The official U.S. government view is that improving the transparency and other aspects of investment climates in Southeast Asian states will provide equal opportunity for U.S. companies to compete with others in those states.

Economic assistance from the United States to Southeast Asian states totals about $400 million per year.[23] It dwarfs Chinese assistance, which usually consists of aid packages in the $3 million range and soft loans of several hundred million tied to specific projects in individual Southeast Asian countries. U.S. assistance programs for Indonesia and the Philippines total more than $200 million annually. The focus on maritime Southeast Asia is appropriate, given U.S. interests in the region.

Washington's response to China's new prominence as a trade partner for Southeast Asian countries has been limited, in part, by domestic political constraints in the United States. The instruments in the American kit bag consists of Trade and Investment Framework Agreements (TIFA), Free Trade Agreements (FTA), continued pressure and targeted economic assistance to promote transparency in the investment climate and legal safeguards for investors in Southeast Asian states,[24] and usually counterproductive sanctions or the threat of sanctions. Unfortunately, TIFAS are no more than agreements to prepare for the negotiation of Free Trade Agreements. Moreover, the United States has only agreed to negotiate Free Trade Agreements with the wealthy states of Singapore, Thailand, and Malaysia. Unlike China's broad China-ASEAN Free Trade Agreement, which leaves the details to be negotiated at a later stage, Congressional restrictions on U.S. Free Trade Agreements require significant reform in the economies of the negotiating partner. As one observer noted, they are "like going to the dentist, good for you but painful."[25]

DIPLOMACY

The United States has been accused of episodic attention, excessive bilateralism, and lacking a "vision" in its relations with Southeast Asia. In reference to the current

American focus on counterterrorism, the accusation has been leveled that "relations between Southeast Asia and the United States were perhaps well described as a policy without a strategy."[26] The United States is routinely compared unfavorably with China, which has smoothly sold its comprehensive strategy for Southeast Asia.

Much of the criticism misses the mark. Much of it is based on assumptions of American patronage that are unrealistic, given America's limited interests in Southeast Asia and the limited diplomatic resources a global power can devote to a specific region of the globe. However, one Singaporean came closer when he said, 'if Washington wishes to support these strategies (hedging by Southeast Asian countries against China's "rise"), it might most effectively focus on diplomatic and economic aspects in extending its influence in the region."[27] The problem is less the absence of a "vision" than a reluctance to define and assign priorities, and to then devote resources to advancing American goals through a coordinated plan.

The strength and balance of America's entrenched position in much of Southeast Asia has encouraged complacency. The United States was the dominant power from the end of World War II; no one questions that it remains the world's sole "superpower," though the idea of distinguishing between "power" and "influence" is beginning to gain currency among some Southeast Asian officials and academics. It is widely assumed to be the most important provider of "security," though the relevance of this "common good" is coming under new questioning with declining perceptions of a threat to security. It is either the first or second largest provider of FDI, the first or second largest trade partner, and the second largest source of official development assistance (ODA) for Southeast Asia as a whole. The United States remains, for most Southeast Asian states, the "least distrusted" external power.[28]

However, the long list of stated American interests in the region includes promoting human rights and democracy, maintaining regional peace and stability, maintaining a U.S. presence and close relations with allies, maintaining freedom of navigation, maintaining trade and investment relations, and so forth. The result is that individual constituencies in the United States push their own agendas, with priorities usually sorted out in an ad hoc fashion based on their impact on individual bilateral relationships.[29] With no accepted order of priorities, the United States can't fashion a strategy that rationally employs the various instruments of influence or power to effectively match means and ends.

U.S. policies for Southeast Asia are also fragmented for structural reasons. Within the State and Defense Departments, and the National Security Council, responsibility for East Asia is in the hands of northeast Asian, principally China and Japan, experts. Southeast Asia is the permanent bureaucratic stepchild. In the Defense establishment, which is focused on traditional, conventional security issues involving Korea and China, Southeast Asia tends to fall to the U.S. Pacific Command. The result is unusually independent U.S. Ambassadors who are, naturally, primarily concerned with their own responsibilities for bilateral U.S. relations with a specific Southeast Asian country.

Policy in Southeast Asia, therefore, often falls between East Asian policy, focused on China and Japan, and bilateral relations with individual Southeast Asian states.

With the exception of counterterrorism, which has received sustained high-level attention, two consequences are the difficulty the United States faces in engaging with multilateral regional institutions, such as ASEAN, and in addressing transnational issues in the region. In addition, the United States faces problems in integrating the economic component of foreign policy, except at the bilateral level, in large part because it assumes that business is the business of business, not governments, a view not widely shared in Asia.

Americans and Southeast Asians seldom share similar views on the utility of multilateral institutions. The American approach to multilateral organizations in East Asia is primarily instrumental.[30] Southeast Asians primarily see multilateral organizations as reflecting aspirations. Americans are generally dismissive of "talk shops." Southeast Asians see these "talk shops" as means to build understanding and confidence. Americans look for an immediate product. Many Southeast Asians are focused on the iterative process, which may or may not lead to a discernible product.

Although the Clinton administration stressed multilateral organizations, primarily APEC, in U.S. relations with East Asia, the Bush administration had initially been, on the whole, dismissive of these organizations. It remains inclined to prefer "coalitions of the willing" to address concrete problems, such as the humanitarian response to the Indian Ocean tsunami. Alternatively, it has sought to employ multilateral mechanisms to address specific, current issues, for example the Bush administration's determined efforts at the 2003 Bangkok APEC Summit to link terrorism and trade, and convince APEC to adopt a security agenda.

The primary result of the American attitude has been a continued decline in Southeast Asian perceptions of America as a "friend" and "partner," particularly in comparison with China. This has not lead to support for the exclusion of the United States from the evolving East Asian multilateral network, but there has also been little effort to include the United States absent clear American interest in participating outside the APEC and ARF mechanisms.

In 2005, officials in Washington began to recognize the utility of being seen to "play the game" if the United States were not to cede a number of diplomatic networks to China. The calculation appears to be that further engagement with ASEAN is simply a cost the United States has to pay. This is a pragmatic decision. It follows on the Secretary of State's decision to avoid the 2005 annual ASEAN/ARF meeting that her predecessors have attended for the past twenty years, a decision that many regional leaders publicly criticized,[31] and the ambivalent response to the Malaysian-hosted East Asian Summit (EAS), in which the United States did not participate.

The wary American reaction to the EAS was based on three assumptions. The first was that the United States could rely on Australian, Japanese, and Indian participation, as well as friends in Southeast Asia, to ensure that China was unable to "highjack" the Summit. The second was that the U.S. Senate would be unlikely to ratify the ASEAN Treaty of Amity and Cooperation (TAC), a requirement for participation in the Summit. The third, which proved prescient, was that the Summit would flounder on Sino-Japanese rivalry, as it did.[32]

With ASEAN itself, Washington's initial response to China's growing economic influence consisted of two initiatives, the anemic "Enterprise for ASEAN Initiative" (EAI), holding out the prospect of bilateral free trade agreements between the United States and a few ASEAN states, and an even less impressive bundling of projects in support of ASEAN integration, cooperation on transnational issues, and strengthening the ASEAN Secretariat under the "ASEAN Cooperation Plan (ACP)."

However, by 2005, the Bush administration was prepared to attempt to complement its bilateral approach with an American version of the "Strategic Partnership" agreements signed between ASEAN and China, among others. The American version, entitled an "Enhanced Partnership," was announced when President Bush met with Southeast Asian leaders whose states are also APEC member "economies" (thus excluding Burma) at the October 2005 Busan (Korea) APEC meeting. The American expectation is a partnership agreement under which concrete issues, such as avian bird flu, can be addressed through a "work plan" with ASEAN. Whether transnational issues can be effectively addressed through ASEAN mechanisms is doubtful, but the American gesture should go some way to assuaging Southeast Asian public and elite desires for affirmation of ASEAN's relevance. In 2006, in anticipation of President Bush's visit to Southeast Asia to attend the November APEC meeting in Hanoi, Washington was prepared to be responsive to Southeast Asian priorities. At APEC, the United States is expected to emphasize trade, a plan to implement the enhanced partnership, and good governance. President Bush will also probably use a visit to Indonesia to symbolize his commitment to a closer relationship with Southeast Asia's largest state.

The one significant weakness in America's broad and balanced portfolio in Southeast Asia is the reputation of the United States. It has had its ups and downs over the past several decades, but has suffered a significant decline since the assumption of power by the Bush administration. The term soft power is routinely employed in Southeast Asia as shorthand to contrast China's accommodation to ASEAN norms with the Bush administrations perceived addiction to unilateral preemption and military solutions to international problems. Part of the problem for the United States is perception. Part of the problem is also a profound unease with the implications of the U.S.-led coalition's removal of Saddam Hussein from power in Iraq, and the continued insurgency in that country.

Polling is unreliable, but it is clear that not only leaders but also ordinary people increasingly see China as the benign, positive force, a reputation that once belonged to the United States. America's reputation and credibility probably reached their lowest levels in the region in thirty years in 2003 when 9 percent of the Thai picked the United States as a friend. Moreover, even though the U.S. credibility now appears to be on the upswing, many Southeast Asian elites continue to view American attention to Southeast Asia as episodic. The American outpouring of assistance, both public and private, in the wake of the Indian Ocean Tsunami, dwarfed China's contribution. It was much appreciated. It led to a demonstrable improvement in America's image. However, one demonstration of the impressive capacity of the U.S. Navy and of the generosity of the American people hasn't entirely overcome years of perceived neglect.

That perception—of a state that failed to play its role as a patron when its "clients" economies came under pressure during the Asian Financial Crisis 1997, of an inattentive giant that interferes haphazardly in states' internal affairs through congressionally mandated sanctions pushed by individual American constituencies, of a power still focused on remnants of the cold war in Asia, of a country launched on a war against terrorism which may hide a campaign against Islam—means that American influence, if not American power, is slowly draining away in Southeast Asia.

However, the residual attraction of the United States, built up over half a century, continues to influence Southeast Asian perceptions, particularly among elites. Many in Southeast Asia's elites received their higher education in the United States, and many appreciate the idealism behind American support for human rights and democracy. And Washington is trying, haphazardly, to adjust. Moreover, it is impossible at this time to distinguish between distrust of the current American administration and growing anti-Americanism as a whole. It does appear, however, that the American Achilles heel in Southeast Asia in the early years of the twenty-first century is America's image in the wake of Iraq rather than the substance of American policy in Southeast Asia itself.

SUMMARY

The United States is entrenched in Southeast Asia, but has yet to fully adjust to the end of the Cold War fifteen years ago. It has the most balanced portfolio of security, economic, and other instruments to influence Southeast Asian policies, but employs the instruments in its portfolio in a haphazard fashion. It provides "security," albeit a common good widely perceived to be of declining value in the era of China's new policies. It is embedded in Southeast Asian economies through investments, though of declining relative importance as a trade partner. The role of the United States as a beacon and model for Southeast Asians has gradually diminished.

Conclusion

A fire-breathing Chinese dragon and an American screaming eagle are not about to confront each other over the jungles, rice paddies, waters and people of Southeast Asia. Instead, the power of an often distracted United States lies quietly beside China's growing but still limited economic, diplomatic, and cultural influence. Moreover, influence is widely shared by several external and almost a dozen indigenous states. Southeast Asian elites remain in control in their own individual countries.

Once Beijing turned its foreign policy toward Southeast Asia on its head, replacing assertiveness with accommodation and the promise of including Southeast Asians in China's dynamic economic growth, it started to push on an open door. After the 1997 Asian Financial Crisis, China transformed itself in most Southeast Asian eyes. China's success accelerated after Sino-U.S. relations improved in 2001 and it sidelined explicit opposition to American policies in the region. China's current policies are largely congruent with Southeast Asian preferences, norms, and perceived interests. China has become a supporter of the political status quo. China's reemergence as a major external player in Southeast Asia now appears natural and inevitable. Chinese success, however, is largely the result of its decision, in Chinese Premier Wen Jiabao's words, to become a "friendly elephant" which asks little from its southern neighbors. Beijing has met its top goals, improved stability on its southern periphery and a Southeast Asian contribution to China's continued economic growth.

However, the romance of the past several years may fade as the relationship evolves. It is not a marriage. Most of Southeast Asia is not drifting into an emerging Sino-centric economic or political order. Moreover, the hard issues—the relative benefits of trade and investment and authority in the energy-rich South China Sea—have been sidelined, not resolved. In addition, China and Southeast Asian states have exercised restraint and avoided stirring nationalist sentiments, but the "nationalism" card remains available to elites seeking to divert domestic challenges. Finally, the international environment in East Asia has been unusually benign, with no indication that bilateral tensions in the U.S.-Chinese relationship have penetrated Southeast Asia and, thus far, a hesitant Japanese response to China's growing weight in regional affairs. The region will continue to require high-level, hands-on attention in Beijing, and a cautious, incremental, and mutually beneficial approach if Beijing is to avoid provoking negative reactions as its network of ties continues to expand.[1]

SOUTHEAST ASIA

From Laos to Indonesia, Southeast Asian reactions to China's rise vary widely. Despite their differences Southeast Asians share several common assumptions with regard to China. Most elites expect China to give more than it receives in return. Second, few states in Southeast Asia think in terms of the grand strategy of great powers. Few possess the complex national security decision-making architecture employed by great powers to coordinate policies. They are, therefore, generally prepared to leave elaborate theories about international relations to the pundits and the resolution of major international issues to the "elephants." Third, none have shown interest in forming a coalition to balance an external power, or to align with China, the United States, or any other outsider. Instead, the priorities are national political stability and economic development, often mingled in the concept of "comprehensive security." Thus "domestic" considerations are often key ingredients in Southeast Asian states' "foreign" policies.[2]

The relationships among these domestic concerns—economic growth, political stability, and regime maintenance—are complex. Too much emphasis on autonomy, as in Myanmar, can strangle the trade and foreign investment necessary for economic growth, which is often a foundation for regime legitimacy in other Southeast Asian states. As the Asian Financial Crisis of 1997 demonstrated, too much openness to international economic forces can lead to the collapse of a corrupt autocracy, in this case in Indonesia. All the original ASEAN states have adopted a democratic model and reaffirmed their commitment to a development model based on foreign investment and export-led growth.[3] The new ASEAN members of Cambodia, Laos, and Myanmar have not made this transition. Vietnam is now attempting to replicate the Chinese experience of continued Communist Party control and market-based economic growth. Southeast Asian elites view China primarily through the prism of China's contribution to their own domestic political and economic interests.

Second, as relatively weak states compared to the United States, China, India, and Japan, Southeast Asian states stress national sovereignty, territorial integrity, the primacy of the principle of noninterference in internal affairs, consensus building, the peaceful resolution of disputes, and multilateral institutions, all of which contribute to constraining the exercise of coercive power. ASEAN has expanded, spawned a plethora of additional regional organizations, and even inspired assertions that the organization has given birth to a unique "culture" of interaction among member states. Whether one accepts or dismisses the normative value of these principles and institutions, they contribute to the goal of preserving as much autonomy as possible for national elites. Southeast Asian governments are pragmatic about the benefits of their "Gulliver strategy" to tie China down.

Third, Southeast Asians have an interest in stressing "soft power," by which they usually mean some mixture of economics and norms of state behavior in a regional system, combined with extensive networking. Diminished, if not entirely stripped, in the Southeast Asian version of soft power is the export of democracy and human rights so prominent in the American heritage.[4] These states would prefer to have external nations seek influence—by conforming to regional norms and providing investment or access to markets—rather than exercise power by demanding internal reform or participation in a coalition organized by the external power.[5] China's avowed peaceful development strategy is cast in similar language and terms.

All Southeast Asian states seek to hedge, or to avoid having to choose one side at the clear expense of another. Southeast Asian states therefore encourage outsiders to remain in the region since their presence contributes to their ability to hedge. At the same time, they discourage, as much as possible, the importation of external conflicts because they seek to avoid pressure to choose one side or another. Southeast Asian governments have enjoyed considerable elbowroom precisely because such tensions as exist in the bilateral U.S.-Chinese relationship have not spilled over into the region. Hedging is at best a general concept and an individual state's ability to hedge is dependent on a state's geography, domestic politics, military and economic resources, and threat perception.[6] But even Myanmar tries a crude version of hedging against its Chinese patron, primarily with India and Russia.

Some Southeast Asian states have ambitions or strategic cultures beyond economic growth and regime maintenance. Precocious Singapore clings to elaborate theories of hedging and the American military; Vietnam's strategic thinking is informed by intermittent Chinese pressure over a thousand years; Thailand holds ambitions to become mainland Southeast Asia's economic hub; and Indonesia retains aspirations for regional leadership.

However, Southeast Asian preferences and aspirations aside, external economic and political realities in the wider East Asian region involve them indirectly but are beyond their power to control. A new division of labor is emerging in East Asia as Southeast Asian countries participate in new trade triangles built on China's rapid industrialization. Taiwan and tensions on the Korean peninsula involve Beijing, Tokyo, and Washington in contentious issues. Down south, everyone wants to avoid being dragged into conflict to the north, but Southeast Asians have little ability to constrain these three regional powers if they insist on injecting their conflicts into Southeast Asia.

CHINA

Beijing's search for stability on China's southern periphery is part of a wider effort to improve ties all along China's borders.[7] It has been particularly successful in Southeast Asia.

Beijing has temporarily placed most contentious issues, such as the South China Sea, on the shelf and limited the issues on which it seeks Southeast Asian political support primarily to Taiwan and, to a lesser extent, Japan. Beijing has abjured overt opposition to the American role in the region. It has deferred to ASEAN on such issues as invitees to the first East Asian Summit (EAS) and largely resisted the temptation to intervene on the behalf of ethnic Chinese Southeast Asians. It has also offered political support to its authoritarian friends in mainland Southeast Asia (supplemented with limited economic assistance), reached out through trade and diplomacy to more important economic partners principally in maritime Southeast Asia, and capped its efforts with enthusiastic participation in multilateral organizations. Close ties with ASEAN also enhance China's influence in the evolving web of Asian multilateral organizations. This strategy is labor intensive, both in terms of senior leaders' time and attention, and in terms of the commitment of Chinese diplomatic resources.

The nature of Southeast Asia's contribution to China's economic development has changed over the past decade, from an early source of foreign direct investment (FDI) to a trade partner increasingly integrated into an evolving East Asian market. Wealthier countries, such as Japan, surpassed Southeast Asia as a source for investment in China during the last century, but trade with Southeast Asia has continued to expand at a phenomenal clip, reaching more than $130 billion in 2005. Moreover, although Beijing runs a trade deficit with Southeast Asia as a whole, early indications are that China continues to solidify its dominance of manufacturing, with various Southeast Asian economies finding often profitable niches as providers of components for Chinese manufactures, of natural resources, and of facilities for Chinese tourists and students. Through mainland Southeast Asia run transportation routes useful in the development of poorer inland Chinese provinces, which should contribute to political stability in China. In addition, though Southeast Asia can only provide a small percentage of China's accelerating energy imports, the bulk of those energy imports must transit Southeast Asian maritime chokepoints.

Taiwan is a fading presence in Southeast Asia. Although Southeast Asian instincts, a decade ago, were to duck any conflict between Beijing and Taipei, until recently Taiwan's political, economic, and cultural connections with ethnic Chinese in Southeast Asia had been a source of influence. However, this influence has declined dramatically over the past five years.[8] Nonetheless, Taiwan retains larger economic investments in Southeast Asia than China. Moreover, Beijing has no room for compromise with Southeast Asians on Taiwan, which provides Southeast Asians with potential leverage.

The fundamental problem for Beijing is that, if its goals in the region become more ambitious, securing them may eventually require some steel in the velvet glove that it has extended to its southern neighbors for almost a decade. Thus far, China has diffused tension in the South China Sea, but it has also insisted that China's sovereignty is indisputable. Limited proven oil reserves in the South China Sea and China's inability to project naval power have argued for moderation, but the temptation to revert to intimidation will grow as China becomes increasingly dependent on imported energy resources transiting Southeast Asia. But attempted coercion would be bound to provoke a negative reaction, and, given Southeast Asian states' wide choice of partners, would probably prove counterproductive. In addition, since September 11, 2001 Beijing has been careful to avoid direct competition with the United States, which would worry Southeast Asians. Potentially more important than the United States, however, would be rising resentment should Southeast Asian economies fail to adjust and fail to profit from their ties to China while China's manufactures continue to hollow out some Southeast Asian industries. Finally, an inevitable tendency to adjust hedging policies as China becomes more influential in the region could also sour some of China's bilateral relationships.

THE UNITED STATES

Entrenched, distracted, usually benign, the United States continues to coast along as the most influential external power in most of Southeast Asia. It retains the most balanced portfolio of security, economic, and political instruments and, when it chooses to do so, can bring more to the table than anyone else. Over the past few years the United States took the lead both to build and support an antiterrorism coalition and to respond to the humanitarian crisis caused by the Indian Ocean tsunami.

However, trade and investment are, in real terms, stagnant. Fading threat perceptions bring into question the continued relevance of America's unique contribution to security in Southeast Asia. The American image declined when the current administration in Washington stressed the unilateral and military aspects of foreign policy, so contrary to professed Southeast Asian norms. Policy and programs are often held hostage by domestic constituencies, and Washington's attention is often filtered through wider global or East Asian lenses. The net result is that the cost to the United States of securing support in the region for its priorities is slowly rising.[9]

No other state will soon dominate the entire region. No other state has the military resources to even contemplate challenging American control, if and when necessary, of strategic sea-lanes between the Pacific and Indian Oceans. A coalition of regional states, supported by the Japan and the United States, is gradually improving maritime security in the Strait of Malacca.

Many pundits once feared that American businesses in Southeast Asia would fall before a Japanese economic juggernaut. In fact, American investment has grown and diversified beyond the extraction of the region's natural resources, and the American market remains the most accessible for most Southeast Asian exports. The China-ASEAN Free Trade Agreement (CAFTA) may, if fully implemented, one day lead to trade diversion to the detriment of the United States. The pattern of "networking" among ethnic Chinese minorities and manufacturing links between China and Southeast Asia may eventually tilt the playing field against some American businesses. However, at this point, there is no evidence that China's economic boom is reducing America's economic stake in Southeast Asia. Indeed, the political reaction in 2005 in the United States that discouraged a Chinese company's acquisition of the American energy company UNOCAL blocked China's most ambitious attempt to invest in Southeast Asian economies.

The American reaction to international terrorism since the September 11, 2001 attacks has both strengthened and complicated its position in the region. Southeast Asian states have cooperated with the United States and their neighbors to suppress regional terrorist organizations linked to the al Qaeda network. But Southeast Asian governments' appreciation for Washington's renewed attention has been tempered by popular distrust of American motives. The Iraq war has precluded the deft diplomacy that might have helped assure these countries of America's interest in their broader concerns while an antiterrorism coalition was also constructed.

The fundamental problem for the United States in Southeast Asia is that expectations surpass America's limited interests in the region. Moreover, in the absence of agreed upon priorities, American influence is often sidelined into secondary concerns. The real challenges are to preserve U.S. predominance in maritime Southeast Asia and to secure the support of the regions' Muslims in the long struggle against terrorism.

CONSEQUENCES

Some Americans, searching for a peer competitor to the United States, assume that China's rise will inevitably lead to a transition of power in which China will challenge the United States, at least in Asia.[10] At that time, Southeast Asians will, it is alleged, be compelled to choose between these two "strategic competitors." Thus, it is argued, inevitably the current ambivalent Beijing-Washington relationship will be transformed into a zero-sum competition, where any gain for China becomes a loss for the United States and vice versa.

But China is not the Soviet Union—a global ideological competitor posing a military threat to America's survival—reborn.[11] And power and influence are widely diffused in Southeast Asia. The reason that American diplomats deny that China and the United States are engaged in strategic competition in Southeast Asia is simple.[12] They aren't.

It is true that improved relations between Beijing and Washington have, at least theoretically, lowered the potential costs for many Southeast Asian states of responding positively to Chinese overtures. However, Southeast Asians have long been adept at picking and choosing what they want from external powers and, thus far, American and Chinese interests and preferences have seldom come into direct conflict in the region.

Instead, China and the United States pursue their different priorities, often with a different mix of foreign policy instruments, largely in different parts of Southeast Asia.

Even a quick review of the goals, methods, and instruments of influence wielded by Beijing and Washington demonstrates how they sit side-by-side, aware of but seldom bumping up against each other. Since the United States possesses overwhelming military power, it stresses traditional security issues. China, incapable of challenging American military forces, has simply turned the tables, questioning not only the relevance of traditional security but also the assumption that China poses a threat.

Southeast Asians hold a wide variety of views on "security," but one Southeast Asian diplomat summed up a widespread view when he said, "I don't care how many more American carrier battle groups transit the Straits. I will only care thirty years from now if a Chinese aircraft carrier goes through the Straits."[13]

If not security, what about economic competition? But even here, the reality is less than a first glance would suggest. The volume of total Southeast Asian-Chinese trade is expected to surpass that of the region with the United States in 2006. However, much of the trade between China and Southeast Asia is processing trade, often by multinational companies with a foot in both China and Southeast Asia, which leads to multiple counting in official statistics. American companies, with a larger stock of investments in Southeast Asia than in China, produce components for their products in both countries. The American market, which takes more finished products, remains the most important for both China and Southeast Asia. Commercial competition may well accelerate in the coming years, but there is no example yet of a Chinese company winning in a head-to-head commercial competition with an American firm. Southeast Asians, meanwhile, trade profitably with and encourage FDI from the United States and China, as well as Japan, Europe, and India.

And the softer end of the power/influence spectrum is even more complicated because there is no agreed means to measure attraction's impact. Southeast Asians want to be courted. As the weaker party in bilateral contacts with external powers, they want the reassurance that comes from deference to the norms they publicly espouse and the multilateralism they use to cloak their individual weaknesses. They seek to preserve as much political autonomy as possible, and resent interference in "internal affairs." Beijing's smooth diplomacy, its promise to include the region in its own economic development, and its support for the political status quo dovetails with Southeast Asian preferences.

The United States, in contrast, is often seen as both distracted and demanding. It at least annually criticizes several Southeast Asian states for failing to meet human rights or other standards. Its demands for cooperation against international terrorists required Indonesian and Thai leaders to take action that they would often have preferred to defer for domestic political reasons. Washington has also demanded internal economic reform as part of the negotiations for bilateral free trade agreements, while Beijing was prepared to sideline contentious issues in forging CAFTA. But the United States continues to hold some valuable "soft power" face cards. Its commitment to basic human rights and democracy in Myanmar shames China. More than a hundred thousand Southeast Asians were at least partially educated in the United States, including the Presidents of Indonesia and the Philippines.

Moreover, Washington has listened to Southeast Asian complaints about disproportionate attention to terrorism and announced its own version of a strategic partnership with ASEAN. America's image appears to be slowly recovering from its low point in 2003. How much more it will do so depends on two factors. First, no one has yet distinguished between popular antagonism to the Bush administration and broader anti-Americanism. Second, Iraq is a public relations fiasco for the United States among the more than 200 million Muslims in Southeast Asia.

In addition to the different instruments of power and influence that China and the United States wield, often in pursuit of different goals, these two countries are focused on different parts of Southeast Asia.

Southeast Asia is divided into mainland (or continental) and maritime (or insular) regions, where geography overlaps with religious, cultural, and domestic political divides. ASEAN's expansion in the 1990s was an attempt to overcome this chasm, and it is now in the interest of Southeast Asian states to place an ASEAN mask over this split, but it is profound.

For most of mainland Southeast Asia, China will loom as the predominant external influence. Thailand retains its ability to bend with the wind, but Myanmar is condemned to deference, if not complete subservience. Vietnam lives in China's shadow. Beijing is the most useful external prop for the authoritarian regimes of Myanmar, Laos, Cambodia. China's basic security interest in Southeast Asia is friendly regimes directly on its southern borders. Southwest China's outlets to the Indian Ocean run through mainland Southeast Asia, which provide transportation routes not only for normal Chinese commercial trade but also potentially for energy imports from the Middle East. The wealthier maritime Southeast Asian states are of growing importance as trade partners, and Beijing has reached out to successfully improve relations with all the states in the region. But maritime Southeast Asia is not part of China's backyard.

American interests are centered in the Strait of Malacca, the world's most important maritime chokepoint, not in Myanmar or Vietnam. The United States will not cede the ability to control strategic sea-lanes. The conflict the United States is now engaged in with violent Islamists will continue to rivet U.S. attention on Indonesia, Malaysia, southern Thailand, and the southern Philippines. American trade and investment, as well as official American economic assistance, are overwhelmingly concentrated in the democracies of maritime Southeast Asia.

The United States may promote democracy and human rights in the authoritarian states of mainland Southeast Asia, and will seek enhanced ties with Vietnam, but it has little reason to challenge China's basic interests. Only those who would place promoting human rights at the forefront of America's goals in Southeast Asia would argue that the United States has a major role to play in Myanmar, Laos, and Cambodia, where U.S. economic and security concerns are marginal.[14] Thus a potentially stable balance of interests and influence, if not traditional power, has emerged between the United States and China in Southeast Asia, with Thailand and Malaysia as transition states.

This balance, against a background of low and decreasing tensions, provides most Southeast Asian states with room to hedge, maneuver, and pick and choose among China, the United States, Japan, and India. Moreover, these states are actors in their own right. As we have seen, they have proactively enmeshed external "powers" in a number of regional or East Asian organizations, promoted norms of behavior, and encouraged FDI and trade. Southeast Asians can point to a strong and generally successful effort to shape the terms under which outsiders participate in their affairs. Thus Southeast Asian states have successfully adjusted to and accommodated the growth of Chinese influence over the past decade. Moreover, Beijing would forfeit much of its influence if it reversed its decade long attempt to woo Southeast Asians and started to throw its weight around in one-on-one relationships. The current balance suits most Southeast Asians just fine.

In fact, in Southeast Asia the focus should be less on China and the United States and more on the implications of China's rise for Taiwan, Japan, and India. Taiwan may be a lost cause for Southeast Asia, given the flow of Taiwanese investment to the Chinese mainland, the fraying of old links between Taiwanese and Southeast Asian leaders, and China's growing influence in the region. Japan is a different matter. It appears that China is stepping into to Japan's old shoes as the most important Asian power in the region.

Japan's economic stake in Southeast Asia remains immense, but for the past decade it has been seen as a player "on autopilot."[15] The primary reason is unassuming and often incoherent policies, which may be institutionalized in Japan's turf-conscious bureaucracies.[16] Japan's new willingness to take on expanded security responsibilities, signs that its economy is emerging from more than a decade in the doldrums, and the hesitant effort to become a "normal country" may eventually lead to a revival of Japanese influence, but its own cultural distinctiveness and ambivalence toward Southeast Asia have further limited the Japanese impact. Another factor is Southeast Asian expectations for the future, which now tend to focus on China. The result is that Japanese private companies' economic stake, in terms of investment and trade, buys the Japanese government remarkably little influence outside the economic sphere, and provides Southeast Asians with little ability to leverage Japan's contribution to secure more from others. Nonetheless, Japan's residual strengths make it a potential competitor that China would not like to push too far.

In addition, India is copying China's strategy for Southeast Asia, albeit with fewer resources. India's "Look East" policy is not designed exclusively to provide Southeast Asians with an alternative to China. New Delhi also wants to promote trade, secure energy supplies, extend its naval power in the Indian Ocean, and participate in the expanding network of East Asian multilateral organizations and free trade agreements. Nonetheless, an active, engaged India provides Southeast Asians with another partner that can be leveraged.

The bottom line is that the image of China and the United States as two states engaged in conflict in Southeast Asia is simplistic and misleading. Instead, they are two of four major external participants in a system that resembles an elaborate and complicated Southeast Asian dance. The music and choreography is usually Southeast Asian and, more often than not, each of the ten members of ASEAN picks his partner for each dance.

THE FUTURE: POTENTIAL AREAS FOR CONFLICT

The crystal ball is murky. Much depends on where the tipping point might be before different Southeast Asian leaders come to believe that China is overplaying its hand. Whether the United States becomes alarmed would probably depend only tangentially on developments in Southeast Asia, as would a Chinese decision that the United States is overreacting to China's "peaceful development." Beijing and Washington will base their views primarily on bilateral issues and developments further north, as will Tokyo. Potential areas of conflict in Chinese-Southeast Asian relations include economics and energy.

China and Southeast Asia are economic competitors, both for FDI and developed export markets in Japan, Europe, and the United States. Many Southeast Asians believe China is sucking up much of the FDI that used to flow to them, but in fact Southeast Asia is attracting more FDI on a per capita basis than China.[17] Wealthier ASEAN countries, such as Singapore, Malaysia, and Thailand, hope to fill niches in an increasingly integrated, Chinese-dominated East Asian economy but their economies may have to undergo wrenching adjustments. Poorer countries should be worried that Chinese economic competition will hollow out their industrial sectors and confine them to colonial economic relationships, but Beijing is going out of its way to give these states a stake in the evolving East Asian economic market. Nonetheless, the difficulty of negotiating bilateral early harvest agreements under the mantle of the CAFTA may be an early sign of problems to come. Despite a recent flurry of agreements, Indonesia, which has traditionally seen itself as the natural leader of ASEAN, harbors concerns about not only China's drive for political influence but also China's potential impact on Indonesia's continued economic development. Absent the perception of a continued "win-win" economic relationship with China, some Southeast Asian states may begin to circle the economic wagons. Moreover, if confronted with economic stagnation, some Southeast Asian politicians might even be tempted to turn to latent anti-ethnic Chinese sentiments to bolster their hold on power. At this point, Southeast Asians are torn between fear that parts of their economies will not be able to compete and appreciation for the boost to their economies that access to China's market continues to provide.

Within the next twenty years, an estimated two-thirds of China's petroleum imports, which will have quadrupled, will flow from the Middle East through Southeast Asian waters. Moreover, China and four Southeast Asian countries claim parts of the natural gas-rich South China Sea. China has already built dams on the Mekong, and plans more, which have had a negative impact downriver in Southeast Asia. China's energy angst, already acute,[18] could easily lead to misjudgments, since the United States and several Southeast Asian countries potentially have a hand on China's energy windpipe. A decade from now, a decision by Beijing to project naval forces into Southeast Asia to protect China's vital energy supply lines could lead to a crisis.

In addition, the CAFTA, if fully implemented, and the emergence of China-centered multilateral institutions excluding the United States, may eventually contribute to rising U.S.-Chinese misunderstanding. Democracy and human rights in Southeast Asia are likely to remain secondary issues in U.S.-Chinese relations unless they lead to regime change in Myanmar or Vietnam, which would present Beijing with concerns about the security of its southern borders. The United States, for its part, will be sensitive to enhanced Chinese security relationships with the Philippines and states bordering on maritime chokepoints further south. Washington is already seeking a closer relationship with Indonesia, the potential leader of any collective regional effort in the future to constrain Chinese influence in Southeast Asia. But China's relationship with the United States is only one factor in the evolution of China's relationships with Southeast Asia. The future of China's increasingly dense and complex ties to its southern neighbors rests primarily in the hands of these Asian states.

Notes

INTRODUCTION

1. The book is agnostic on the debate over whether Chinese policy is driven primarily by external constraints and opportunities or domestic change. See Nan Li's article, "The Evolving Chinese Conception of Security and Security Approaches." In *Asia-Pacific Security Cooperation, National Interests and Regional Order*, edited by see Seng Tan and Amitav Archarya. New York: M.E. Sharpe, 2004. It argues that the latter better explains revisions of China's foreign policy.

2. The Philippines, Malaysia, and Brunei have overlapping territorial claims among themselves and with China in the South China Sea.

CHAPTER 1

1. It should also be noted that ethnic Chinese played a larger than proportional role in many of these insurgencies in the region.

2. In 2005 the Association of Southeast Asian Nations (ASEAN) includes Brunei, Cambodia, Indonesia, Laos, Malaysia, Myanmar, the Philippines, Singapore, Thailand, and Vietnam. Vietnam was admitted in 1995, Laos and Myanmar in 1997, and Cambodia in 1999.

3. "Southeast Asia states remained silent or, as in the Thai and Malaysian cases, noted simply that it was an 'internal affair.'" Shambaugh, "China Engages Asia, Reshaping the Regional Order." *International Security*, 29(3) (Winter 2004/2005): 67. In fact, Singapore criticized the Chinese government's resort to force.

4. Cambodia, Laos, Myanmar, and Vietnam were not yet members of ASEAN.

5. In mid-1997, several Asian currencies began to collapse under the twin burdens of crony capitalism and the pressure of international speculators, a process that became known as the Asian Financial Crisis. Three ASEAN countries were sliding into harsh economic recessions that would see Thailand's GDP drop by 10% and Indonesia's by 13%, and would lead to the removal of Southeast Asia's longest-running authoritarian regime in Indonesia.

6. Michael A. Glosny, "Heading Toward a Win-Win Future? Recent Developments in China's Policy Toward Southeast Asia." *Asian Security*, 2(1) (2006): 1; David Shambaugh, "China Engages Asia, Reshaping the Regional Order," 64–99. In March 2004, in response to questions about China's relations with ASEAN, Premier Wen Jiabao described China as a "friendly elephant."

7. In essence, the "ASEAN Way" emphasizes consultation not to resolve a specific issue but to gradually build agreement on a set of norms, values, and procedures. It is predicated on the assumption that states support the status quo.

8. IMF Direction of Trade Statistics. However, another source explains: "Senior Chinese officials are aware that prevailing trade data showing China's central role in Asian trade networks tend to overestimate China's importance. The trade figures dealing with China count the full value of a product as it crosses Chinese boundaries, sometimes several times, before being completed. The actual value added by China in each of these transfers is obviously less than would appear from the stated value seen in the trade figures. Over half of China's trade in 2004 was this so-called processing trade." Sutter, "China's Rise: Implications for U.S. Leadership in Asia," Policy Studies 21, East-West Center, Washington, DC, 2006, 3. In addition, about two-thirds of Chinese-ASEAN trade may be conducted by international companies, which may lead to multiple counting as products pass in and out of China and ASEAN countries before the "finished" product is sold elsewhere. Finally, components imported from elsewhere in Asia account for between 50% and 65% of the value of China's exports.

9. The distinction between "influence" and "power" is not addressed in these discussions, but in this book the term "influence" means more than the "attraction" often associated with so-called "soft power" and less than the ability to convince others to do what they would not normally do as a consequence of the use of the military or economic components of "power." This issue will be considered in Chapters 2 and 7.

10. China has undertaken a concerted campaign to secure Southeast Asian support against "Anti-Beijing Groups." Beijing is adamant that Southeast Asian governments should not tolerate the activities of anti-Chinese individuals such as the Dalai Lama or groups such as the Falun Gong, banned in China since 1999. As with Chinese pressure to cut links between Taiwan and Southeast Asia, China has isolated the Dalai Lama and ensured that Southeast Asian leaders do not permit visits. As for the Falun Gong, shortly after new Thai Prime Minister Taksin assumed office in 2001, "the Chinese government and its embassy went to great lengths to exert pressure on the Taksin government" to ban the "evil cult." (Sutter, *China's Rise in Asia*, 197. Thai officials also blocked a convention planned by Falun Gong adherents. In April 2003, as Chinese Premier Wen Jiabao was about to visit Bangkok, Thai police detained and subsequently deported a foreign Falun Gong member. According to the Indonesian press, in 2005 Jakarta did permit a demonstration by radical Indonesian Muslim groups condemning Chinese oppression of their Uighur Muslim brethren in Xinjiang.

11. Chen Jie, "Taiwan's Diplomacy in Southeast Asia: Still Going South" and Samuel C.Y. Ku, "The Changing Political Economy of Taiwan's and China's Relations with Southeast Asia." In *China and Southeast Asia: Global Changes and Regional Challenges*, edited by Ho Khai Leong and Samuel C.Y. Ku. Institute of Southeast Asian Studies, Singapore, 2005.

12. Chen, "Taiwan's Diplomacy in Southeast Asia," 233.

13. Statistics on Taiwanese investment in Southeast Asia vary widely. According to the ASEAN statistical database (Table 6.2) "Foreign Direct Investment in ASEAN by Source Country/Region as of 31 December 2005," Taiwan (ROC) investment in ASEAN declined from $2.524 billion in 2001 to $1.186 billion in 2004. Taiwan's cumulative investment in Southeast Asia may total only about $9 billion in 2005.

14. Chen, "Taiwan's Diplomacy in Southeast Asia," 251.

15. Percival interview with senior strategic studies institute official, Kuala Lumpur, September 2004.

16. Beijing may be largely indifferent to Taiwanese companies' investments in Southeast Asia unless such investments also influence Southeast Asian political leaders' relations with Taiwan. Beijing's goal is to sever official, not economic, links between Taiwan and Southeast Asian states.

17. Chen, "Taiwan's Diplomacy in Southeast Asia," 251.

18. Sutter, "*China's Rise in Asia*," 197.

19. *Central News Agency*, May 20, 2005. Also see Santo Darmosumarto, "Understanding the One China Policy and Indonesia's Ties with Taiwan," *Jakarta Post*, July 28, 2006.

20. See Teo Kah Beng, "Singapore," *Betwixt and Between, Southeast Asian Strategic Relations with the U.S. and China*. IDSS Monograph No. 7, 2005, p. 45, or Teo Chu Cheow, "Sino-Singapore Relations Back on Track," China Brief, 5(16) (July 19, 2005): 3–5.

21. Percival interview with a Singaporean strategic studies institute political/military expert, August 2005.

22. Robert Sutter, "China's Regional Strategy and America." In *Power Shift, China and Asia's New Dynamics*, edited by David Shambaugh. Berkeley: University of California Press, 2005, 292.

23. Ibid., 294.

24. For example, in 1998 China "cooled its rhetoric" calling for the elimination of U.S. alliances when ASEAN states "privately but sternly" told Beijing that its relations with Southeast Asia could only prosper if China refrained from pushing for the severance of bilateral security arrangements with the United States in the region. Shambaugh, "China Engages Asia, Reshaping the Regional Order," 70.

25. American officials' commentary on U.S.-China relations has not been entirely consistent since 2001. Former Secretary of State Colin Powell called Chinese-U.S. relations the best in decades, while his successor has adopted a more cautious line. Deputy Secretary of State Zoellick has called on China to become a responsible "stakeholder" in the international system, a term also employed by President Bush during Hu Jintao's April 2006 visit to the United States. Also see Steven Weisman, "U.S. and Australia Take Different Tones on China's Rising Power." *New York Times*, March 16, 2006.

26. For an alternative view, which stresses traditional security issues, see Mohan Malik, "China's Strategy of Containing India," *Power and Interest News Report*, February 6, 2006.

27. Lam Peng-Er argues that Japan has played a larger political role in Southeast Asia than in its more immediate Northeast Asian neighborhood because its relations with Southeast Asia are "less bedeviled by unresolved issues of history." Southeast Asian countries are more open to Japanese diplomatic initiatives, and the Southeast Asian region does not "have intractable security problems of the same magnitude as Northeast Asia." See "Japan-Southeast Asia Relations: Trading Places." *Comparative Connections*, 1st Quarter, 2002.

28. "Neither Beijing nor Tokyo is intentionally pursuing a policy of confrontation. Except for a minority of nationalist elites in each country, the political establishments in Japan and China want to stop the downward spiral because their top policy agenda is domestic economic reform, not regional expansion." Minxin Pei and Michael Swaine, *Simmering Fire in Asia: Averting Sino-Japanese Strategic Conflict*, Policy Brief 44, Carnegie Endowment for International Peace, November 2005, 4.

29. David Kang writes, "East Asian states see China as a responsible state, and do not fear Chinese aggrandizement . . . East Asian states have responded differently to Japanese power than they have to Chinese power. Throughout East Asia, and particularly in northeast Asia, Japanese moves are seen as more threatening and less trustworthy than are Chinese moves . . . Japanese attempts to lead East Asia have historically been relatively unsuccessful, and led to resistance and resentment in East Asia." "East Asian Integration: Some Underlying Factors," Remarks Prepared for a Bureau of Intelligence and Research, Department of State, Workshop on East Asian Integration, March 10, 2006, 3–4.

30. Chinese warnings about the potential for a revival of Japanese militarism usually fall on deaf ears in Southeast Asia, but Southeast Asian states generally oppose Japanese policies that could be portrayed as "anti-Chinese" or the injection of Chinese-Japanese disputes into the region.

31. Japan received little credit for its aid in response to the Asian Financial Crisis. Aid to Southeast Asia totaled $2.5 billion in 1998. See James Borton, "Japanese Aid Brings Dividends, Division." 2003, *Asian Times Online*, http://www.atimes.com/atimes/Japan/EF20Dh03.html.

32. Japan provides about 60% of total ODA to Southeast Asia and more than half of bilateral aid to most individual Southeast Asian countries. However, Japanese ODA and concessionary loans are widely perceived in Southeast Asia to be designed in large part to support private Japanese firms investing in or trading with Southeast Asia. Moreover, billions of dollars of Japanese aid, either bilateral or channeled through the Asian Development Bank, have gone into development schemes in the greater Mekong river region that primarily benefit China. Percival interviews with officials and strategic studies institute experts in Hanoi, Bangkok, Jakarta, Kuala Lumpur, and Singapore, September 2004, March 2005, and August 2005.

33. Cumulative outflows of Japanese Foreign Debt Investment in Southeast Asia from 1951 to 2004 totaled $83.626 billion, according to Professor Hugh T. Patrick, Weatherhead East Asia Institute, Columbia University, New York. http://www.mof.go.jp/english/elc008.htm.

34. Japan's ODA budget has fallen 34% since its peak in 1995. IMF Direction of Trade Statistics show ASEAN-Japan trade at $120 billion in 2003, down from about $125 billion in 1995; the ASEAN Statistical Yearbook shows Japanese annual investment falling from $51/2 billion in 1995 to $2 billion in 2003. According to Professor Hugh T. Patrick, Columbia University, "Japan's Official Development Assistance to, and FDI in, Southeast Asia Countries", paper presented at a March 20, 2006, Conference hosted by the Bureau of Intelligence and Research, Department of State, Washington, D.C., "Japanese FDI in 2004 to China amounted to $4.6 billion, and to all of Southeast Asia only $2.8 billion."

35. Lam Peng-Er, "Japan-Southeast Asia Relations Trading Places? The Leading Goose & Ascending Dragon." *Comparative Connections*, 1st Quarter 2002: 6–7.

36. See Department of State, Office of Research, "Among Urban Southeast Asian Publics, US Image Improves Markedly Following Tsunami Relief," March 31, 2005.

37. Percival interviews with senior officials and diplomats, Bangkok, Singapore, and Washington, D.C., August and September 2005. In the end, only Singapore among all the Southeast Asian states supported Japan's bid for a permanent seat on the United Nations Security Council.

38. Anecdotal evidence suggests that Vietnam, among ASEAN states, is probably most supportive of an enhanced Japanese role in Southeast Asia.

39. Percival interview with a senior diplomat, Singapore, August 2005. For additional information on Japan's role in Southeast Asia, see Bronson Percival, "Japan-Southeast Asia Relations: Playing Catch-up with China," *Comparative Connections*, 8(3), October 2006.

40. China's close relationship with Myanmar is often ascribed a strategic significance for the United States that is not warranted. The mythology of Myanmar's significance in China's comprehensive strategy for Southeast Asia is addressed later in this book.

41. Sutter, *China's Rise in Asia*, 199.

42. When China acceded to the ASEAN Treaty of Amity and Cooperation (TAC) in 2003, Beijing and ASEAN obliquely criticized the United States when they announced that they had agreed to cooperate with China "while upholding the authority and central role of the UN."

43. Percival interview with a senior U.S. diplomat, Bangkok, August 2005.

44. Official comment, as reported in the Hong Kong press, was moderate.

45. See Bronson E. Percival, *Indonesia and the United States: Shared Interest in Maritime Security*. The United States-Indonesia Society, Washington, DC, June 2005.

46. Robert Ross. *A Realist Policy for Managing US-China Competition*, Policy Analysis Brief, The Stanley Foundation, November 2005, 7. In addition, China's decision to avoid the kind of strident criticism that had characterized its reaction to closer U.S. military and other sensitive ties with Asian governments prior to 2001 may have provided such Asian states as the Philippines and Singapore with a freer hand to pursue closer strategic relationships with the United States.

47. Kavi Chongkittavorn, "ASEAN-China Ties in 2020: Stronger and Deeper?" *The Nation*, November 28, 2005.

48. Dana R. Dillon and John J. Thacik, Jr. *China and ASEAN: Endangered American Primacy in Southeast Asia*, Backgrounder Published by the Heritage Foundation, No. 1886, October 19, 2005, 5.

49. See individual country sections in Chapters 3 and 4.

50. In one move that was widely interpreted to include an element of anti-Americanism, Beijing raised the status of Philippine President Arroyo's visit to China after she bowed to domestic political pressures, shrugged off American opposition, and withdrew the token Filipino military force from Iraq in 2005.

51. Several constituencies in the United States have raised concerns about the implications of China's growing influence in Southeast Asia: Human rights organizations point to China's support for authoritarian regimes in several Southeast Asian countries. Business leaders have cited a "China threat" even while Washington focused on counterterrorism in the region (for example, the President of the U.S./ASEAN business council was quoted in an October 9, 2003, in a *New York Times* article as stating, "I do feel the Chinese Monroe Doctrine is being built here in the region. As the Chinese get their act together and play on the world stage, this region is the first of a series of concentric circles."). Some analyst have tried to suggest that China's military modernization, though now directed toward potential conflict in the Taiwan Strait, could eventually be reoriented to threaten Southeast Asia.

CHAPTER 2

1. This is not a book about international relations theory, and an exhaustive review of theory will not be undertaken. The goal is simply to pick up different "schools of thought," which might be thought of as different pairs of glasses, and to hold them up to see where they apply in Southeast Asia. Some pairs of glasses will not be used because they are not helpful. The America-centric concept of "soft power" is analytically useless in Southeast Asia, but the term is so common that the idea must be addressed. To transform this idea into an explanatory concept, we need to place it in an Asian context, separate it from economics, and

address it through the lens of who benefits in Southeast Asia. We do so in a separate chapter (Chapter 7).

2. David Shambaugh, "China Engages Asia: Reshaping the Regional Order." *International Security*, 29, no. 3 (Winter 2004/2005): 66.

3. Goh, *Meeting the China Challenge: The U.S. in Southeast Asian Regional Security Strategies*, Policy Studies 16, East-West Center, Washington, DC, 2005, ix.

4. "Realists" might argue that China's "power" is not yet sufficient to cause these results.

5. Also see Robert Ross, *A Realist Policy for Managing US-China Competition*. Policy Analysis Brief, The Stanley Foundation, November 2005.

6. Robert Ross, "The Geography of Peace: East Asia in the Twenty-First Century." *International Security*, 23, no. 4 (Spring 1999): 84–86.

7. Ross, *A Realist Policy for Managing US-China Competition*, 3.

8. Ibid., 4.

9. In the 2006 version of his unpublished manuscript "Balance of Power Theory and the Rise of China," Ross acknowledges that "The military rise of China in East Asia and the corresponding decline of U.S. military power vis-à-vis third countries is not uniform throughout the region. China is balancing U.S. power, but is only doing so in the Korean and Taiwan theaters, regions abutting improve Chinese mainland-based capabilities. Elsewhere in East Asia China is not a rising power and it is not balancing U.S. power. In the region's maritime theaters the distribution of power is stable as China has yet to challenge U.S. military supremacy" (page 14) but then he goes on to state that maritime Southeast Asian countries are "consolidating defense cooperation with the United States" (page 39) to balance against "this region's growing dependence on the Chinese economy."

10. Shannon Tow, "Southeast Asia in the Sino-U.S. Strategic Balance." *Contemporary Southeast Asia*, 26, no. 3, 2004: 437.

11. Ibid., 455.

12. See Vuving, "Vietnam's Conduct of its Relations with China: Balancing, Bandwagoning, Accepting Hierarchy, or a Fourth Configuration?" Paper presented at the conference, "Vietnam as an Actor on the International Stage," School of Advanced International Studies, Johns Hopkins University, Washington, DC, April 29, 2005.

13. Robert Ross, Unpublished Manuscript, "Balance of Power Theory and the Rise of China: Accommodation and Balancing in East Asia," 20.

14. Ross, *A Realist Policy for Managing US-China Competition*, 7.

15. See David C. Kang, "Hierarchy and Stability in Asian International Relations." *American Asian Review*, 19, no. 2 (Summer 2001): 121–160; David C. Kang "Getting Asia Wrong, The Need for New Analytical Frameworks." *International Security*, 27, no. 4 (Spring 2003): 57–85.

16. Brantly Womack, "China and Southeast Asia: Asymmetry, Leadership and Normalcy." *Pacific Affairs*, 76, no. 4 (Winter 2003–2004): 531.

17. Goh, "Meeting the China Challenge," 2.

18. Though both seek to extract resources and support by "playing off" external powers against each other, much as some Southeast Asian and other states did during the long Cold War.

19. Ibid., 29.

20. Ibid., 27.

21. Ibid., 45.

22. Robert Sutter, *China's Rise in Asia, Promises and Perils*. Oxford: Rowan & Littlefield, 2005, 181.

23. Michael A. Glosny, "Heading Toward a Win-Win Future? Recent Developments in China's Policy Toward Southeast Asia." *Asian Security*, 2(1) (2006): 14.

24. Economists often overemphasize Japan's ability to compete with China in Southeast Asia because they fail to recognize the limitations of economic ties.

25. Etel Solingen, "ASEAN Cooperation: The Legacy of the Economic Crisis." *International Relations of the Asia-Pacific*, 5 (2005): 3. This conceptual construct was devised by Solingen to explain ASEAN cooperation in the wake of the Asian Financial Crisis.

26. One of the most difficult issues in assessing Chinese influence in Southeast Asia is separating the reality of Chinese-Southeast Asian economic relationships from the "hype" that has accompanied the rapid expansion of these ties. This is true in part because Southeast Asians tend to lump economics and "soft power" together. Chapters 6 and 7 disentangle the elements of both economics and "soft power."

27. Joseph Nye, *Soft Power: The Means to Success in World Politics*. (New York: Public Affairs, 2004), x.

28. Ibid., 83–89. China, Japan, India, Thailand, and South Korea are mentioned.

29. Solingen, quoting Archarya, "ASEAN Cooperation," 5.

CHAPTER 3

1. Southeast Asian specialists are well aware of the region's diversity. In relation to China, the region might be divided in several ways. For the purposes of this book, the division between mainland (or continental) and maritime (or insular) Southeast Asia has been stressed, but Vietnam might be considered a separate category on its own, given the intensity of the Vietnamese-Chinese relationship for the past two thousand years. In fact, Vietnamese academics suggested to the author that Vietnam would more accurately be identified as part of a Chinese influenced East Asia than as part of Southeast Asia. A third approach is to separate the original ASEAN-6, who (with the exception of Brunei) are democracies, from the new ASEAN members of Cambodia, Laos, Myanmar (Burma), and Vietnam (CLMV). Scholars of Chinese history, moreover, point out that China has traditionally divided Southeast Asia as follows: (a) the states maintaining overland relations differentiated among themselves (Vietnam vs. Myanmar, for example) and (b) these states differentiated from the maritime kingdoms of Southeast Asia, which were themselves divided on an east-west line with Java and the Malay peninsula included in a category that stretched to the European kingdoms. One key is that trade was the basis for China's relationships with maritime Southeast Asia, as it remains today. For further discussion of China's traditional views of the division of Southeast Asia, see Wang Gungwu, "China and Southeast Asia," *Power Shift, China and Asia's New Dynamics*. . 187–199. Also see Martin Stuart-Fox, *A Short History of China and Southeast Asia*.

2. They also provide alternatives to traditional transportation routes from Southwestern China through Vietnam to the sea.

3. Kao Kim Hourn and Sisowath Doung Chanto, "ASEAN-China Cooperation for Greater Mekong Sub-Region Development." In *ASEAN-China Relations, Realities and Prospects*, edited by Saw Swee Hock, Sheng Lijun, and Chin Kin Wah (Singapore: Institute for Southeast Asian Studies, 2005), 323.

4. Wasant Techawongtham, "Don't Mess with the Mighty Mekong." *The Bangkok Post*, November 8, 2002. Also see Peter Goodman, "Manipulating the Mekong." *Washington Post*, E1, December 30, 2004.

5. According to the Mekong River Commission, the fish catch in Cambodia dropped by 50% in 2004. Jane Perlez, "In Life on the Mekong, China's Dams Dominate." *New York Times*, March 19, 2005.

6. Although the analogy has not been highlighted elsewhere, Bangkok may look to China to moderate Burmese behavior in much the same way that Seoul looks to Beijing to moderate North Korean behavior. However, since the internal dynamics of the North Korean and Myanmar regimes are so opaque, in neither case is the depth of Beijing's leverage clear.

7. Percival interview with a former senior U.S. diplomat, Washington, D.C., September 2004.

8. Elizabeth Economy, "China's Rise in Southeast Asia: Implications for the United States." *Journal of Contemporary China*, 14, no. 44 (2005): 423 (also repackaged as "China's Rising in Southeast Asia: Implications for Japan and the United States," at JapanFocus.org.) Myanmar's politics are so opaque that it is difficult to judge Beijing's influence with the military junta or to know whether it attempted to persuade the regime to take steps to promote national reconciliation in the interests of political stability. There are some reports that Beijing may have talked directly with the military regime in 2004 and 2006 to encourage "national reconciliation."

9. In July 2005, China's Foreign Minister Li Zhaoxing left an ASEAN Summit early to meet with Myanmar's leadership, presumably to reassure Myanmar of China's continued support.

10. Although after meeting with Chinese Premier Wen Jiaboa in February 2006, Myanmar's leadership said that China would block "attempts to put Burma on the U.N. Security Council's agenda." See Gary Bass, "China's Unsavory Friends." *Washington Post*, April 23, 2006 and Glenn Kessler, "U.S. Sees Burma as Test Case in Southeast Asia." *Washington Post*, December 28, 2005, p. A18, and "Burma Disputes Report that Led to U.N. Action." *Washington Post*, February 15, 2006, A17.

11. Many observers believe China maintains a radar station or some form of communications facility on Coco Island, a foothold that has been sometimes described as a base. More recent speculation has it that China is contemplating a "string of pearls" to protect China's shipping from the Persian Gulf. This "string of pearls" would allegedly include naval bases at Sittwe in Myanmar and Gwadar harbor in Pakistan, which China is now helping to improve near the Iranian border and the Persian Gulf. For a less sanguine view, see "The Emerging Cold War on Asia's High Seas," *Power and Interest News Report*, February 13, 2006.

12. Some experts believe Beijing's approach to Myanmar includes a long-term strategic appreciation of China's vulnerability to the interruption of its imported energy supplies, which now flow primarily through the Strait of Malacca between Indonesia and Malaysia. They believe China wants to "slip the Malacca straits noose," and looks to Myanmar as the best alternative to do so. In the absence of access to the Chinese leadership's thinking of this issue, it is difficult to assess the importance of this geo-economic strategic component in China's policy toward Myanmar. However, it is clear that the construction of oil and natural gas pipelines through Myanmar is an expensive proposition. Moreover, such pipelines could not substitute for energy transported on ships, and would thus only partially alleviate China's "Malacca problem." Nonetheless, China's National Development Reform Commission has "approved plans to build a pipeline from Sittwe on Myanmar's coast to Yunnan." Jane Perlez, "Myanmar Is Left in the Dark, An Energy Rich Orphan," *New York Times*, November 17, 2006.

13. Alan Sipress, "Asia Keeps Burmese Industry Humming." *Washington Post*, January 7, 2006.

14. Percival interview with a former U.S. diplomat, Bangkok, August 2005.

15. One observer claimed that Taiwan remained the largest investor in Cambodia in 2003. See Julio Jeldres, "China-Cambodia: More Than Just Friends." *Asian Times*, September 16, 2003.

16. Southeast Asian diplomats have alleged that they have seen Chinese officials hand Cambodians their talking points at ASEAN plus meetings. Percival interview with an official, Bangkok, August 2005.

17. Jane Perlez. "In Life on the Mekong, China's Dams Dominate." *New York Times*, March 19, 2005.

18. Paul Marks, "China's Cambodia Strategy." *Parameters*, Autumn 2000: 4. In 2005, the number of ethnic Chinese in Cambodia is usually estimated at between three and four hundred thousand.

19. Elizabeth Becker, "International Business: Low Cost and Sweatshop Free." *New York Times*, May 12, 2005.

20. Some observers believe that China's aid may rival Japan's. Because China neither participates in donor coordination mechanisms nor reports its aid to international bodies that track this information, it is extremely difficult to measure China's aid to a country such as Laos.

21. Ethnic Chinese were estimated to number no more than 10,000 in 1990, but the border is porous and observers claim that substantial Chinese migration has taken place into northern Laos.

22. See Ian Storey, "China and Vietnam's Tug of War Over Laos." *China Brief*, Jamestown Foundation, June 7, 2005.

23. Ibid.

24. "Vietnamese officials, whether in the precolonial period or the contemporary, rarely speak openly about a 'China threat.' As one writer has observed 'fear and distrust of China must surely be the most important emotional foundation of Vietnamese foreign policy... yet that feeling, quite realistic in view of recent experience, is veiled when officials speak." See Carlyle A. Thayer, "Vietnamese Perceptions of the China Threat." In *The China Threat: Perception, Myths and Reality*, edited by Herbert Yee and Ian Storey New York: Routledge, 2002, 1.

25. Ramses Amer, "Assessing Sino-Vietnamese Relations Through the Management of Contentious Issues." *Contemporary Southeast Asia*, 26, no. 2 (2004): 333.

26. Wang Gungwu, "China and Southeast Asia." In *Power Shift, China and Asia's New Dynamics*, edited by David Shambaugh. Berkeley: University of California Press, 2005, 190.

27. Although China's Ambassador to Vietnam stated "China had become the No. 1 trading partner of Vietnam." *People's Daily Online*, September 2, 2005.

28. See Alexander L. Vuving, "Vietnam's Conduct of its Relations with China: Balancing, Bandwagoning, Accepting Hierarchy, or a Fourth Configuration?" Paper presented at the conference, "Vietnam as an Actor on the International Stage," School of Advanced International Studies, Johns Hopkins University, Washington, DC, April 29, 2005.

29. Apparently the Vietnamese national assembly has yet to ratify this agreement.

30. According to Vietnam's Defense Minister, Vietnam "occupies 31 of the islets in the Spratlys, while the other five claimants held only a few." Malcolm Brailey. "Vietnam's Defense Policy: Combining Tradition with Transformation." IDSS Commentary, Singapore: Institute of Strategic and International Studies, 2004, 3.

31. Percival interview with a Vietnamese scholar, Hanoi, August 2005.

32. *Wenweipo News*, November 1, 2005.

33. This resentment was apparently a factor in the removal of the Vietnamese Communist Party's General Secretary in April 2001. See Jurgen Haacke, "The Significance of Beijing's Bilateral Relations: Looking 'Below' the Regional Level in China-ASEAN Ties." In *China and Southeast Asia, Global Changes and Regional Challenges*, edited by Ho Khai Leong and Samuel C.Y. Ku. Singapore: Institute of Southeast Asian Studies, 2005, 125.

34. David Shambaugh, "Return to the Middle Kingdom? China and Asia in the Early Twenty-First Century." In *Power Shift, China and Asia's New Dynamics*, edited by David Shambaugh. Berkeley: University of California Press, 2005. 34.

35. Ibid.

36. Le Linh Lan, "The Changing Roles of the U.S. and China in Southeast Asia." *Betwixt and Between, Southeast Asian Strategic Relations with the U.S. and China*. IDSS Monograph No. 7, 2005, 3.

37. Percival interview with a former senior official, Washington, D.C., March 2006.

38. Henry J. Kenny, *Shadow of the Dragon: Vietnam's Continuing Struggle with China and Its Implications for the United States*. Washington, DC: Brassey's, 2002, 86.

39. Southeast Asian government statistics compiled by Taiwan's Investment Commission, Ministry of Economic Affairs, quoted in Chen Jie, "Taiwan's Diplomacy in Southeast Asia: Still Going South?" In *China and Southeast Asia, Global Changes and Regional Challenges*, edited by Ho Khai Leong and Samuel C.Y. Ku. Institute of Southeast Asian Studies, Singapore, 2005.233.

40. Percival interview with an expert at a foreign policy institute, Hanoi, August 2005.

41. Le Linh Lan, "The Changing Roles of the U.S. and China in Southeast Asia," 79.

42. David Shambaugh, "China Engages Asia, Reshaping the Regional Order." *International Security*, 29, no. 3 (Winter 2004/2005): 81.

43. Compared to economic assistance in 2004 alone from Japan ($870 million), the World Bank ($621 million), and the ADB ($197 million).

44. ASEAN Secretariat, "International Visitor Arrivals in ASEAN,"2005. www.aseansec.org.

45. Percival interview with a senior official at an academic institute, Hanoi, August 2005.

46. Amer, "Assessing Sino-Vietnamese Relations Through the Management of Contentious Issues," 337.

47. Percival interview with a Vietnamese official, August 2005.

48. Shambaugh, "China Engages Asia, Reshaping the Regional Order," 81.

49. The International Court recently awarded ownership of two islands in dispute between Malaysia and Indonesia on the basis of Malaysia's "exercise of authority." See Bruce Vaughn, "China-Southeast Asia Relations: Trends, Issues, and Implications for the United States," CRS Report for Congress, Updated February 2005.

50. Thai and Malaysian China policies are similar. Some scholars argue that Kuala Lumpur–Beijing ties are based on a firmer foundation than Bangkok-Beijing ties because Malaysia, under former Prime Minister Mahathir's leadership, made a conscious decision to seek a closer relationship with Beijing. Others argue that Thai ties to China are more deeply rooted, include a security component absent in the Malaysian case, and are not impeded by domestic political considerations involving a distinct and relatively large ethnic Chinese minority, as in Malaysia.

51. Percival interview with a senior diplomat, Bangkok, August 2005.

52. Lyall Breckon and Dr. H.J. Kenny, *China's Growing Presence in Southeast Asia: Implications for the United States*. Alexandria, VA: Project Asia, Center for Naval Analyses, April 2004, 23.

53. Michael R. Chambers, "The Chinese and Thais are Brothers: The Evolution of Sino-Thai Friendship." *Journal of Contemporary China*, 14, no. 45 (November 2005): 623.

54. Percival interviews with senior diplomats, Singapore, August 2005.

55. Bradley Mathews, "Bangkok's Fine Balance: Thailand's China Debate." In *Asia's China Debate*, edited by Satu Limaye. Asia-Pacific Center for Security Studies Special Assessment, December 2003, 14–16.

56. Michael Vatikiotis, "Catching the Dragon's Tail: China and Southeast Asia in the 21st Century." *Contemporary Southeast Asia*, 25, no. 1, April 2003: 7.

57. According to IMF figures, trade jumped from $6.6 billion in 2000 to $17.3 billion in 2004. The ASEAN Trade Statistics Database Shows 2004 Thai exports at $7.09 billion and imports at $8.17 billion.

58. Chambers, "The Chinese and Thais are Brothers," 619.

59. Mathews, "Bangkok's Fine Balance," 14–16.

60. Breckon and Kenny, *China's Growing Presence in Southeast Asia*, 23.

61. Chambers, "The Chinese and Thais are Brothers," 621.

62. Percival interview with an official, Bangkok, August 2005.

CHAPTER 4

1. According to 2004 IMF Direction of Trade Statistics, China's trade with ASEAN in 2004 totaled $103 billion. Of that trade, $80.055 billion, or 77%, was with maritime Southeast Asia.

2. Beijing supported the primarily ethnic Chinese Communist insurgency in Malaya (until 1989) and, at least rhetorically, the Indonesian Communist Party (until 1965).

3. With the exception of Brunei.

4. Ethnic Malay Muslims are a majority in four southern provinces of Thailand.

5. At the same time, improved relations with China are often explained in Malaysia as partly motivated by a desire to "balance" American power.

6. Kuala Lumpur is not about to quickly adopt another Asian country as a model, as happened when Mahathir dropped Japan in favor of China. On the other hand, Malaysia has not yet undertaken a serious review of its current policy. When it does so, Malaysia's close identification with the wider Muslim world and its traditional desire to balance outsiders may lead to a cooling of the current bilateral relationship with China.

7. The potential influence of domestic politics on Malaysia's China policy is complicated. Shee Poon Kim writes in his *Political Economy of Mahathir's China Policy: Economic Cooperation, Political and Strategic Ambivalence* that "Mahathir hoped his (August 1999) visit to Beijing could help him gain popularity from the Chinese community to compensate for his loss of support from Malay voters as a result of the trial and imprisonment of former Deputy Prime Minister Anwar Ibrahim." He adds that Chinese voters in mixed constituencies helped the Mahathir-led United Malays National Organization (UMNO) limit the gains of the opposition Islamic party despite a shift of Malay votes toward the Parti Islam-se Malaysia in the subsequent national election. On the other hand, while a well-placed observer told the author in March 2005 that there was "no indication that they (China) are playing games with the ethnic Chinese communities," UMNO must avoid the perception in the politically dominant Malay community that it is kowtowing to either China or Malaysia's ethnic Chinese.

8. Percival interview with a Malaysian editor, Kuala Lumpur, March 2005.

9. Joseph Chinyong Liow, "Balancing, Bandwagoning, or Hedging? Strategic and Security Patterns in Malaysia's Relations with China, 1981–2003." In *China and Southeast Asia, Global*

Changes and Regional Challenges, edited by Ho Khai Leong and Samuel C.Y. Ku. Singapore: Institute of Southeast Asian Studies, 2005, 292–293.

10. "Dr. Mahathir's World Analysis," quoted in Lee Poh Ping, "Malaysia and a Rising China." Conference on "Contending Perspectives: Southeast Asian and American Views of a Rising China." Institute of Defence and Strategic Studies and The National Bureau of Asian Research (NBR), Singapore, August 2005.

11. Breckon, Lyall and Dr. H. J. Kenny, *China's Growing Presence in Southeast Asia: Implications for the United States*. Alexandria, VA: Project Asia, Center for Naval Analyses, April 2004, 27.

12. In July 1998, Taiwan's leader visited Malaysia; in December 1998, Malaysia's Minister of Transport traveled to Taiwan. Beijing expressed concern about both visits. See Ronald Montaperto, "Find New Friends, Reward Old Ones, But Keep All In Line." *Comparative Connections*, July–September 2004: 6.

13. According to IMF trade statistics, Malaysian exports to Taiwan were $4.148 billion and imports $5.698 in 2004.

14. Percival interview with a senior official of a Malaysian strategic studies institute, Kuala Lumpur, March 2005.

15. Statistics vary. ASEAN Trade Statistics show Malaysian exports as (2003) $6.43, (2004) $8.38 vs. Malaysian imports from China as (2003) $6.73, (2004) $10.34, but Solingen, International Monetary Fund: China's imports from Malaysia s (2003), $13.987, China's exports to Malaysia (2003) $6.141, in billions of U.S. dollars. IMF statistics show total trade jumping from approximately $18 billion (2003) to $26 billion (2004).

16. Zakaria Haji Ahmad, "Malaysia," *Betwixt and Between, Southeast Asian Strategic Relations with the U.S. and China*. IDSS Monograph No. 7, 2005, 56.

17. Wayne Arnold, "With Eye to China, Malaysians Ponder Revaluation." *New York Times*, July 8, 2005.

18. Professor Lee Poh Ping, Conference on "China's Relations with Malaysia" hosted by the School for Advance International Studies, Johns Hopkins University and the Carnegie Endowment for International Peace, Washington, D. C., September 27, 2005.

19. Tan Khee Giap, "ASEAN and China: Relative Competitiveness, Emerging Investment-Trade Patterns, Monetary and Financial Integration." Paper presented at IDSS/NBR Conference in Singapore, August 2005.

20. Percival interview with Professor Heng Pek Koon, American University, Washington, D. C., January 2005.

21. Percival interview with Professor Heng Pek Koon, American University, Washington, D. C., January 2005.

22. Percival interview with a Malaysian editor, Kuala Lumpur, March 2005.

23. Percival interviews with officials and a former U.S. diplomat, Kuala Lumpur, March 2005, and Washington, D. C., April 2005.

24. Allegedly, one often hears a quote from the Quran, apparently that, "if you want knowledge, go even to China." Percival interview with a Malaysian editor, Kuala Lumpur, March 2005.

25. Percival interview with a senior U.S. diplomat, Kuala Lumpur, March 2005.

26. Percival interview with a diplomat, Kuala Lumpur, March 2005.

27. Percival interviews with government and strategic studies institute officials, Kuala Lumpur, March 2005.

28. J. N. Mak, "The Chinese Navy and the South China Sea: A Malaysian Assessment," 150, quoted in Shee Poon Kim, "The Political Economy of Mahathir's China Policy: Economic

Cooperation, Political and Strategic Ambivalence." International University of Japan, IUJ Research Institute Working Paper 2004–06, Asia Pacific Series, 2003.

29. Liow, "Balancing, Bandwagoning, or Hedging?" 295.

30. "Badawi raps US-Japan View of China as threat," *Kyodo News Agency*, June 2, 2005.

31. Montaperto, "Find New Friends, Reward Old Ones, But Keep All In Line," and Yasin Khan, "Malaysia to Buy Chinese Missiles for Technology Transfer," August 1, 2004, www.defencetalk. com

32. "China, Malaysia to Boost Trade, Defense Cooperation," BBC Monitoring via COMTEX, September 3, 2005.

33. Percival interview with a U.S. official, Washington, D. C., September 2004.

34. Teo Kah Beng, "Singapore," *Betwixt and Between, Southeast Asian Strategic Relations with the U.S. and China*. IDSS Monograph No. 7, 2005, 41.

35. Breckon and Kenny, *China's Growing Presence in Southeast Asia*, 30.

36. This overemphasis on the United States also lets Southeast Asian states "off the hook" in terms of their role in resisting Chinese pressures, since the United States is so often presumed to be on call to "balance" China.

37. As Evelyn Goh put it, "Singapore's policy makers constantly try to make their country 'useful' to the major powers in their quest for security." See Goh, "Singapore's Reaction to a Rising China, Deep Engagement and Strategic Adjustment." In *China and Southeast Asia, Global Changes and Regional Challenges*, edited by Ho Khai Leong and Samuel C.Y. Ku. Singapore: Institute of Southeast Asian Studies, 2005," 311.

38. Singapore Ambassador Chan Heng Chee at a Johns Hopkins School of Advanced International Studies Conference, Washington, D. C., April 25, 2005.

39. Eric Teo Chu Cheow, "Sino-Singapore Relations Back on Track." *China Brief*, The Jamestown Foundation, 5, no. 16 (July 19, 2005): 3

40. Percival interview with an analyst at a strategic studies institute, Singapore, August 2005.

41. Teo Kah Beng, "Singapore," 44.

42. Ibid., 47.

43. Ibid., 44.

44. Singapore Ambassador Chan, Johns Hopkins/SAIS Conference, April 25, 2005.

45. Goh, "Singapore's Reaction to a Rising China," 312.

46. Percival interviews with several Singaporean officials and academics, Singapore, August 2005.

47. In August 2005, the author shared a faculty hotel in Singapore with a Chinese delegation of local officials from Jianxi. Also see "Singapore University Conducts Courses for PRC Officials." *Singapore Straits Times*, April 12, 2005.

48. The training facilities in Taiwan are apparently those used by the Japanese Army before they overran Singapore in 1942.

49. Percival interview with a government official, Singapore, August 2005.

50. Percival interview with an Indonesian official, Jakarta, September 2004.

51. Hadi Soesastro, "China-Indonesia Relations and the Implications for the United States," *USINDO Report*, November 7, 2003, 2 (Conference Cosponsored by the United States-Indonesia Society and the Sigur Center at The George Washington University).

52. Percival interview with a diplomat, Jakarta, September 2004.

53. Chinese maps show a dotted line in the South China Sea to distinguish Chinese territory. Waters near the Natuna islands that have long been viewed as Indonesian appear to fall within this dotted line.

54. Percival interview with a government official, Washington, D. C., February 2006.

55. China has also signed strategic partnership agreements with the U.S., Russia, and India.

56. Ronald Montaperto, "Dancing with China: (In a Psyche of Adaptability, Adjustment, and Cooperation)." *Comparative Connections*, April–June 2005: 7.

57. For additional analysis of Indonesia's post-Suharto foreign policy, see Anne Marie Murphy, "Indonesia and the World." In *Indonesia, the Great Transition*, edited by John Bresnan. Rowman & Littlefield, Lanham, MD, 2005.

58. Indonesian CSIS Executive Director Dr. Hadi Soestrasto at a Washington conference on China-Indonesia relations, November 2003. See note 51.

59. The Indonesian Foreign Ministry had used this argument throughout the 1980s, when it was engaged in a running debate with the Indonesian Armed Forces over reestablishing diplomatic relations with China.

60. See Eric Teo Chu Cheow, "Assessing the Sino-Indonesian Strategic Partnership." *PACNET*, 25 (June 23, 2005).

61. "Indonesia and China Forge Strategic Partnership." *The Straits Times*, July 29, 2005.

62. The text of the China-Indonesia Joint Statement of July 29, 2005, suggests that Beijing convinced Jakarta to avoid endorsing Japan's bid for a UN Security Council seat; on the other hand, Yudhoyono may have told Japanese Prime Minister Koizumi that Indonesia wouldn't "go to far" with China. Percival interview with a diplomat, Jakarta, August 2005.

63. Daniel Novotny conducted 45 interviews in Indonesia with prominent members of the nation's foreign policy elite about their perceptions of external threats facing Indonesia. He concluded, "Indonesian leaders generally believe the nation will increasingly have to maneuver between the United States and China who will vigorously compete for influence in the region." Daniel Novotny, *Indonesian Foreign Policy: Rowing Between Two Reefs*. Departments of Indonesian Studies and International Relations, UNSW, Sydney, Australia, September 2005.

64. Santo Darmosumarto, "Understanding the One China Policy and Indonesia's Ties with Taiwan," *Jakarta Post*, July 28, 2006.

65. Anthony L. Smith, "From Latent Threat to Possible Partner: Indonesia's China Debate," In *Asia's China Debate*, edited by Satu Limaye. Asia-Pacific Center for Security Studies Special Assessment, Chapter 7, December 2003, 4.

66. Santo Darmosumarto, "Understanding the One China Policy and Indonesia's Ties with Taiwan," Jakarta Post, July 28, 2006. IMF statistics show Indonesian exports of $2.854 billion and imports of $1.24 billion in 2004.

67. International Monetary Fund, Direction of Trade Statistics, 2005.

68. Xinhua's China Economic Information Service, December 14, 2005. Indonesia's President, on the other hand, was reported to have acknowledged that China has become an "agent of dynamism" in the region, but "stressed that ASEAN needed to continue moving towards regional integration." *The Star* (Malaysia), Internet Version, December 12, 2005.

69. *Bisnis Indonesia*, May 17, 2005. Subsequently, China offered $54 million to develop a fisheries port in Indonesia, *Asia Pulse*, March 22, 2006.

70. Alan Sipress, "Indonesia's Illegal Coal Mines Feed China: Demand Transforms Island Nation's Lightly Regulated South Kalimantan Province." *The Washington Post*, September 21, 2005.

71. China has provided $7.5 million for tsunami relief, according to Xinhua. Whether this is in addition to the pledged $20 million is not clear. "China Gives Indonesia 7.5 M dollars for homes for Aceh Tsunami Survivors," Xinhua News Agency, February 9, 2006.

72. Smith, "From Latent Threat to Possible Partner," 5 (see note 65).

73. Phelim Kyne, "Interview: Indonesia, China Embrace Doesn't Spook Taiwan," DowJones Newswires, July 14, 2005.

74. See Ian Storey, "Progress and Remaining Obstacles in Sino-Indonesian Relations." *Jamestown Brief,* V, no. 18, (August 16, 2005).

75. *Agence France Press,* December 15, 2005. Exactly what has happened remains unclear but rising world prices for LNG have apparently led Indonesia to request an increase in the price at which the LNG from the Tangguh field will be delivered to China.

76. "The Chinese Foreign Ministry issued statements that Indonesia should protect ethnic Chinese—although China quickly backed away from these statements soon after they were made." Smith, "From Latent Threat to Possible Partner," 6.

77. Jane Perlez, "China's Reach: Chinese Move to Eclipse U.S. Appeal in South Asia." *The New York Times,* November 18, 2004.

78. Howard W. French. "Another Chinese Export is all the Rage: China's Language." *The New York Times,* January 11, 2006.

79. Percival interview with a diplomat, Jakarta, September 2004.

80. See "Indonesia: The Happy Chinese." *The Economist,* February 4, 2006, 40.

81. Percival interview with a diplomat, Jakarta, March 2005.

82. Hostility toward the United States had grown within sectors of the Indonesian military leadership, and was one factor in Indonesia's military leaders' less antagonistic view of China.

83. Percival interview with a senior military officer, Jakarta, September 2004.

84. Edward Cody, "Shifts in Pacific Force U.S. Military to Adapt Thinking." *The Washington Post,* September 17, 2005.

85. David S. Isby, "Indonesia Announces Missile and Rocket Co-operation with China." *Jane's Missiles and Rockets,* October 1, 2005.

86. China and the Philippines, among others, have overlapping claims to part of the Spratly islands. A Chinese-Filipino bilateral agreement preceded this tripartite agreement and caused some alarm in Hanoi. In fact, the bilateral agreement was confined to waters off Palawan and the Chinese have yet to invest as of 2006.

87. *People's Daily On-Line.* "China, Philippines Issue Joint Statement." April 29, 2005.

88. Herman J. Kraft, "The Philippines," *Betwixt and Between, Southeast Asian Strategic Relations with the U.S. and China.* IDSS Monograph No. 7, 2005, 13.

89. Rumor has it that Beijing has suggested to Manila that provincial-level officials were behind this "mistake."

90. Carl Baker, "China-Philippine Relations: Cautious Cooperation," Special Assessment Series, Asia-Pacific Center for Security Studies, October 2004, 2–7

91. "Philippines-Taiwan Labor Relations Grow." *The Manila Times,* December 24, 2004.

92. Ebias, Jun and Ian C. Sayson, Bloomberg News, *International Herald Tribune,* April 27, 2005.

93. "Overview of Sino-Philippine Relations," www.china-embassy.org.ph/eng/zfgx/zzgx/t180703.html, 3.

94. Ebias and Sayson, Bloomberg News, *International Herald Tribune,* April 27, 2005.

95. "China, Philippines Sign $1.5 B in Deals." *United Press International,* April 27, 2005.

96. See Abola and Manzano, "The Challenges and Opportunities in China-Philippine Economic Relations," AT 10 Research Conference, Tokyo, February 2004, 12–15.

97. Kraft, "The Philippines," 15.

98. Jane Perlez, "China Competes with West in Aid to its Neighbors," *New York Times,* September 18, 2006.

99. See "Fishing in Troubled Waters" section of "Making the Rounds." *Comparative Connections*, 2 nd Quarter 2001:3.

100. ExpertLink, March 21, 2005.

101. Kraft, "The Philippines,"15.

102. *Xinhua News*. "Country Conducts Maritime Exercise with the Phillipines." October 10, 2004.

103. Banlaoi, *Philippines-China Defense and Military Cooperation, Problems and Prospects*, Paper presented at the International Conference on 30 years of China-Philippine Relations entitled "Charting New Directions in a Changing Global Environment," October 22, 2005.

104. "Since (1999), the size of U.S. participation in joint exercises has steadily expanded, doubling between 2003 and 2004. In addition, the focus of the exercises has expanded beyond antiterrorist activities to include participation in amphibious exercises in the vicinity of the Spratly Islands, which both Beijing and Manila claim as their territory. In late 2004, the U.S. and Philippine air forces conducted joint exercises using the former U.S. base at Clark airfield. Since 2001 annual U.S. military assistance to the Philippines increased from $1.9 million to a projected $126 million in 2005, and the Philippines is now the largest recipient of U.S. military assistance in East Asia. Manila is also planning to purchase U.S. fighter planes. Whereas for most of the 1990s the Philippines was hostile to the U.S. military, it is now a "major non-NATO ally with an expanding U.S. presence on its territory." Robert Ross. "A Realist Policy for Managing US-China Competition." The Stanley Foundation, *Policy Analysis Brief*, November 2005, 7.

105. For additional information on China-Brunei ties see Ian Storey, "China's Thirst for Energy Fuels Improved Relations with Brunei." The Jamestown Foundation, *China Brief*, 5, no. 24 (November 22, 2005).

106. In response to a press story quoting East Timor Foreign Minister and Nobel Peace Prize Laureate Ramos-Horta to the effect that China was East Timor's "closest ally," Ramos-Horta wrote a letter to the *Sydney Morning Herald* stating that "No two countries are more important to East Timor than our two closest neighbors, Australia and Indonesia, and my President and Government has spared no effort in cementing this very important relationship." http://www.etan.org/et2002 c/july/07–13/11china.htm.

107. I am indebted to Prof. Ian Storey, Asia Pacific Center for Strategic Studies, for the detailed information on China's ties to East Timor.

CHAPTER 5

1. ASEAN admitted Vietnam in 1995, and planned to admit Cambodia, Laos, and Myanmar in 1997. As a consequence of an internal coup, Cambodia's admission was postponed until 1999. Many observers predicted a decline in ASEAN solidarity as a consequence of the authoritarian domestic political systems and strategic orientations of the new members, with whom China is particularly influential. For example, see James Clad, "Fin de siecle, Fin de ASEAN."

2. From the mid-1990s to 2003, China's policy for the ARF, ASEAN+1 (China), and ASEAN+3 (China, Japan, and the Republic of Korea) was managed by the same division of the Chinese Foreign Ministry. Kuik Cheng-Chwee, "Multilaterialism in China's ASEAN Policy: Its Evolution, Characteristics, and Aspiration." *Contemporary Southeast Asia*, 27, no. 1 (2005): 104.

3. Because Myanmar is an issue in U.S. relations both with ASEAN countries and with China, some scholars and officials tend to assume that Myanmar is equally prominent in Chinese-ASEAN relations. This assumption may not be warranted. Although ASEAN states' policies with regard to Myanmar vary considerably, generally they lie between Beijing's opposition to interference in Myanmar's internal affairs and the increasingly stringent sanctions on Myanmar imposed by the United States. These sanctions have had the unintended consequence of complicating Washington's relationship with ASEAN as a regional organization, and thus with those ASEAN member states who oppose sanctions as a means to place pressure on the Myanmar regime. Many Southeast Asian academics and officials, and American experts on Southeast Asia, argue that current U.S. sanctions should be modified both because they are an impediment to improved U.S.-ASEAN relations and because there is no evidence that they have influenced the Myanmar regime. However, there is little evidence, even among such Southeast Asian states such as Malaysia and Indonesia that have pushed for national reconciliation in Myanmar, that ASEAN states are as prepared to criticize and press China on Myanmar as they are to take Washington to task.

4. Beijing has also asked little from Southeast Asian states through bilateral mechanisms, but it has preferred to employ its bilateral ties to press for support for China's Taiwan policies and in its rivalry with Japan.

5. It did, however, participate in the Bandung nonaligned conference in 1955.

6. Kuik, "Multilaterialism in China's ASEAN Policy," 106.

7. Nan Li, "The Evolving Chinese Conception of Security and Security Approaches." In *Asia-Pacific Security Cooperation, National Interests and Regional Order*, edited by see Seng Tan and Amitav Archarya. New York: M.E. Sharpe, 2004, 65.

8. ARF's procedures have led some to suggest that it is "irrelevant" as a security organization. See Heller, "The Relevance of the ASEAN Regional Forum (ARF)."

9. Breckon, Lyall and Dr. H. J. Kenny. *China's Growing Presence in Southeast Asia: Implications for the United States*. Alexandria, VA: Project Asia, Center for Naval Analyses, April 2004, 14.

10. The 1976 Treaty of Amity and Cooperation is a legal document that articulates ASEAN norms for international relations. For additional information, see Donald E. Weatherbee, *International Relations in Southeast Asia, the Struggle for Autonomy*. Oxford: Rowman & Littlefield, 2005, 126–28.

11. See *China's New Security Concept: Reading Between the Lines*, by David Finkelstein, CNAC Project Asia monograph, April 1999.

12. Breckon and Kenny, *China's Growing Presence in Southeast Asia*, 15.

13. This was part of a campaign against the "three evils"—terrorism, separatism, and hegemonism. But Gao Zhiguo says the "three forces" are terrorism, separatism, and extremism." Gao Zhiguo, "South China Sea: Turning Suspicion into Mutual Understanding and Cooperation." In *ASEAN-China Relations, Realities and Prospects*, edited by Saw Swee Hock, Sheng Lijun, and Chin Kin Wah. Singapore: Institute for Southeast Asian Studies, 2005, 338).

14. Nan Li, "The Evolving Chinese Conception of Security and Security Approaches," 61.

15. ASEAN has "strategic partnerships" with China, Japan, India, and the Republic of Korea. In addition, the United States has proposed an "enhanced partnership" with ASEAN, which Washington expects to become more substantive and "functional" than some of the "strategic partnerships" that ASEAN has already signed.

16. Breckon and Kenny, *China's Growing Presence in Southeast Asia*, 17.

17. Ibid.

18. The Boao Forum for Asia (BFA), named for a resort town on Hainan Island, held its first annual meeting in April 2002, bringing together some 2,000 current and former high-ranking officials, scholars, and businessmen. China hopes that the BFA will evolve into an Asian version of the annual World Economic Forum in Davos, Switzerland.

19. Unpublished address to the Asia Society—Texas by Singaporean Ambassador Chan, Houston, Texas, February 3, 2006.

20. Percival interview with a senior official, Singapore, August 2005.

21. Ralph A. Cossa, Simon Tay, and Lee Chung-min, "The Emerging East Asian Community: Should Washington be Concerned?" *Issues and Insights*, 5, no. 9, Pacific Forum CSIS, Honolulu, Hawaii, August, 2005, 13.

22. Percival interviews with several Southeast Asian and U.S. officials, August 2005.

23. Percival interview with a former senior U.S. official, Washington, D. C., November 2005.

24. Percival interview with a senior U.S. official, Washington, D. C., January 2006. For example, an East Asia "avian flu" initiative followed the APEC Summit "avian flu" initiative by three weeks.

25. Alan D. Romberg. "The East Asia Summit: Much Ado About Nothing—So Far." This essay originally appeared in the December 2005 issue of *Freeman Report* by the Center for Strategic and International Studies in Washington, DC, and was then posted at the Henry L. Stimson Foundation, www.stimson.org.

26. Ibid.

27. Percival interview with a senior U.S. official, Washington, D. C., January 2006.

28. Percival interview with a senior official, Singapore, August 2005. Romberg also notes "a 'perceptible shift' of attention and solicitude in the region from Japan to China." "The East Asia Summit: Much Ado About Nothing—So Far."

29. China and Vietnam claim all the islands on grounds of longstanding occupation and use, citing historical records and physical evidence. The Philippine claim to the Spratlys is based on exploration by a Philippine national in the 1956, and was only made official in 1978. Malaysia and Brunei claim a smaller number of islands that lie within what they claim as their Exclusive Economic Zones under the Law of the Sea. The United States takes no position on the validity of any of these claims, but calls for peaceful resolution of differences and insists that freedom of navigation not be infringed.

30. Over half of the world's merchant fleet (by tonnage) passes through the South China Sea.

31. Vietnam became an ASEAN member in 1995, transforming the South China Sea dispute into primarily an issue between ASEAN and China.

32. Baviera, "The South China Sea Disputes after the 2002 Declaration: Beyond Confidence Building." In *ASEAN-China Relations, Realities and Prospects*, edited by Saw Swee Hock, Sheng Lijun, and Chin Kin Wah. Institute for Southeast Asian Studies, Singapore, 2005, 347.

33. Although not in the South China Sea, in 2005 the Indonesian and Malaysian navies confronted each other over disputed islands, even though the issue had been referred to the international court and decided in Malaysia's favor.

34. For additional information on ASEAN perceptions of the South China Sea dispute, see Ralph Emmers, "What Explains the De-Escalation of the Spratly's Dispute," *IDSS Commentaries*, Singapore: Institute of Defense and Security Studies, December 5, 2006.

35. Baviera, "The South China Sea Disputes after the 2002 Declaration," 348.

36. Gao, "South China Sea," 34.

37. Baviera, "The South China Sea Disputes after the 2002 Declaration," 347.

38. Teo Chu Cheow, "ASEAN+3: The Roles of ASEAN and China." In *ASEAN-China Relations, Realities and Prospects*, edited by Saw Swee Hock, Sheng Lijun, and Chin Kin Wah. Singapore: Institute for Southeast Asian Studies: 2005, 49.

39. Cai Peng Hong, "Non-Traditional Security and China-ASEAN Relations: Co-operation, Commitments and Challenges." Chapter 6 in *China and Southeast Asia, Global Changes and Regional Challenges*, edited by Ho Khai Leong and Samual C.Y. Ku. Singapore: Institute of Southeast Asian Studies, 2005, 161.

40. Breckon, "SARS and a New Security Initiative from China." *Comparative Connections*, April–June 2003, 2.

41. Teo Chu Cheow, in "ASEAN+3: The Roles of ASEAN and China," claims that with "SARS the confidence to consume, invest, trade, service and interact was seriously at stake" and that East Asian "consumption-based" economic growth was thus threatened. However, see *The Economist*, October 15, 2005, article, "In Search of Elusive Domestic Demand," for further information on Southeast Asian economies continued dependence on exports, rather than domestic consumption.

42. Bronson E. Percival, *Indonesia and the United States: Shared Interest in Maritime Security*. The United States-Indonesia Society, Washington, DC, June 2005, 21.

43. In Manila in September 2003, Beijing also proposed that a counterterrorism "alliance" be established between the Philippines, Indonesia, and Malaysia, and the members of the Shanghai Cooperation Organization, established in 2001 by China, Kazakhstan, the Kyrgyz Republic, Russia, Tajikistan, and Uzbekistan.

44. "The Rebuilding Starts," *The Economist*, February 5, 2005, 42. China's pledged contribution ranked 13th among international donors. Its actual deliveries totaled $22 million, according to the *China Daily* of January 19, 2006. A subsequent article claimed that China had contributed $7.5 million, but it is not clear whether his is part of the $22 million, or additional funding.

45. Percival interview with senior officials, Singapore, March 2005.

46. Sheng Lijun, "China-ASEAN Cooperation against Illicit Drugs from the Golden Triangle," *Asian Perspectives*, 30(2), 2006, 121.

47. The U.S.-Thai Cobra Gold military exercise and cooperation among four ASEAN members to suppress piracy in the Malacca Strait are among the few examples of "multilateral" military cooperation. The first meeting of the ASEAN Defense Ministers was held in June 2006.

48. In June 2003, at the ASEAN Ministerial in Phnom Penh, China proposed the establishment of a New Security Policy Conference, comprised of senior military as well as civilian officials, through the ARF.

CHAPTER 6

1. Trade statistics should be treated with caution for several reasons. First, they vary considerably depending on the source, which include the IMF direction of trade data, Chinese statistics, ASEAN statistics, Asian Development Bank (ADB) statistics, and so forth. The IMF statistics appear to be the most reliable. Second, whether and when Hong Kong should be considered part of China in calculating trade and foreign direct investment is a complicated and contentious issue. Third, some experts believe the volume and value of China's trade with Southeast Asia is exaggerated because so much of it is "processing trade," which often leads

to double and triple counting. "Senior Chinese officials are aware that prevailing trade data showing China's central role in Asian trade networks tend to overestimate China's importance. Over half of China's trade in 2004 was this so-called processing trade." Sutter, "China's Rise: Implications for U.S. Leadership in Asia." *Policy Studies*, 21 (2006), East-West Center, Washington, DC, 3.

2. UNCTAD FDI Inflows records $60.630 billion for China, with another $34.035 for China–Hong Kong, compared to $25.662 billion for Southeast Asia in 2004. However, in 2005, FDI inflows to Southeast Asia totaled $38 billion, compared to $53 billion to China.

3. ASEAN Secretariat statistics for 2003 show U.S. investment in Southeast Asia at more than ten times Chinese investment in Southeast Asia. In 2003, total American investment in Southeast Asia was seven times larger than American investment in China.

4. Although information on the investment plans of foreign firms is unavailable, anecdotal evidence suggest that some Japanese politicians would like to see Japanese companies consider "covering their bets," that is their investments in China, by increasing their investment in Vietnam and Indonesia.

5. According to several officials and diplomats in Singapore, in 2005 the Chinese Embassy in Singapore initially sought to intervene on a particularly sensitive commercial issue, but then reversed its approach and left the decision to the Singapore courts.

6. China mixes official aid, low-cost loans and forgiveness of debts in packages that are often labeled as "aid." The debate about the amount of "aid" China extends to Southeast Asian countries revolves, in part, around debate over the definition of "aid."

7. See Etel Solingen on the role of "internationalizing" domestic political coalitions in Southeast Asia in "From 'Threat' to 'Opportunity'? ASEAN, China and Triangulation." Conference on "Contending Perspectives: Southeast Asian and American Views of a Rising China." Institute of Defence and Strategic Studies and The National Bureau of Asian Research (NBR), Singapore, August 2005.

8. "South-East Asia's Economies, In Search of Elusive Domestic Demand." *The Economist*, October 15, 2005.

9. See "Taksin Helps Himself." *The Economist*, January 28, 2006, and Jane Perlez, "Bold Thai Leader Faces Growing Criticism." *New York Times*, March 14, 2004.

10. Individual countries have often placed national interests above regional economic integration through the ASEAN Free Trade Area (AFTA). Southeast Asian countries have also begun protecting domestic industries in connection with the CAFTA by placing them on lists of "sensitive" products, suggesting that CAFTA may also stumble in fully implementing the goals of the agreement. See Thomas Fuller, "Unified-Market Plan Gains Steam in Asia," *International Herald Tribune*, August 23, 2006, for information on Southeast Asian efforts to strengthen their own free trade zone.

11. Chinese statistics appear to often anticipate and thus overstate the rate at which trade has grown between China and Southeast Asia. Asian Development Bank (ADB) statistics are based on information provided by individual countries and are interesting as a means of comparison. The most reliable statistics, on which Table 6.1 is based, are IMF direction of trade statistics.

12. Hong Kong statistics have been included in Table 6.1. According to the Hong Kong Trade and Industry Department, 40% of exports to Hong Kong in 2002 were re-exported from Hong Kong to the mainland.

13. John Ravenhill, "Is China an Economic Threat to Southeast Asia?," *Asian Survey* 46(5) (2006): 669.

14. U.S. Census Bureau statistics record 2004 ASEAN exports to the U.S. at $88.206 billion, with ASEAN imports at $47.891 billion, for a total of slightly more than $136 billion. In 2004 the U.S. was ASEAN's largest trading partner. The most commonly cited figure for U.S.-ASEAN trade in 2005 is $144 billion.

15. IMF statistics show ASEAN-China trade at $103 billion in 2004, or 10% of ASEAN's trade. Asian Development Bank country figures for 2004 show ASEAN exports to China at $44.721 and imports from China at $49.734 billion. These statistics show 7.9% of ASEAN exports and 9.9% of ASEAN imports to or from China.

16. Total trade derived from adding exports and imports in IMF Direction of Trade Statistics (DOTs), as was the trade between Hong Kong and the individual Southeast Asian country, working from the IMF direction of trade statistics for 2005.

17. "China has been guilty of lowering standards through its (politically motivated but economically weak) 'free' trade agreements, and ASEAN in particular has been an accomplice." See "APEC 2005: Economic Takes Center Stage", *PacNet* 50, November 2005.

18. Initiated in 1992, the AFTA has been slow to get off the ground because ASEAN states have not been prepared to sacrifice national interests to construct an integrated market that might have competed with China. In 2006, ASEAN leaders were floating proposals to accelerate the integration of ASEAN economies. See Thomas Fuller, "Southeast Asia Group Seeks to Accelerate a Trade Zone," *New York Times*, August 23, 2006.

19. "The framework agreement provides three phases in its implementation of CAFTA: The first phase involves the implementation of an "early harvest" program between 2004 and 2006 for 5 ASEAN countries (Indonesia, Malaysia, Singapore, Thailand, and Vietnam) and up to 2010 for new members and the Philippines (which was accepted by China). This would concern the product coverage for tariff reduction and elimination, implementation timeframes, rules of origin, trade remedies, and emergency measures applicable to the program.

The second phase includes the list of "normal track" items, not covered by the "early harvest" program for which parties could phase out tariff rates at the end of the framework agreement, from 2005 to 2010 for 5 ASEAN countries, and 2010 to 2015 for the new members and the Philippines.

The last phase includes the "sensitive track" items that are to be kept at a minimum. These items concern industries that need time to adjust, and for them, inclusion in the FTA would be step by step, and respectively applied rates, reduced and eliminated with timeframes to be mutually agreed between the parties." See "China-Southeast Asia Relations: The ASEAN-China Free Trade Agreement" by Corazon Sandoval Foley, Department of State, Bureau of Intelligence and Research, Washington, D. C., September 19, 2005.

20. Ong Keng Yong, as reported by Xinhua, "ASEAN Secretary General Says China an Important Partner," October 29, 2003.

21. "China-Southeast Asia Relations: The ASEAN-China Free Trade Agreement" by Corazon Sandoval Foley, Department of State, Bureau of Intelligence and Research, September 19, 2005.

22. Ibid., 4.

23. The ASEAN-China Expert Group on Economic Cooperation was established in 2001 to study the implications of China's accession to the World Trade Organization.

24. Kathie Krumm and Homi Kharas, editors. *East Asia Integrates: A Trade Policy Agenda for Shared Growth* (Advance Edition). Washington, DC: The World Bank, 2003.

25. See ASEAN Statistical Yearbook, 2004.

26. ASEAN Statistical Yearbook, 2004, 97.

27. The U. S. Department of Energy predicts that Southeast Asia will provide 40% of China's growing LNG imports by 2025, but industry sources have questioned the U.S. Department of Energy's methodology. Percival interview with Mikkal E. Herberg, The National Bureau of Asian Research, November 2005.

28. Percival interviews with academics and officials, Bangkok, March 2005.

29. For a discussion of the impact of termination of the Multi-Fiber Agreement on Asian countries, see *The Far Eastern Economic Review*, November 27, 2003.

30. "China-Southeast Asia Relations: The ASEAN-China Free Trade Agreement" by Corazon Sandoval Foley, Department of State, Bureau of Intelligence and Research, September 19, 2005, 5.

31. See John Ravenhill, "Is China an Economic Threat to Southeast Asia?," *Asian Survey* 46(5) (2006): 653–674, for additional information on China's economic relationship with Southeast Asia.

32. UNCTAD World Investment Report, 2005.

33. "Overseas Chinese Firms Awarded," *News Guangdong*, December 15, 2003. While Chinese in Southeast Asia are part of a new wave of investment in China, their share of total investment is declining.

34. Stephen Frost, "Chinese Outward Direct Investment in Southeast Asia: How Big are the Flows and what does it mean for the Region?" *The Pacific Review*, 17, no. 3 (2004): 5.

35. UNCTAD, "Country Fact Sheet: China," 2005 and see footnote 37.

36. UNCTAD, Table 1, *Spotlight on ASEAN*, February 10, 2003, for 1996 figures; and *World Investment Report 2003 (WIR 2003)*, Annex Table B.1, "FDI inflows, by host region and economy, 1991–2002," September 2003, for 2001 figures. 2004 figures from UNCTAD country reports. 2005 data from the *World Investment Report* shows FDI inward flows to Southeast Asia for 2001 at $18.758 billion.

37. By way of historical comparison, in 1980, Southeast Asian states attracted a high of over 60% of all FDI inflows into East Asia, and 4% of the world's FDI, while China received virtually no FDI. By 1985, ASEAN and China's shares were comparable at between 4 and 3% each. By 1995, China had overtaken ASEAN at about 11% and 8% respectively. After the Asian Financial Crisis of 1997, the gap widened rapidly.

38. Michael A. Glosny, "Heading Toward a Win-Win Future? Recent Developments in China's Policy Toward Southeast Asia." *Asian Security*, 2(1) (2006): 17.

39. *IBRD World Indicators, 2001.*

40. See Wayne Arnold, "International Business; Not All Roads Lead to China," *New York Times*, February 28, 2006.

41. "Asia and the Pacific: Rates of return on FDI, selected economies, 1999–2001." *UNCTAD World Investment Report (WIR) 2003*, Annex Table A.II.2.

42. See Tan Khee Giap, "ASEAN and China: Relative Competitiveness, Emerging Investment-Trade Patterns, Monetary and Financial Integration." Conference on "Contending Perspectives: Southeast Asian and American Views of a Rising China." Institute of Defence and Strategic Studies and The National Bureau of Asian Research (NBR), Singapore, August 2005.

43. Friedrich Wu, Pao Tiang Siaw, Yeo Han Sia, and Puah Kok Keong, "Foreign Direct Investment to China and Southeast Asia: Has ASEAN Been Losing Out?" Ministry of Trade and Industry, Government of Singapore, 2002.

44. However, an old UNCTAD report, written in 2002, ascribed much of the downturn in FDI flows to ASEAN to increased investment in China.

45. Lu Fuyuan, Ministry of Commerce, People's Republic of China, "Interview on the 5th ASEM Economic Ministers Meeting," April 12, 2003; Chana Kanaratanadilok, Assistant to the Director-General of Business Economics, Ministry of Commerce, Thailand, "ASEAN-China Trade and Economic Cooperation," 2002.

46. Krumm and Kharas, *East Asia Integrates*.

47. Comment by China's Ambassador to the United States, Asia Society Texas Annual Dinner, Houston, Texas, February 2006.

48. The "Malaysia-China Forum 2004" estimated Malaysian investment in China at $3.1 billion.

49. UNCTAD, *Spotlight on ASEAN*, Table 2.

50. Frost, "Chinese Outward Direct Investment in Southeast Asia," 6.

51. ASEAN Secretariat, Statistics, Table 6.2. Foreign Direct Investment in ASEAN by Source Country/Region as of December 31, 2005. According to these statistics, Hong Kong invested $204.5 million (2002), $100.1 million (2003) and $344.9 million (2004).

52. "Intraregional FDI flows in developing Asia: 1999–2001," *UNCTAD World Investment Report*, 2003, Table II-1.

53. As mentioned in the previous chapter, the Chinese government announced in a January 2006 *China Daily* report that the Chinese government's contribution for Tsunami relief totaled $22 million.

54. Cambodia Development Resource Institute, "Flash Report on the Cambodian Economy," December 2002. www.mef.gov.kh/publications/pub_flashreport.html.

55. Voice of Vietnam, Hanoi, July 24, 2002 (FBIS).

56. Mikkal E. Herberg, "China's Search for Energy Security and Implications for Southeast Asia." Conference on "Contending Perspectives: Southeast Asian and American Views of a Rising China," Singapore, August 2005, 7.

57. According to Zweig and Jianhai, "China's Global Hunt for Energy." Foreign Affairs, September/October 2005, Vietnam supplied 4.4% of China's crude imports, Indonesia 2.8%, and Malaysia, 1.4%.

58. Simon Wordell, "No Progress on Cepu, According to Indonesian Oil Company," Global Insights and Daily Analysis, November 23, 2005.

59. Herberg, "China's Search for Energy Security and Implications for Southeast Asia," 10.

60. Ibid., 17.

61. Ibid., 3.

62. Nonetheless, Indonesia did seek to renegotiate the price for delivery of LNG to China in early 2006. See Shawn Donnan and Enid Tsui, "CNOOC Cuts Order from BP's Tangguh," *Financial Times*, December 16, 2005.

63. Thai officials reportedly expressed some concern about the implications in private, and the Chinese Foreign Ministry issued a strong statement at one point about the politicization of a commercial issue by Americans.

64. Herberg, "China's Search for Energy Security and Implications for Southeast Asia," 6.

65. Ibid., 15., quoting "South China Sea Region," Country Analysis Brief, Energy Information Administration, U.S. Department of Energy, September 2003.

66. China's Premier Wen Jiaboa has been quoted in public as lamenting China's "Malacca problem," or growing dependence on energy supplies from the Middle East and Africa that transit Southeast Asian maritime choke points.

CHAPTER 7

1. See Joseph Nye, *Soft Power: The Means to Success in World Politics.* New York: Public Affairs, 2004.

2. Brantly Womack, "Dancing Alone: A Hard Look At Soft Power," 1. Available at japan-focus.org, November 16, 2005.

3. For example, an argument could be made that elements of "soft power" have contributed to China's increasingly successful isolation of Taiwan in Southeast Asia. One argument would be that the ethnic Chinese communities in Southeast Asia are increasingly oriented to China and Hong Kong, rather than to Taiwan. On the other hand, Taiwan's relative economic role in Southeast Asia has also declined rapidly compared to China's, and Beijing has pressed to severe political links between Taiwan's government officials and their Southeast Asian counterparts.

4. Even predominantly ethnic Chinese Singapore is sensitive to its position as a small island surrounded by a "Malay Muslim sea."

5. Some thoughtful observes question the reality of Chinese influence in Southeast Asia. If influence is demonstrated by convincing people or countries to do something they would not usually do, and if China has asked little of Southeast Asians, where is the evidence of Chinese influence? However, there is no rule that influence needs to be expended, instead of accumulated, to demonstrate that it exists.

6. Though most international relations scholars leaning toward "realist" interpretations might be tempted to claim that China has accomplished little more than picking off "low-hanging fruit" in its "charm offensive" in the region.

7. Joshua Kurlantzick, "China's Chance." *Prospect Magazine*, 108 (March 2005).

8. "Nye himself once told me Defense Secretary Rumsfeld's response to the concept" was "I don't know what soft power is." James Taub, "The Way We Live Now, Idea Lab; The New Hard-Soft Power." *New York Times*, January 30, 2005.

9. Elizabeth Economy, "China's Rise in Southeast Asia: Implications for the United States." *Journal of Contemporary China*, 14(44) (2005): 420 (also repackaged as "China's Rising in Southeast Asia: Implications for Japan and the United States," at JapanFocus.org.).

10. Percival interview with a senior official in Singapore, August 2005.

11. The only Southeast Asians the author has ever heard express concern about the possibility that China's growing influence might undermine democracy in Southeast Asia were Filipino academics and journalists.

12. "Lee Kuan Yew Reflects." *Time Asia*, December 5, 2005.

13. Ibid.

14. Alastair Ian Johnston, "Socialization in International Institutions: The ASEAN Way and International Relations Theory." In *International Relations Theory and the Asia-Pacific*, edited by John Ikenberry and Michael Mastanduno. New York: Columbia University Press, 2003, 107.

15. In addition, China has pledged to establish a $15 million Asia Cooperation Fund to pay for the participation of Chinese officials in regional cooperation. See "Initiatives at the ASEAN Summit in November 2004," by John Andre, U.S. Department of State.

16. Economy, "China's Rise in Southeast Asia," 1.

17. See Keith Bradsher and Elisabeth Rosenthal, "China Plans Billions of Poultry Vaccinations." *New York Times*, November 15, 2005, Howard W. French, "Bird by Bird, China Tackles Vast Flu Task," *New York Times*, December 2, 2005.

18. Official U.S. tsumani-related assistance totaled $841 million ($400 million to Indonesia alone), with another $1.8 billion in private U.S. tsunami donations, compared to approximately $83 million from China, of which apparently only $22 million has been delivered.

19. Jane Perlez, "China Moves to Eclipse U.S. Appeal in South Asia." *New York Times*, November 18, 2004.

20. China's budget for "Confucian Institutes" is $12 million. "Instead of building expensive new headquarters in each city, the institutes team up with local partners, taking space in their buildings or getting foreign governments to pay for their housing. Instead of sending teachers who will instruct foreigners directly, the institute sends teacher trainers who can help upgrade the skills of local Chinese teachers." Howard W. French. "Another Chinese Export Is All the Rage: China's Language." *New York Times*, January 11, 2006.

21. Lyall Breckon and Dr. H. J. Kenny, *China's Growing Presence in Southeast Asia: Implications for the United States*. Alexandria, VA: Project Asia, Center for Naval Analyses, April 2004, 55.

22. Andy Xie, Morgan Stanley analyst, to Xinhua, as reported by www.china.org, Hong Kong, September 10, 2001.

23. Wayne Arnold, "Chinese on a Grand Tour." *New York Times*, October 21, 2005.

24. China National Tourist Office, New York, 2002. http://www.cnto.org/chinastats.asp.

25. The ASEAN Secretariat, "International Visitor Arrivals in ASEAN," 2004. However, the same statistics demonstrate that China still trails Japan (3,481,186) as a source of tourists to ASEAN countries.

26. Ibid.

27. "Chiang Mai Agreement: 3M Chinese Tourists a Year Targeted." *The Nation*, September 22, 2005.

28. The Indonesian section (Chapter 4) claims 84,000 Chinese tourists visited in 2004.

29. China National Tourist Office, online statistics. http://www.cnto.org/chinastats.asp.

30. Simon Montlake. "Chinese Tourists: Asia's New 'Ugly Americans'?" *The Christian Science Monitor*, January 1, 2006.

31. The 2002 Chinese estimate of tourist spending would indicate an average expenditure of $1,060 per tourist. As the poorest of the major destinations for Chinese tourists, Vietnam may derive the largest percentage of its foreign exchange from Chinese tourism, though it is a cheaper destination than, for example, Singapore. According to Wayne Arnold's *New York Times* article "Chinese on a Grand Tour," "most tourists from China sign up for $250 package tours that whisk them through as many as five countries in a week."

32. Perlez,"Chinese move to Eclipse U.S. Appeal in Southeast Asia."

33. Glosny, quoting statistics from the PRC Ministry of Foreign Affairs in "Stabilizing the Backyard: Recent Developments in China's Policy towards Southeast Asia,"32

34. Perlez, "China Moves to Eclipse U.S. Appeal in South Asia."

35. Glosny, quoting statistics from the PRC Ministry of Foreign Affairs in "Stabilizing the Backyard: Recent Developments in China's Policy towards Southeast Asia," 31.

36. The Taiwanese DPP has cut subsidies for Southeast Asian Chinese to study in Taiwan. Joshua Kurlantzick, Conference on "China's Soft Power in Southeast Asia," Carnegie Endowment for International Peace, Washington, D. C., June 13, 2006.

37. Percival interview with U.S. Embassy official, Jakarta, March 2005.

38. Perlez, "China Moves to Eclipse U.S. Appeal in Southeast Asia."

39. Joseph Kahn, "China Has An Ancient Mariner to Tell You About." *New York Times*, July 20, 2005.

40. "Chairman's Statement of the 8th ASEAN-China Summit," held in Vientienne, Laos, November 29, 2004, paragraph 12.

41. As Glosny notes, "Given that many of the singers, actors, and directors are from Taiwan or Hong Kong, whether or not the popularity of these movies and singers should count as soft power for mainland China is still a debatable point."

42. Teo Chu Cheow, "China's Rising Soft Power in Southeast Asia," CSIS Pacific Forum, PacNet, Number 19 A, May 3, 2004, 2.

43. Perlez, "China Moves to Eclipse U.S. Appeal in South Asia

44. Economy, "China's Rise in Southeast Asia," p. 410.

45. Percival interview with Professor Leo Suryadinata, Institute of Southeast Asian Studies, Singapore, March 2005. Suryadinata argues that in the Chinese-Southeast Asian relationship "soft power" is not the same as that articulated by Joseph Nye. Instead, "soft power" in Southeast Asia means "networking" that "integrates" China and Southeast Asia. This networking is not values-based. Instead, Chinese culture emphasizes mutual obligations for members of the network.

46. "According to scholar Hong Liu, in 2001, top officials from Beijing's Overseas Chinese Affairs Office visited more than 20 countries to hold meetings with leaders of Chinese communities," Discussion with Joshua Kurlantzick, Carnegie Endowment for International Peace. Also found in Kurlantzick's unpublished draft document entitled "ceip policy brief Jan 2005," 7.

47. According to Forbes 2004 list of the 10 richest men in Southeast Asia, 8 are ethnic Chinese. "Special Report: Southeast Asia's Richest." August 25, 2004.

48. "It (China) would only protect the 'overseas Chinese' if this initiative coincided with the highest priority of China's national interest such as national security, territorial integrity and the survival of the regime." Leo Suryadinata, "China and Ethnic Chinese in ASEAN: Post Cold-War Development." In Saw Swee-Hock, Sheng Lijun, and Chin Kin Wah, *ASEAN-China Relations, Realities and Prospects*, Singapore, 2005, 356.

49. "1999 estimates indicate a population of 23 million ethnic Chinese in Southeast Asia. They comprise 80% of the Chinese population outside China. In terms of percentage of national populations, Singapore has the highest percentage (77%), followed by Malaysia (25%), and Brunei (16%). However, in absolute numbers, Indonesia has the largest population (6.3 million), followed by Malaysia (5.5 million) and Thailand (5.2 million)." Leo Suryadinata, "Ethnic Chinese in Southeast Asia and their Economic Role." In *Chinese Populations in Contemporary Southeast Asian Societies, Identities, Interdependence and International Influence,* edited by M. Jocelyn Armstrong, R. Warwick Armstrong, and Kent Mulliner. Richmond, VA: Curzon Press, 2001. Limpe estimates 800,000 to 1 million ethnic Chinese in the Philippines in 2002. Irene C. Limpe, "The Transformation of Ethnic Identities Among Chinese an Chinese Meztizos in the Philippines." Paper presented at the Yale University Inaugural Conference on Southeast Asian Studies.

50. Reliable estimates of the number of ethnic Chinese in Myanmar, Laos, Cambodia, and Vietnam are not available. The most common estimates of the populations involved are 1 million in Myanmar and 300,000 in Cambodia. There has also been significant immigration of ethnic Chinese into Laos since Suryadinata estimated that population at 10,000 in 1990.

51. Percival interview with Prof. Leo Suryadinata, March 2005. He said that scholars need to be careful in estimating the flow of recent ethnic Chinese migrants to Southeast Asia because new migrants to Singapore, Malaysia, and Indonesia are both legal and illegal, and not just from China but also from Hong Kong. Ethnic Chinese are also returning to Vietnam.

52. See Wang Gungwu, "Chinese Ethnicity in New Southeast Asian Nations," *Ethnic Relations and Nation-building in Southeast Asia: the Case of the Ethnic Chinese*. ISEAS, Singapore, 2004.

53. "The 1980 nationality law, introducing the first citizenship law since the birth of the PRC, stating that China will only recognize one citizenship." Leo Suryadinata, "China and Ethnic Chinese in ASEAN: Post Cold-War Development," 358.

54. Beijing strongly protested Hanoi's efforts to force ethnic Chinese to become Vietnamese citizens in the late 1970s, which led many ethnic Chinese to flee Vietnam. But the deteriorating Chinese-Vietnamese relationship was not based primarily on the fate of ethnic Chinese, but on international considerations following Vietnam's invasion of Cambodia.

55. Breckon and Kenny, "China's Growing Presence in Southeast Asia," 21.

56. Leo Suryadinata, "China and Ethnic Chinese in ASEAN: Post Cold-War Development," 361.

57. Ibid., 362.

58. Her husband, businessman Taufiq Keimas, led an Indonesian trade delegation to China in 2002. Also see Leo Suryadinata,, "Postscript on Post-Suharto Sino-Indonesian Relations." *Pribumi Indonesians, the Chinese Minority and China*. Singapore: Marshall Cavendish Academic, 2005.

59. "Chinese Indonesians Ready for Elections." *Jakarta Post*, February 24, 2004.

60. Ethnic Chinese are rapidly becoming re-sinicized. This is largely a result of the government policy that is based on race and indigenism. However, the rise of China, the resurgence of ethnicity worldwide, and the spread of democratic ideals are also responsible for the re-sinicization of the Chinese in Malaysia. See Leo Suryadinata, "Peranakan Chinese Identities in Singapore and Malaysia: A Re-examination." In *Ethnic Chinese in Singapore and Malaysia: A Dialogue between Tradition and Modernity*. Singapore: Times Academic Press, 2002.

61. Percival interview with a Malaysian expert, Washington, D. C., January 2006. The Malaysian Chinese Association (MCA)-sponsored Tunku Abdul Rahman University teaches in English, but there are also three post-secondary "colleges" that teach in Mandarin in Kuala Lumpur, Penang and Johore Bahru.

62. Percival interviews with Malaysian and Singaporean academics, August and December 2005.

63. Teo Chu Cheow, "China's Rising Soft Power in Southeast Asia." *PACNET*, No. 19 A, May 3, 2004, p. 2.

64. Ibid., 2.

65. Leo Suryadinata, "China and Ethnic Chinese in ASEAN: Post Cold-War Development," 364.

66. Womack, "Dancing Alone," 4.

67. Corazon Sandoval Foley, Bureau of Intelligence and Research, Department of State, at a conference partially sponsored by this Bureau in Washington, DC, November 2005.

68. "Asian Views of China." Office of Research, Opinion Analysis, Department of State. Washington, DC, November 9, 2005, 6.

69. "American Character Gets Mixed Reviews: U.S. Image Up Slightly, but Still Negative." The Pew Global Attitudes Project. Released June 23, 2005. http://pewglobal.org/reports/display.php?Report=247.

70. Wayne Arnold, "Chinese on a Grand Tour." *New York Times*, October 21, 2005.

71. Percival interviews with officials and academics in Malaysia and former U.S. officials in Washington, D. C., 2005. Illegal Chinese migration to the region is raising increasing concern, and stories haveappeared in the press in Malaysia and Indonesia about Chinese girls

participating in the sex trade. These stories take on a domestic interethnic element when the Chinese government protests strip searches and other offensive measures by local police of Chinese women in these countries. In the most widely publicized case, the Chinese woman who was alleged to have been strip-searched by the police was eventually identified not as an ethnic Chinese woman but as a Malaysian ethnic Malay citizen.

CHAPTER 8

1. This is not to argue that Washington has been continuously and equally neglectful of the region from 1975 to 2001. American interest in the region has naturally waxed and waned, as larger ideological or strategic issues have played out in Southeast Asia. The domestic controversy in the United States as a result of the Vietnam War, and the American-supported South Vietnamese regime's collapse in 1975, weakened America's reputation in the region and led to much speculation about American withdrawal from Southeast Asia as a whole. The closure of U.S. military bases at Subic and Clark in the Philippines in late 1980s/early 1990s left a sour taste in the mouths of many senior Pentagon and other American officials, which was only gradually replaced as the United States turned to a policy of "places not bases" to maintain a security presence. The reputation of the United States suffered another blow when Washington, in the eyes of many Southeast Asians, failed to come to the Thai economy's rescue during the Asian Financial Crisis of 1997–1998. It is also important to recognize that one of the constant refrains in Southeast Asia is and has long been that the United States does not pay sufficient attention to the region.

2. The exception in the new century has been the Southeast Asian component of the global war on terrorism.

3. A secondary concern is access to airbases and the ability to "stage" forces and supplies through Thailand and Singapore.

4. US-ASEAN Business Council Statistics, based on U.S. Department of Commerce data.

5. An alternative view stresses the strategic significance of Myanmar to China, and then argues that it must therefore also be significant for the United States. Arguments advanced in support of Myanmar's strategic importance appear to often reflect a familiarity with the history of World War II in Asia. Then Burma mattered because the allies had lost control of the Strait of Malacca with Singapore's surrender in February 1942, and the only way supplies could be sent to a China blockaded and partially occupied by Japanese Imperial forces was through Burma, or by flying supplies over the "hump" from India to China. With this history in the background, an argument is advanced that China sees Myanmar as a strategically crucial alternative for the import of essential energy supplies, should a confrontation with the United States lead Washington to close the Strait of Malacca to Chinese energy imports. But the argument holds little water. In the highly unlikely event that a U.S.-Chinese confrontation is so serious that Washington closes the strait to Chinese energy imports, it would also control coastal traffic off Myanmar. In the meantime, until China constructs oil and natural gas pipelines through Myanmar, the idea that Myanmar offers a more secure energy transportation route for China is premature. Even then it would not serve as a serious alternative to transport by sea through the Malacca or Lombok (Indonesia) straits. This is not to deny that Americans, and others, may have a moral responsibility to attempt to alleviate the suffering of Myanmar's citizens, but for the United States, Myanmar is, at most, a strategic sideshow. It is precisely because Myanmar is such a sideshow that little internal opposition existed within the U.S. government to raising human rights violations in Myanmar with China in late 2005 and early 2006 and to

pushing to have the military regime's violation of basic human rights in Myanmar discussed in the U. N. Security Council.

6. Indonesia, Malaysia, the Philippines, Singapore, and Thailand.

7. Catharin E. Dalpino, *The Bush Administration in Southeast Asia. Two Regions? Two Policies?* Washington, DC: The Brookings Institution, 116.

8. See Thom Shanker, "Rumsfeld Issues a Sharp Rebuke to China on Arms." *New York Times*, June 4, 2005. The July 2005 U.S. Department of Defense's White Paper also paints an alarming picture of Chinese intentions and capabilities.

9. Glenn Kessler, "U.S. Seeks Improved SE Asia Ties; Zoellick Trip is Aimed at Building Economic, Political Links." *Washington Post*, April 30, 2005.

10. "The Bush administration's emphasis on allies and friends partly reflected its views of China—which seemed contradictory. The first was to regard China, in U.S. secretary of state Colin Powell's words, as a 'competitor, a potential regional rival,' and the second was to treat it as a less central player in U.S. policy towards Asia." Satu P. Limaye, "Recalibration Not Transformation, U.S. Security Policies in the Asia-Pacific." Chapter 12 in *Asia-Pacific Security Cooperation, National Interests and Regional Order*, edited by See Seng Tan and Amitav Archarya. New York: M.E. Sharpe, 2004, 207.

11. The extension of non-NATO ally status had more to do with the need to announce results, or "deliverables" in State Department jargon, for President Bush's APEC trip to Bangkok in 2003 than with countering terrorism or enhancing Thailand's security. The U.S. may also have wished to reward Thailand for allowing a secret detention and interrogation center for captured al Qaeda terrorists until June 2003. See the *Washington Post* of November 2, 2005, 1.

12. PBS Documentary on the American Civil War.

13. Robert Ross, *A Realist Policy for Managing US-China Competition.*, Policy Analysis Brief, The Stanley Foundation, November 2005, 7.

14. Dalpino, The Bush Administration in Southeast Asia. Two Regions? Two Policies? 109.

15. Limaye, "Recalibration Not Transformation, U.S. Security Policies in the Asia-Pacific," 212.

16. The ambivalence is even clear among Southeast Asia "experts," with those who are vested in mainland Southeast Asia and some U.S. business leaders stressing the "China threat."

17. Intelligence liaison and cooperation against terrorists was also low-key and effective, and the United States strongly encouraged cooperation among traditionally suspicious individual Southeast Asian services. The high-profile arrest of Jemaah Islamiyah's operations chief in Thailand, while a counterterrorism coup of considerable significance, led to repeated public Indonesian demands that the United States turn Hambali, an Indonesian citizen, over to the Jakarta for trial by Indonesia.

18. The current U.S. antiterrorism military actions and presence in Southeast Asia "should not be permanent, should not be large scale, and should not change the current international relations in the region." See "Developing ASEAN-China relations" (ISEAS), 6.

19. IMF Direction of Trade Statistics.

20. US-ASEAN Business Council. http://us-asean.org.

21. See Chapter 6.

22. "U.S. investment in ASEAN at the end of 2003 stood at slightly over $88 billion, according to figures from the U.S. Department of Commerce . . . Along with this rapid growth has been an increasing diversification of U.S investment in the region. In the mid-1980s, much of American investment was in the oil and gas sector; in the mid-1980s, for example, such investment accounted for more than half of the total U.S. investment presence in the region. This has changed steadily since then, and manufacturing and services now account for

the largest share of U.S. investment activity in ASEAN. The Commerce Department data for the year-end 1999 shows that 36% of U.S. investment in the region is concentrated in the manufacturing sector, while an equal amount is in services and other related industries. The remaining 28% of U.S. investment in the region is in the petroleum sector." See US-ASEAN Business Council's Web site, www.us-asean.org.

23. The United States and Japan have agreed on a "strategic development alliance," which will focus on Indonesia and Pakistan. Percival interview with a U.S. official, Washington, DC, December 2005.

24. With Vietnam, Cambodia, and Laos, the U.S. has bilateral investment treaties.

25. Comment by a senior U.S. official at a conference sponsored in part by the Bureau of Intelligence and Research, Department of State, Washington, DC, November 2005.

26. Rommel C. Banlaoi, "Southeast Asian Perspectives on the Rise of China; Regional Security After 9/11," *Parameters* (Summer 2003), quoted in Elizabeth Economy, "China's Rise in Southeast Asia: Implications for the United States." *Journal of Contemporary China*, 14(44) (2005): 411

27. Percival interview with an official, Singapore, August 2005.

28. The United States has been characterized as the "least distrusted" or "most trusted" external power for at least a decade. The first use of this phrase is often ascribed to former Singaporean Prime Minister Lee Kuan Yew, Mentor Minister, Singapore.

29. "In some ways the administration has outdone the Clinton administration by allowing special interests to take an increasing hold on relations. This is less the result of disagreement within the administration than within the Republican party . . . the conservative right in Congress increasingly influences policy toward the "other" (mainland) Southeast Asia." Dalpino, *The Bush Administration in Southeast Asia. Two Regions? Two Policies?* 115

30. This is not a universal U.S. attitude. For example, NATO and the OAS are valued as organizations, not simply for the immediate "product" of their work. On the other hand, the United States, as a global power, does not have the surplus of government officials with the appropriate rank to "cover" innumerable meetings half way across the world in East Asia. The United States will never be either willing or able to compete equally with a regional power, such as China, in conducting attentive, personal diplomacy through multilateral mechanisms in East Asia.

31. Joe Brinkley, "Rice, in Southeast Asia, Draws Fire for Plan to Avoid Forum." *The New York Times*, July 12, 2005.

32. Percival interviews with U.S. officials, December 2005, January and March 2006.

CONCLUSION

1. China's influence is based neither on the exercise of military or economic power to threaten Southeast Asian states, nor the "soft power" of attraction. Instead, China's "influence" depends on China's contribution to the economic growth and political stability of Southeast Asian regimes and on Southeast Asians' expectations that additional benefits will be derived from closer relations with China in the future.

2. Indonesia's decision to sever relations with China for twenty-five years is a classic example of the primacy of domestic politics.

3. This commitment is modified to allow elites in these states to reserve control over some resources, through state corporations, affirmative action, crony capitalism, corruption or other means, to reward domestic governing coalitions and promote political stability.

4. The only Southeast Asian state that criticized the resort to violence to suppress civilian demonstrations in 1999 in Tiananmen in Beijing was Singapore. ASEAN states' ambivalence with regard to the promotion of democracy has been repeatedly demonstrated with regard to Myanmar since its accession to ASEAN.

5. This preference has not prevented Southeast Asian contributions to UN and other peacekeeping forces, or the dispatch of small, symbolic Thai and Filipino military contingents to Iraq.

6. For example, Vietnam's hedging with regard to China is shaped by shared borders, shared leadership by Communist Parties, conflicting claims in the South China Sea, and a thousand of years of close but unequal relations, as well as a recent war. Indonesia, on the other hand, shares none of Vietnam's constraints in its relationship with China.

7. Not to belabor the obvious, but as explained in the introduction this book does not speculate on the possibility of a major upheaval within China, which could theoretically lead to a radical revision of Chinese policy in Southeast Asia.

8. As discussed previous, through its "Go South" informal diplomatic campaign, Taiwan sought to compete aggressively with China in Southeast Asia until the election of Chen Shui-bian. Since 2000, annual Taiwanese investment in Southeast Asia has fallen by more than half and old links between Southeast Asian and Taiwanese political leaders have atrophied. Beijing has successfully pressed for a virtual embargo on contacts between Southeast Asian Cabinet Ministers and their Taiwanese counterparts, and even contacts between officials are diminishing. In addition, Southeast Asia's ethnic Chinese look less to Taiwan, and more to China and Hong Kong, for cultural inspiration and ethnic Chinese networks than they did in the 1990s.

9. The conventional assumption is that China's rise has encouraged Singapore, the Philippines, and Thailand to draw closer to the United States, at least in terms of solidifying security and military to military ties. However, there is no evidence that Singapore or Thailand have strengthened these ties with the United States in response to China's rise, as explained elsewhere in this book. Moreover, China's increasing influence is widely perceived in Southeast Asia to provide additional options for Southeast Asians should they be inclined to resist American preferences.

10. The alleged analogy to Germany's post-1870 rise is often used to buttress this argument. See Avery Goldstein, "An Emerging China's Emerging Grand Strategy, A Neo-Bismarkian Turn? In *International Relations Theory and the Asia-Pacific*, edited by G. John Ikenberry and Michael Mastanduno, 57–106 (New York: Columbia University Press, 2003).

11. See Henry A. Kissinger, "China: Containment Won't Work." *Washington Post*, June 13, 2005.

12. Glenn Kessler, "U.S. Seeks Improved SE Asia Ties: Zoellick Trip is Aimed to Build Economic, Political Links." *Washington Post*, April 30, 2005.

13. Percival interview with foreign ministry official, Singapore, August 2005.

14. For the United States, repression in Myanmar is largely a symbolic human rights issue. Washington will not compromise its global reputation by moderating its current policies in a probably forlorn attempt to gain influence with the current Myanmar regime, which has repeatedly exploited Beijing's opposition to external inference in internal affairs to block ASEAN's ambivalent efforts to press for reform. ASEAN, individual Southeast Asian governments, and China have often disagreed on the promotion of basic human rights and political freedoms in that country.

15. Percival interview with a senior official, Singapore, August 2005.

16. See William W. Grimes, "Institutionalized Inertia: Japanese Foreign Policy in the Post-Cold World." In *International Relations Theory and the Asia-Pacific*, edited by G. John Ikenberry and Michael Mastanduno, 353–386 (New York: Columbia University Press, 2003).

17. Percentage of FDI inflow into Developing Asia-Pacific: 1990, ASEAN-5 (31.2%), China (15.6%), 2003, ASEAN-5 (14.4%), China (49.9%).

18. China's Premier Wen Jiabao has been quoted in public as lamenting China's "Malacca problem," or growing dependence on energy supplies from the Middle East and Africa that transit Southeast Asian maritime choke points.

Selected Bibliography

Abramowitz, Morton and Steven Bosworth. *Chasing the Sun: Rethinking East Asia Policy.* New York: The Century Foundation Press, 2006.

———. "Adjusting to the New Asia." *Foreign Affairs* 82(4) (July/August 2003): 119–131.

Acharya, Amitav. *Constructing a Security Community in Southeast Asia, ASEAN and the Problem of Regional Order*. London: Routledge, 2001.

———. *Seeking Security in the Dragon's Shadow: China and Southeast Asia in the Emerging Asian Order*. IDSS Working Paper No. 44, Singapore: Institute of Defence and Strategic Studies, March 2003.

Alagappa, Muthiah. *Asian Security Order: Instrumental and Normative Features*. Stanford, CA: Stanford University Press, 2003.

Amer, Ramses. "Assessing Sino-Vietnamese Relations Through the Management of Contentious Issues." *Contemporary Southeast Asia*, 26(2) (2004): 320–345.

"Asia's China Debate," Special Assessment Series, Honolulu, Hawaii: Asia-Pacific Center for Security Studies, December 2003.

Ba, Alice. "China and ASEAN: Renavigating Relations for a 21st Century Asia." *Asian Survey*, 43(4) (July/August 2003): 622–647.

———. "The Politics and Economics of "East Asia." In *China and Southeast Asia, Global Changes and Regional Challenges*, edited by Ho Khai Leong and Samuel C.Y. Ku. Singapore: Institute of Southeast Asian Studies, 2005.

———. "Southeast Asia and China." *Betwixt and Between, Southeast Asian Strategic Relations with the U.S. and China*. IDSS Monograph No. 7, Singapore: Institute of Defence and Strategic Studies, 2005, 93–108.

Baker, Carl. "China-Philippines Relations: Cautious Cooperation." Special Assessment Series, Asia-Pacific Center for Security Studies, October 2004.

Banlaoi, Rommel C. "Southeast Asian Perspectives on the Rise of China: Regional Security After 9/11." *Parameters* (Summer 2003): 98–107.

Barnett, Thomas P.M. "The Chinese Are Our Friends," *Esquire*, November 1, 2005. Available at: http://www.keepmedia.com/pubs/Esquire/2005.

Baviera, Aileen S.P. "The South China Sea Disputes After the 2002 Declaration: Beyond Confidence Building." In *ASEAN-China Relations, Realities and Prospects*, edited by Saw Swee Hock, Sheng Lijun, and Chin Kin Wah. Singapore: Institute for Southeast Asian Studies, 2005.

Bert, Wayne. *The United States, China and Southeast Asian Security, A Changing of the Guard?* New York: Palgrave MacMillan, 2003.

———. "Burma, China and the U.S.A." *Pacific Affairs*, 77(2) (Summer 2004): 263–282.

Breckon, Lyall. "SARs and a New Security Initiative from China." *Comparative Connections*, April–June 2003.

———. "A New Strategic Partnership Is Declared." *Comparative Connections*, October–December 2003.

———. "A Lull, and Some Complaints." *Comparative Connections*, January–March 2004.

Breckon, Lyall and Dr. H.J. Kenny. *China's Growing Presence in Southeast Asia: Implications for the United States*. Alexandria, VA: Project Asia, Center for Naval Analyses, April 2004.

Cai Peng Hong. "Non-Traditional Security and China-ASEAN Relations: Co-operation, Commitments and Challenges." Chapter 6 in *China and Southeast Asia, Global Changes and Regional Challenges*, edited by Ho Khai Leong and Samual C.Y. Ku. Singapore: Institute of Southeast Asian Studies, 2005.

Cao Yunhua. "U.S.-ASEAN, Japan-ASEAN Relations and Their Impacts on China." In *ASEAN-China Relations, Realities and Prospects*, edited by Saw Swee Hock, Sheng Lijun, and Chin Kin Wah. Singapore: Institute for Southeast Asian Studies, 2005.

Chan, Steven. "Is There a Power Transition between the U.S. and China? The Different Faces of National Power." *Asian Survey*, 45 (September/October 2005): 687–701.

Chanda, Nayan. *Southeast Asia After September 11*. Yale Center for the Study of Globalization, 117–130.

Chang Pao-min. "Sino-Vietnamese Relations: Prospects for the Twenty-first Century." In *Vietnamese Foreign Policy in Transition*, edited by Carlyle A. Thayer and Ramses Amer. Singapore: ISEAS, 1999.

Chambers, Michael R. "The Chinese and Thais Are Brothers: The Evolution of Sino-Thai Friendship." *Journal of Contemporary China*, 14(45) (November 2005): 597–627.

Chen Jie. "Taiwan's Diplomacy in Southeast Asia: Still Going South?" In *China and Southeast Asia, Global Changes and Regional Challenges*, edited by Ho Khai Leong and Samuel C.Y. Ku. Singapore: Institute of Southeast Asian Studies, 2005.

Cheung, Gordon C. K. "Chinese Diaspora as a Virtual Nation: Interactive Roles Between Social and Political Capital." *Political Studies*, 52(4) (December 2004):664–684.

"China's Growing Influence in Southeast Asia: Interim Findings." *INSS Staff Report*, Institute for National Security Studies, National Defense University, April 21, 2004.

"China and Southeast Asia." *Policy Bulletin*. The Stanley Foundation, 44th Strategy for Peace Conference, October 2003.

"China-Indonesia Relations and the Implications for the United States: A Joint Conference Report Cosponsored by the United States—Indonesia Society and the Sigur Center for Asian Studies of the Elliott School of International Affairs at The George Washington University." Washington, DC: November 7, 2003.

Chirathivat, Suthiphand. "China's Rise and its Effect on ASEAN-China Trade Relations." Conference on "Contending Perspectives: Southeast Asian and American Views of a Rising

China." Singapore: Institute of Defence and Strategic Studies and The National Bureau of Asian Research (NBR), August 2005.

Chulacheeb Chinwanno. "Thailand." *Betwixt and Between, Southeast Asian Strategic Relations with the U.S. and China*. IDSS Monograph No. 7, 2005, 61–72.

Clad, James. "Fin de siecle, fin de l'ASEAN." Available at http://www.atimes.com/sea-asia/BC08Ae01.html.

Cole, Bernard D. *Oil for the Lamps of China—Beijing's 21st Century Search for Energy*. McNair Paper 67, Institute for National Security Studies, National Defense University. Washington, DC: 2003.

Cossa, Ralph A. "The East Asian Community and the United States: An American Perspective." One of three articles in Ralph A. Cossa, Simon Tay, and Lee Chung-min, "The Emerging East Asian Community: Should Washington Be Concerned?" *Issues and Insights*, 5(9), Pacific Forum CSIS, Honolulu, Hawaii, August, 2005: 1–12.

Da Cunha, Derek. "Southeast Asian Perceptions of China's Future Security Role in Its "Backyard." Available at http://www.rand.org/publications/CF/CF137/CF137.chap6.pdf.

Dalpino, Catharin E. "The Bush Administration in Southeast Asia. Two Regions? Two Policies?" *George W. Bush and Asia: A Midterm Assessment*, edited by Robert M. Hathaway and Wilson Lee. Washington, DC: Woodrow Wilson Center for International Scholars, (2003):103–116. Available at http://wwics.si.edu/topics/pubs/ACF2A4.pdf.

———. "U.S.- Southeast Asia Relations: Summitry Hints of a More Activist Approach." *Comparative Connections*, April–June 2005.

Devare, Sudhir. *India & Southeast Asia, Towards Security Convergence*. Singapore: Institute of Southeast Asian Studies, 2006.

Developing ASEAN-China Relations, Realities and Prospects. A Brief Report of the ASEAN-China Forum. Singapore: Institute of Southeast Asian Studies, 2004.

Dillon, Dana R. and John J. Tkacik, Jr. *China and ASEAN: Endangered American Primacy in Southeast Asia*. Backgrounder Published by the Heritage Foundation, No. 1886, October 19, 2005.

Economy, Elizabeth. "China's Rise in Southeast Asia: Implications for the United States." *Journal of Contemporary China*, 14(44) (2005): 409–425.

Emmers, Ralf. "Regional Hegemonies and the Exercise of Power in Southeast Asia: A Study of Indonesia and Vietnam." *Asian Survey*, 45(4): 645–665.

Evans, Grant, Christopher Hutton, and Kuah Khun Eng. *Where China Meets Southeast Asia, Social and Cultural Change in the Border Regions*. Singapore: Institute of Southeast Asian Studies, 2000.

Foley, Corazon Sandoval. *China-Southeast Asia Relations: The ASEAN-China Free Trade Agreement*. Washington, DC: Department of State, Bureau of Intelligence and Research, September 19, 2005.

———. *China-Southeast Asia Relations: ASEAN Hedging Strategy*. Washington, DC: Department of State, Bureau of Intelligence and Research, 2005.

Foot, Rosemary. "China in the ASEAN Regional Forum: Organizational Processes and Domestic Modes of Thought." *Asian Survey* 38(5) (1998): 425–440.

"Foreign Direct Investments to China and Southeast Asia: Has ASEAN Been Losing Out?" *Economic Survey of Singapore*, 3rd Quarter, 2002.

Frost, Ellen. "Re-Engaging with Southeast Asia." *PacNet 37*, July 26, 2006

Frost, Stephen. "Chinese Outward Direct Investment in Southeast Asia: How Big Are the Flows and What Does It Mean for the Region?" *The Pacific Review*, 17, no. 3 (2004): 323–340.

Gao Zhiguo."South China Sea: Turning Suspicion into Mutual Understanding and Cooperation." In *ASEAN-China Relations, Realities and Prospects*, edited by Saw Swee Hock, Sheng Lijun, and Chin Kin Wah. Singapore: Institute for Southeast Asian Studies, 2005.

Glosny, Michael A. "Heading Toward a Win-Win Future? Recent Developments in China's Policy Toward Southeast Asia." *Asian Security*, 2(1) (2006): 24–57.

Goh, Evelyn. *Betwixt and Between, Southeast Asian Strategic Relations with the U.S. and China*. IDSS Monograph No. 7. Singapore: Institute of Defence and Strategic Studies, 2005.

———. *Great Powers and Southeast Asian Regional Security Strategies: Omni-Enmeshment, Balancing and Hierarchical Order*. IDSS Working Paper No. 84. Singapore: Institute of Defence and Strategic Studies, 2005.

———. *Meeting the China Challenge: The U.S. in Southeast Asian Regional Security Strategies*. Policy Studies 16, East-West Center, Washington, DC, 2005.

———. "Singapore's Reaction to a Rising China, Deep Engagement and Strategic Adjustment." In *China and Southeast Asia, Global Changes and Regional Challenges*, edited by Ho Khai Leong and Samuel C.Y. Ku. Singapore: Institute of Southeast Asian Studies, 2005.

Gomez, Edmund Terence and Hsin-Huang Michael Hsiao, eds. *Chinese Business in Southeast Asia*. New York: Routledge Curzon, 2004.

Goodman, David S.G. "Are Asia's 'Ethnic Chinese' a Regional Security Threat?" *Survival*, Winter 1997/1998.

Grimes, William W. "Institutionalized Inertia, Japanese Foreign Policy in the Post-Cold War World." In *International Relations Theory and the Asia-Pacific*, edited by G. John Ikenberry and Michael Mastanduno. New York: Columbia University Press: 2003.

Haacke, Jurgen. "The Significance of Beijing's Bilateral Relations: Looking 'Below' the Regional Level in China-ASEAN Ties." In *China and Southeast Asia, Global Changes and Regional Challenges*, edited by Ho Khai Leong and Samuel C.Y. Ku. Singapore: Institute of Southeast Asian Studies, 2005.

Hassan, Mohamed Jawhar, "Strengthening Cooperation in the ASEAN Regional Forum: An ASEAN View." In *ASEAN-China Relations, Realities and Prospects*, edited by Saw Swee Hock, Sheng Lijun, and Chin Kin Wah. Singapore: Institute for Southeast Asian Studies, 2005.

He Shengda and Sheng Lijun. "Yunnan's Greater Mekong Sub-Region Strategy." In *ASEAN-China Relations: Realities and Prospects*, edited by Saw Swee Hock, Sheng Lijun, and Chin Kin Wah Singapore: Institute for Southeast Asian Studies, 2005.

Heller, Dominik. "The Relevance of the ASEAN Regional Forum (ARF) for Regional Security in the Asia-Pacific." *Contemporary Southeast Asia*, 27 (1) (2005): 123–145.

Herberg, Mikkal E. "China's Search for Energy Security and Implications for Southeast Asia." Conference on "Contending Perspectives: Southeast Asian and American Views of a Rising China," Singapore, August 2005.

Ho Khai Leong. "ASEAN +1 or China +1." In *China and Southeast Asia, Global Changes and Regional Challenges*, edited by Ho Khai Leong and Samuel C.Y. Ku. Singapore: Institute of Southeast Asian Studies, 2005.

Hund, Markus. "ASEAN Plus Three: Toward a New Age of Pan-Asian Regionalism? A Skeptics Appraisal." *Pacific Review*, 16(3) (2003): 383–417.

John, Eric. "The US and Indonesia: Toward a Strategic Partnership." Speech by US Department of State Deputy Assistant Secretary, Washington, DC, December 20, 2005.

Johnston, Alastair Ian. "Socialization in International Institutions: The ASEAN Way and International Relations Theory." In *International Relations Theory and the Asia-Pacific*, edited by G. John Ikenberry and Michael Mastanduno. New York: Columbia University Press, 2003.

Kagan, Robert. "The Illusion of "Managing" China." *The Washington Post*, May 15, 2005.

Kang, David C. "Hierarchy and Stability in Asian International Relations." *American Asian Review*, 19(2) (Summer 2001): 121–160.

———. "Getting Asia Wrong, The Need for New Analytical Frameworks." *International Security*, 27(4) (Spring 2003): 57–85.

Kao Kim Hourn and Sisowath Doung Chanto. "ASEAN-China Cooperation for Greater Mekong Sub-Region Development." In *ASEAN-China Relations, Realities and Prospects*, edited by Saw Swee Hock, Sheng Lijun, and Chin Kin Wah. Singapore: Institute for Southeast Asian Studies, 2005.

Kaplan, Robert D. "How We Would Fight China," *The Atlantic Monthly*, June 2005.

Kenny, Henry J. *Shadow of the Dragon: Vietnam's Continuing Struggle with China and Its Implications for the United States*. Washington, DC: Brassey's, 2002.

Kerrey, J. Robert and Robert A. Manning. *The United States and Southeast Asia: A Policy Agenda for the New Administration*. Report of an Independent Task Force Sponsored by the Council on Foreign Relations, 2001.

Kraft, Herman J. "The Philippines." *Betwixt and Between, Southeast Asian Strategic Relations with the U.S. and China*. IDSS Monograph No. 7, 2005, 9–28.

Ku, Samuel C. Y. "The Changing Political Economy of Taiwan's and China's Relations with Southeast Asia: A Comparative Perspective." In *China and Southeast Asia, Global Changes and Regional Challenges*, edited by Ho Khai Leong and Samuel C.Y. Ku. Singapore: Institute of Southeast Asian Studies, 2005.

Kuik, Cheng-Chwee. "Multilateralism in China's ASEAN Policy: Its Evolution, Characteristics, and Aspiration." *Contemporary Southeast Asia*, 27(1) (2005): 102–122.

Kurlantzick, Joshua. "How China Is Changing Global Diplomacy," *New Republic Online*, June 27, 2005.

———. "China's Charm: Implications of Chinese Power." *Policy Brief 47*, Carnegie Endowment for International Peace, June 2006.

Lam Peng-Er. "Japan-Southeast Asia Relations: Trading Places? The Leading Goose & Ascending Dragon." *Comparative Connections*, 1st Quarter 2002.

Lanti, Irman G. "Indonesia." *Betwixt and Between, Southeast Asian Strategic Relations with the U.S. and China*. IDSS Monograph No. 7, 2005, 29–38.

———. "Indonesia in Triangular Relations with China." Conference on "Contending Perspectives: Southeast Asian and American Views of a Rising China." Singapore: Institute of Defence and Strategic Studies and The National Bureau of Asian Research (NBR), August 2005.

Leavitt, Sandra R. "The Lack of Security Cooperation between Southeast Asia and Japan, Yen Yes, Pax Nippon No." *Asian Survey*, 45(2) (2005): 216–240.

Lee, Chung-Min. "China's Rise, Asia's Dilemma." *The National Interest*, no. 81 (Fall 2005).

———. "East Asian Community and the United States: A Contrarian Perspective." One of three articles in Ralph A. Cossa, Simon Tay, and Lee Chung-min, "The Emerging East Asian Community: Should Washington Be Concerned?" *Issues and Insights*, 5, no. 9, Pacific Forum CSIS, Honolulu, Hawaii, August, 2005: 29–33.

Lee, K.H. and C.B. Tan. *The Chinese in Malaysia*. Kuala Lumpur: Oxford University Press, 2000.

Lee Poh Ping. "Malaysia and a Rising China." Conference on "Contending Perspectives: Southeast Asian and American Views of a Rising China." Singapore: Institute of Defence and Strategic Studies and The National Bureau of Asian Research (NBR), August 2005.

Lee Poh Ping and Lee Kam Hing. "The Rise of China as an Economic Power and Southeast Asia's Chinese Economy and Business with Special Reference to Malaysia." Unpublished Paper. Presentation at ISEAS Conference on "Ethnic Chinese Economy and Business in Southeast Asia in the Era of Globalization," Singapore, April 2005.

Limaye, Satu P. "Recalibration Not Transformation, U.S. Security Policies in the Asia-Pacific." Chapter 12 in *Asia-Pacific Security Cooperation, National Interests and Regional Order*, edited by See Seng Tan and Amitav Archarya. New York: M.E. Sharpe, 2004, 206–222.

Lindsey, Tim and Helen Pausacker, eds. *Chinese Indonesians, Remembering, Distorting and Forgetting*. Singapore: Institute of Southeast Asian Studies, 2005.

Linh Lan, Le. "The Changing Roles of the U.S. and China in Southeast Asia." *Betwixt and Between, Southeast Asian Strategic Relations with the U.S. and China*. IDSS Monograph No. 7, 2005, 73–82.

Liow, Joseph Chinyong. "Balancing, Bandwagoning, or Hedging? Strategic and Security Patterns in Malaysia's Relations with China, 1981–2003." In *China and Southeast Asia, Global Changes and Regional Challenges*, edited by Ho Khai Leong and Samuel C.Y. Ku. Singapore: Institute of Southeast Asian Studies, 2005.

Malik, Mohan. "Eyeing the Dragon: India's China Debate." In *Asia's China Debate*, edited by Satu Limaye. Asia-Pacific Center for Security Studies Special Assessment, December 2003.

Marks, Paul. "China's Cambodia Strategy." *Parameters*, Autumn 2000: 92–108.

Mathews, Bradley. "Bangkok's Fine Balance: Thailand's China Debate." In *Asia's China Debate*, edited by Satu Limaye. Asia-Pacific Center for Security Studies Special Assessment, December 2003.

Mathews, Vergese. "China-Cambodia Ties: A Special Bond Blooms." *The Straits Times*, Singapore, October 23, 2004.

Medeiros, Evan and Taylor Favel. "China's New Diplomacy." *Foreign Affairs* 82(6) (November/December 2003): 22–35.

Montaperto, Ronald. "Smoothing the Wrinkles." *Comparative Connections*, April–June 2004.

———. "Find New Friends, Reward Old Ones, but Keep All in Line." *Comparative Connections*. July–September 2004.

———. "Thinking Globally, Acting Regionally." *Comparative Connections*, October–December 2004.

———. "Assurance and Reassurance." *Comparative Connections*, January–March 2005.

———. "Dancing with China: (In a Psyche of Adaptability, Adjustment, and Cooperation)." *Comparative Connections*, April–June 2005.

Morrison, Wayne M. *Thailand-U.S. Economic Relations: An Overview*. Congressional Research Service Report for Congress, March 28, 2003.

Nan Li. "The Evolving Chinese Conception of Security and Security Approaches." In *Asia-Pacific Security Cooperation, National Interests and Regional Order*, edited by see Seng Tan and Amitav Archarya. New York: M.E. Sharpe, 2004.

Novotny, Daniel. *Indonesian Foreign Policy: Rowing Between Two Reefs*. Departments of Indonesian Studies and International Relations, University of New South Wales, Australia, 2005.

Nye, Joseph S. *Soft Power: The Means to Success in World Politics*. New York: Public Affairs, 2004.

Osborne, Milton. "The Paramount Power, China and the Countries of Southeast Asia." *Lowy Institute Paper No. 11*. New South Wales, Australia: Lowy Institute for International Policy, 2006.

Ott, Marvin C. "China and Southeast Asia." Report No. 15, SAIS Policy Forum Series, April 2002.

———. "The Great Reverse—Part II." *Yale Global*, September 6, 2004.

———. "China's Strategic Reach into Southeast Asia." Presentation to the U.S.-China Commission, Washington, DC, July 22, 2005.

———. "Southeast Asian Security Challenges: America's Response." *Strategic Forum*, No. 222, Washington, DC: Institute for National Strategic Studies, National Defense University, October 2006. Available at http://www.ndu.edu/inss.

Pei, Minxin and Michael Swaine. *Simmering Fire in Asia: Averting Sino-Japanese Strategic Conflict*. Policy Brief 44, Carnegie Endowment for International Peace, November 2005.

Percival, Bronson E. *Indonesia and the United States: Shared Interest in Maritime Security*. The United States-Indonesia Society, Washington, DC, June 2005. Available at: http://www.usindo.org.

———. "China's Influence in Southeast Asia: Implications for the United States." Presentation to the U.S.-China Commission, Washington, DC, July 22, 2005.

———. "The Friendly Dragon Looks South: China, America and Southeast Asia in the New Century," Presentation to the Asia Society—Texas 2006 Ambassador's Forum & Corporate Conference.

———. "Japan-Southeast Asia Relations: Playing Catch-up With China," *Comparative Connections*, 8(3), October 13, 2006.

Pollack, Jonathan D. "The United States and Asia in 2003, All Quiet on the Eastern Front?" *Asian Survey*, 44(1): 1–13.

———. "The United States and Asia in 2004, Unfinished Business." *Asian Survey*. 45(1): 1–13.

Ravenhill, John. "Is China an Economic Threat to Southeast Asia?" *Asian Survey*, 46(5): 653–674.

Ross, Robert. *A Realist Policy for Managing US-China Competition*. Policy Analysis Brief, The Stanley Foundation, November 2005.

———. "The Geography of Peace: East Asia in the Twenty-First Century." *International Security*, 23(4) (Spring 1999): 81–118.

Rowan, Joshua P. "The U.S.-Japan Security Alliance, ASEAN, and the South China Sea Dispute." *Asian Survey*, XLV(3) (May/June 2005): 414–436.

Samuels, Richard J. "Soft Power in East Asia." Paper prepared for a conference on "Asia's Search for a Security Community and American Common Sense." Washington, DC, October 20, 2004.

Saunders, Phillip C. "China's Global Activism: Strategy, Drivers, and Tools." *Institute for National Strategic Studies, Occasional Paper 4*, Washington, DC: National Defense University Press, October 2006

Saw Swee-Hock, Sheng Lijun, and Chin Kin Wah. *ASEAN-China Relations, Realities and Prospects*. Singapore: Institute for Southeast Asian Studies, 2005.

See Seng Tan and Ralf Emmers. *An Agenda for the East Asia Summit: 30 Recommendations for Regional Cooperation in East Asia*. Singapore: Institute of Defence and Strategic Studies, November 2005.

Shambaugh, David. "China Engages Asia, Reshaping the Regional Order." *International Security*, 29(3) (Winter 2004/2005): 64–99.

———. *Power Shift, China and Asia's New Dynamics*. Berkeley: University of California Press, 2005.

———. "Return to the Middle Kingdom? China and Asia in the Early Twenty-First Century." In *Power Shift, China and Asia's New Dynamics*, edited by David Shambaugh. Berkeley: University of California Press, 2005.

Shee, Poon Kim. "The Political Economy of Mahathir's China Policy: Economic Cooperation, Political and Strategic Ambivalence." International University of Japan, IUJ Research Institute Working Paper 2004–06, Asia Pacific Series, 2003.

Sheng Lijun. "China's Influence in Southeast Asia." *Trends in Southeast Asia Series, 4*, Singapore: Institute of Southeast Asian Studies, 2006.

Simon, Sheldon W. "U.S.-Southeast Asia Relations: Misses and Hits." *Comparative Connections*, July–September 2005.

Siriluk Masviriyakul. "Sino-Thai Strategic Economic Development in the Greater Mekong Subregion (1992–2003). *Contemporary Southeast Asia*, 26(2) (2004): 302–319.

Sisowath, Doung Chanto. "Cambodia." *Betwixt and Between, Southeast Asian Strategic Relations with the U.S. and China*. IDSS Monograph No. 7, 2005, 83–92.

Smith, Anthony L. "From Latent Threat to Possible Partner: Indonesia's China Debate." In *Asia's China Debate*, edited by Satu Limaye. Asia-Pacific Center for Security Studies Special Assessment, December 2003.

Solingen, Etel. "Southeast Asia in a New Era, Domestic Coalitions from Crisis to Recovery." *Asian Survey*, 44(2) (2004) 182–212.

———. "ASEAN Cooperation: The Legacy of the Economic Crisis." *International Relations of the Asia-Pacific*, 5 (2005):1–29.

———. "From 'Threat' to 'Opportunity'? ASEAN, China, and Triangulation." Conference on "Contending Perspectives: Southeast Asian and American Views of a Rising China." Singapore: Institute of Defence and Strategic Studies and The National Bureau of Asian Research (NBR), August 2005.

Sree Kumar, Sharon Siddique, and Yuwa Hendrick-Wong. *Mind the Gaps: Singapore Business in China*. Singapore: Institute of Southeast Asian Studies, 2005.

Storey, Ian. "China's Rising Political Influence in Southeast Asia." Conference on "Contending Perspectives: Southeast Asian and American Views of a Rising China." Singapore: IDSS/NBR Conference, August 2005.

Stuart-Fox, Martin. *A Short History of China and Southeast Asia: Tribute, Trade and Influence*, Crows Nest, Australia: Allen & Unwin, 2003.

———. "Southeast Asia and China: The Role of History and Culture in Shaping Future Relations." *Contemporary Southeast Asia*, 26(1) (2004): 116–139.

Sukma, Rizal. *Indonesia and China: The Politics of a Troubled Relationship*. London: Routledge, 1999.

Suryadinata, Leo. "Ethnic Chinese in Southeast Asia and their Economic Role," in *Chinese Populations in Contemporary Southeast Asian Societies, Identities, Interdependence and International Influence*, edited by M. Jocelyn Armstrong, R. Warwick Armstrong, and Kent Mulliner. Richmond, VA: Curzon Press, 2001.

———. *China and the ASEAN States, the Ethnic Chinese Dimension*. Singapore: Marshall Cavendish International, 2005.

———. *Pribumi Indonesians, the Chinese Minority and China, A Study of Perceptions and Policies*. Singapore: Marshall Cavendish International, 2005.

Sutter, Robert. *China's Policy Priorities and Recent Relations with Southeast Asia*. Report Number Seven, Johns Hopkins School of Advance International Studies Policy Forum Series, October 1999.

———. "China's Rise and US Leadership in Asia." Paper for a conference sponsored by the State Department, October 20, 2004.

———. "China's Regional Strategy and America." in *Power Shift, China and Asia's New Dynamics*, edited by David Shambaugh. Berkeley: University of California Press, 2005.

———. *China's Rise in Asia, Promises and Perils*. Oxford: Rowan & Littlefield, 2005.

———. "China-Southeast Asia Relations: Emphasizing the Positive; Continued Wariness." *Comparative Connections*, October-December 2005.

———. "China's Rise: Implications for U.S. Leadership in Asia." *Policy Studies*, 21 (2006), East-West Center, Washington, DC.

———. "Why Rising China Can't Dominate Asia." *PacNet Newsletter 45*, September 8, 2006.

Takeda, Yusuhiro. "Japan's Compound Approach to Security Cooperation." In *Asia-Pacific Security Cooperation, National Interests and Regional Order*, edited by see Seng Tan and Amitav Archarya. New York: M.E. Sharpe, 2004.

Tamamoto, Masaru. "Ambiguous Japan: Japanese National Identity at Century's End." In *International Relations Theory and the Asia-Pacific*, edited by G. John Ikenberry and Michael Mastanduno.New York: Columbia University Press, 2003.

Tan Khee Giap. "ASEAN and China: Relative Competitiveness, Emerging Investment-Trade Patterns, Monetary and Financial Integration." Conference on "Contending Perspectives: Southeast Asian and American Views of a Rising China." Singapore: Institute of Defence and Strategic Studies and The National Bureau of Asian Research (NBR), August 2005.

Tay, Simon S.C. "An East Asian Community and the United States." In Ralph A. Cossa, Simon Tay, and Lee Chung-min, "The Emerging East Asian Community: Should Washington Be Concerned?" *Issues and Insights*, 5(9), Pacific Forum CSIS, Honolulu, Hawaii, August 2005.

Teo Chu Cheow, Eric. "China's Rising Soft Power in Southeast Asia." *PACNET*, No. 19A, May 3, 2004.

———. "ASEAN+3: The Roles of ASEAN and China." In *ASEAN-China Relations, Realities and Prospects*, edited by Saw Swee Hock, Sheng Lijun, and Chin Kin Wah. Singapore: Institute for Southeast Asian Studies: 2005.

———. 2005. "Assessing the Sino-Indonesian Strategic Partnership." *PACNET*, 25 June 23, 2005.

———. "Sino-Singaporean Relations Back on Track." *China Brief*, The Jamestown Foundation, 5(16) (July 19, 2005): 3–5.

Teo Kah Beng. "Singapore." *Betwixt and Between, Southeast Asian Strategic Relations with the U.S. and China*. IDSS Monograph No. 7, 2005, 39–50.

Thayer, Carlisle A. "China Consolidates Long-Term Regional Relations." *Comparative Connections*, 4th Quarter, 1999.

———. "Making the Rounds." *Comparative Connections*, 2nd Quarter 2001.

———. "Vietnamese Perceptions of the China Threat." In *The China Threat: Perception, Myths and Reality*, edited by Herbert Yee and Ian Storey. New York: Routledge, 2002.

Tow, Shannon. "Southeast Asia in the Sino-U.S. Strategic Balance." *Contemporary Southeast Asia*, 26(3) (2004): 434–459.

Tow, William T. "Convergent Security Revisited, Reconciling Bilateral and Mulitlateral Security Approaches." In *Asia-Pacific Security Cooperation, National Interests and Regional Order*, edited by see Seng Tan and Amitav Archarya. New York: M.E. Sharpe, 2004, 19–32.

"U.S. Policy in Southeast Asia: Fortifying the Foundation, A Report and Recommendations from the Southeast Asia in the Twenty-First Century: Issues and Options for US Policy Initiative." The Stanley Foundation, 2003–2005.

Vatikiotis, Michael. "Catching the Dragon's Tail: China and Southeast Asia in the 21st Century." *Contemporary Southeast Asia*, 25(1) (April 2003): 65–78.

———. "In Asia's Chinese Disapora, Are Loyalties Divided?" *International Herald Tribune*, August 24, 2005.

Vaughn, Bruce. "China-Southeast Asia Relations: Trends, Issues, and Implications for the United States." *CRS Report for Congress*, Updated February 8, 2005.

Vuving, Alexander L. "Vietnam's Conduct of Its Relations with China: Balancing, Bandwagoning, Accepting Hierarchy, or a Fourth Configuration?" Paper presented at the conference on, "Vietnam as an Actor on the International Stage." School of Advanced International Studies, Johns Hopkins University, Washington, DC, April 29, 2005.

Wang Gungwu. "China and Southeast Asia, The Context of a New Beginning." In *Power Shift, China and Asia's New Dynamics*, edited by David Shambaugh. Berkeley: University of California Press, 2005.

———. "The Cultural Implications of the Rise of China on the Region." In *The Rise of China and a Changing East Asian Order*, edited by Kokubun Ryosei and Wang Jisi Tokyo: Japan Center for International Exchange, 2004.

Wang Jisi. "China's Search for Stability with America." *Foreign Affairs*, 84(5) (September/October 2005): 39–48.

Weatherbee, Donald E. *International Relations in Southeast Asia, the Struggle for Autonomy*. Oxford: Rowman & Littlefield, 2005.

Womack, Brantly. "China and Southeast Asia: Asymmetry, Leadership and Normalcy." *Pacific Affairs*, 76(4) (Winter 2003–2004): 529–548.

———. "Dancing Alone: A Hard Look at Soft Power. "Available at japanfocus.org, November 16, 2005.

———. *China and Vietnam: The Politics of Asymmetry*. Unpublished manuscript expected to be published by Cambridge University Press.

Yuan, Jing-dong. "China-ASEAN Relations: Perspectives, Prospects and Implications for U.S. Interests." Available at http://www.StrategicStudiesInstitute.army.mil/, October 2006.

Zakaria, Haji Ahmad. "Malaysia." *Betwixt and Between, Southeast Asian Strategic Relations with the U.S. and China*. IDSS Monograph No. 7, 2005: 51–60.

Zweig, David and Bi Jianhai, "China's Global Hunt for Energy." *Foreign Affairs*, 84(5), September/October 2005. Available at http://www.cfr.org/publications/8957/chinas_global_hunt_for_energy.html.

Index

About the Author

BRONSON PERCIVAL, a former diplomat and professor at the U.S. Naval War College, has worked and now writes on radicalism and terrorism in Asia, national security issues in Southeast Asia, and maritime security. During his career with the U.S. Foreign Service, he reported from countries spanning an arc from Lebanon to Indonesia. After 9/11, Percival returned to the Department of State to help analyze and design policies to counter terrorism in Southeast Asia. He is now the senior advisor for Southeast Asia and Terrorism in Asia at the Center for Strategic Studies, The CNA Corporation, in Alexandria, Virginia. Percival was educated at the University of California-Berkeley, the National War College, and the University of Chicago.